Robert Scott

Sermons Preached before the University of Oxford

Robert Scott

Sermons Preached before the University of Oxford

ISBN/EAN: 9783743441699

Manufactured in Europe, USA, Canada, Australia, Japa

Cover: Foto ©Lupo / pixelio.de

Manufactured and distributed by brebook publishing software (www.brebook.com)

Robert Scott

Sermons Preached before the University of Oxford

SERMONS

PREACHED BEFORE THE

UNIVERSITY OF OXFORD,

BY ROBERT SCOTT, D.D.,

MASTER OF BALLIOL COLLEGE, AND PREBENDARY OF EXETER.

———

LONDON:

JOHN MURRAY, ALBEMARLE STREET.

1860.

OXFORD:

PRINTED BY JAMES WRIGHT, PRINTER TO THE UNIVERSITY.

ADVERTISEMENT.

THE following Sermons have no claim to the scientific
or systematic character which usually distinguishes University Discourses.

But, even in an Academical Congregation, there are
many who thankfully receive more humble and more
practical teaching. They have sins to repent of; they
have a work to do; they have crosses to bear. They
need warning, and encouragement, and sympathy. They
need, from time to time, to have their minds recalled
from other studies to careful and reverent meditation on
the Word of GOD.

It was especially to such persons that these Sermons
were originally addressed. And the Author has been
assured that they have been useful to some of those who
heard them.

May the same blessing attend their publication in the
present Volume!

CONTENTS.

SERMON V.

THE BOND BETWEEN TEACHER AND DISCIPLE.

1 THESSALONIANS ii. 19, 20.

SERMON VI.

THE PORTRAIT OF CHRISTIAN LOVE.

1 CORINTHIANS xiii. 1.

SERMON VII.

THE PHARISEE AND THE SADDUCEE.

ST. MATTH. XVI. 12.

SERMON VIII.

THE PUBLICAN.

St. Luke xviii. 13.

SERMON IX.

THE RICH MAN AND LAZARUS.

St. Luke xvi. 31.

SERMON X.

THE REVELATION OF IMMORTALITY.

Isaiah xxxviii. 18, 19.

SERMON XI.

FORGIVENESS WITH CHASTISEMENT.

2 Samuel xii. 13.

SERMON I.

SERMON I.

SMALL AND GREAT TRIALS.

Preached on Act Sunday, July 2, 1854.

JEREMIAH xii. 5.

If thou hast run with the footmen, and they have wearied thee, then how canst thou contend with horses? and if in the land of peace, wherein thou trustedst, they wearied thee, then how wilt thou do in the swelling of Jordan?

IT is no unwise rule, that we should suspect a fallacy when we hear a truism. For a truism that is popular, is, most commonly, only *a half truth.* And a half truth is almost always false in fact; and most frequently mischievous in application. For if that which it asserts is true, that which it implies or leaves to be inferred will commonly be found to be false.

Among the examples of that popular style

B

of moralizing, which thus sails under false colours, it is worth while to mark the very common saying, that No one knows what his next neighbour's sufferings may be. Not as if the truth of the assertion can be questioned; but because, on the very ground of its truth, the false inference tacitly connected with it is the more mischievous.

Truly, indeed, "the heart knoweth his own bitterness, and a stranger doth not intermeddle with his joy."[1] Truly there is a compensation, even in this life of trial, which does much to equalize human conditions under all the contrasts of outward station and circumstance. But does this guide us to the real meaning of the saying, as it passes current in the mouths of men? Is it meant to rouse our attention to the amount of hidden sorrow around us; to make us more watchful in seeking out our neighbours' sufferings, and more energetic in relieving them? I very much fear that its tendency is more often to harden our hearts to the wretchedness to which we cannot shut our eyes, and to encourage us to luxuriate in our own sentimental distresses.

[1] Prov. xiv. 10.

The truth is, that we are apt to flatter ourselves, each among all the mercies of his lot, that we are hardly dealt with, and ought to be unhappy. We flatter ourselves, I say; for there is a morbid delight in thinking so, which is most strangely common. We do not wait even for the gourd, of which we have been exceeding glad, to wither, before we maintain that "we do well to be angry, even unto death."[2]

And this is the folly which is also wickedness :—wickedness, for it is a rebellious murmuring against HIM who has done great things for us :—folly, for it is a profligate waste of the strength which HE has given us to be trained and exercised by small trials until it is fit to sustain greater. In running with the footmen we suffer ourselves to be wearied. How then shall we contend with horses ?

And yet herein is contained the strongest proof of the ever watchful mercy and providence of GOD, which spares us, for the most part, His severest visitings. Very acute pain or suffering or misfortune is the exception, not

[2] Jonah iv. 9.

the rule. Extreme anguish of spirit not only arises from causes comparatively few, but has this especial comfort attendant on it, that it can hardly fail of throwing us upon HIM who careth for us, and thus of proving the medicine rather than the sickness of the soul.

We inherit, indeed, the liability to all these things; and the times come when they actually visit us. But for the most part it is not so.

Without referring to purely spiritual evils (which manifestly do not belong to this subject), let us think only of the temporal ills which we continually deprecate in our Church's Litany. How many of these there are, which, in truth, we never recognise as hanging over ourselves! How many, from which we have always been, and seem still to be, so entirely free, that we scarcely know against what we are praying!

There is the prayer for deliverance "from lightning and tempest; from plague, pestilence, and famine; from battle and murder, and from sudden death;" said in one breath; perhaps forgotten in the next!

And yet we are liable to these,—all of us, always! But because the LORD has kept them afar off, we have forgotten them! Is not this to have forgotten Him?

And this requires the more especial consideration; because, as we in this place seem to be beyond others fenced off from the toil and moil of the outward world, we have the more temptation to spare ourselves the wholesome reminiscences of our brotherhood and its sympathies, nay, of our nature and its liabilities.

Now, there are times in most years, when *tempests* by sea and land remind us Whose word they are fulfilling. Yet, when we say the prayer, do we not need to ask ourselves whether we appreciate the trials which the LORD's daily compassions have spared us?

Famine, such has been His unmerited kindness to us, *we* have not seen : fulness of bread has rather been our temptation. And yet we have known its horrors in the neighbouring island, among those who are bound to us by the closest ties of national unity, the plainest duties of Christian brotherhood. And of scarcity and general distress we have lessons all too frequent around our very doors.

Pestilence has not indeed been let loose amongst us in its fury : we have not known what it is to see a thousand fall beside us, and ten thousand at our right hand. And yet we have seen enough, in the very streets and by-lanes of our city, to suggest to us "the terror by night, and the arrow that flieth by day; the pestilence that walketh in darkness, and the sickness that destroyeth in the noonday;"[3] enough to make us think, when we feel the scourge of whips so heavy, how awful the scourge of scorpions would have been.

And there are other forms of ill, of which for many years we have not had to con-tend with so much as the semblance, yet which we have seen taking their course amongst the nations of Europe;—the evil which David deprecated[4], and which we have been spared, of falling into the hands of *man*, instead of into the hand of GOD. We have been, after all, in the land of peace, wherein we trusted; while there are those who have been in the swelling of Jordan! GOD help them!

And now that there are threats and warn-ings of the heavier trials,—when the sword is unsheathed, the famine scarcely averted, the

3 Psalm xci. 5, 6, 7.   4 2 Samuel xxiv. 13, 14.

pestilence felt in all the exaggerated terrors of an unseen presence walking in darkness in our land, what has been our preparation? How have we used the time of training under our lighter burdens? In running with the footmen, we have been wearied, and in the land of peace! If the sun is but withdrawn and the heavens are overcast, we are down-hearted! If the sun is glowing, and the air sultry, we flag! We would have no trial, no training, no race set before us! We seek the prize, but shun the contest! We long for the Sabbath rest, but will not earn it by the six days' toil! And therefore, if GOD does so much as touch us with a little finger, we wince and cry, as though we were set up to be the mark of all his arrows. It seems a simple, almost a foolish thing to say, that our lot has been free from the worst evils of life. And yet even this must be urged again and again, so long as men will practically deny it; until they are made to feel and brought to confess how tenderly GOD's mercy has dealt with themselves.

It is with our mind's eye as with that of our body. We measure things, not by their size, but by their distance. · We magnify a hundred fold that which touches us,—loss of property, sickness, affliction. Be it ever so slight, we hold it close to our eyes, we dwell on it, we gloat over it, till it expands under our gaze, and hides every thing else from us. A man's hand *there* will hide a mountain on the horizon : and even though our own sorrows were as handbreadths, and those of our neigh- bours mountain-high, still to our perception the proportions are reversed.

But now we are brought to a turning point, a point where the line seems strongly marked between the past and the future. And looking back, and looking forward, we are called upon not merely as deciding a speculative question, but with all the pressure of a practical judg- ment, to answer the inquiry in the text. All are called upon, who have dwelt so long as our nation has, in a land of peace wherein they trusted. *We* are called upon even more than all others, because ours has been, not only the tranquillity of the city of GOD, but the deeper and holier stillness of His sanctuary. How can we contend with horses ? How shall we do in the swelling of Jordan ? Do we think that we shall have averted the greater troubles, by making a great noise about the less? Do we think that to have repined at the less, is the discipline by which we shall gain strength to bear the greater? We know that we are exposed to the risk of all; but HE only knows on whom they will be permitted to fall.

Did it occur to none of those who saw our nation's fleet rehearsing in their Sovereign's presence the dread game which has turned so soon to earnest, to ask in his heart, which of them were to return in their pride, and which were to prove the power of war and of the elements? And when *we* dismiss year after year the precious objects of our care, to embark, as on a summer sea, in all the brightness of youth and energy and high hope, do none of us feel an anxiety for their chequered future, a longing for an insight into the varied perils of their several courses, that we might warn them, I will not say for their whole future career, but even, were it only for the space of their summer holy-day, against each one's particular hazards?

And though this may not be, yet we

may warn them, if we are alive to the warning ourselves, that there is ONE who alone knows what trials, what sufferings are to search the spirit of each; ONE who sees which of them are to learn from others the lesson of life's uncertainty and the world's treachery, and which are to have it written on their own foreheads and in their own hearts; ONE only, with whom it rests that each shall or shall not have the most severe of worldly ills to struggle with; ONE who alone could tell what in mercy HE conceals, until with the hour of agony comes the angel of consolation.

Again, we may warn them, before they go forth from beneath our hands, what will be the part of the wise pilgrim as he goes on his journey. Will it be, when the roads grow rough and the heavens seem overcast, to sit him down to weep and wail by the wayside on the milestone which was meant to mark his onward progress? Rather, surely, to gird up his loins and step out the more firmly and resolutely, calling on HIM who has promised to be his guide and support; fixing his eyes and his thoughts upon the goal of his pilgrimage.

And to him who does this, though the way may wax rougher and steeper, and the storms may beat wildly round, there will be a Saviour ever present to bear up his feet; as really present, as manifestly present to his spiritual sense, as in the pillar of cloud and flame to the Israelites in the wilderness. He that has not given way to weariness in the land of peace, will not be forsaken amid the swellings of Jordan.

And all these interferences, the petty annoyances as well as the more serious afflictions of life, are sent to serve His purposes, to try us, and, if we thwart them not, to do us good at the latter end. No event, whether it seem good or evil, befalls us, in which we may not recognise His hand: no blessing so slight, but we must thank HIM for it; no trial so petty, but we must receive it *as a trial*, and thank HIM for that also. Trifling as it may seem, it will not be so trifling, that we may not serve HIM acceptably by enduring it aright. It will not be so trifling, that it may not, if well used, bring us a step nearer Heaven: and if it be but one step, it is what all this world's goods could never buy.

Therefore it must be accepted and endured with the full consciousness of what it is, and whence it comes ; accepted and endured with the feelings as well as on the principles of Christianity. For we must not keep our Christianity for great occasions and great trials alone, like a suit of mourning to be worn when some terrible calamity befalls us. It must be put on and worn day by day. We must labour in it, that our labours may be blest; we must rest in it, that our holy-day may be a Sabbath to the LORD. If we neglect to use it in the struggles of every-day life, it will not stand us in stead when our heavy afflictions come upon us. If we seek not this strength in the land of peace, it will be all the more hard to find it amid the swellings of Jordan. And what shall supply its place, if it be lacking there ?

And there will be an easy safeguard against the danger of our seeming to ourselves to do some great thing for the LORD in bearing this or that which he lays upon us. That very petition of our Litany to which reference has been already made, may at once remind us of the real and substantial evils by which those of our own flesh and blood are continually visited, and may teach us to measure our own trials by a truer standard; to add humility to patience; to join thanksgiving for what we are spared, with fortitude under what we have to endure.

And thus by little and little will be revealed to us the true place which these slighter trials and difficulties hold in the dispensation of GOD; and we shall learn to see how the less are connected with the greater. The heathen story of the athlete, who developed his bodily strength by carrying day by day a living and growing burden, becomes a Christian parable. Our heavenly FATHER has many trials in store for HIS children, before HE has trained and proved them to the full, and established for them their claim to the prize of their high calling. And these come upon us, for the most part, gradually. HE is faithful, and will not tempt us above that we are able. HE makes us run with the footmen in the first place. HE lays a light cross, an easy yoke upon us. Yet still it *is* a cross, it *is* a yoke: and we must take it up daily, and bear it after HIM. And to those who strive in earnest to fulfil

this their duty, it not only becomes itself less
irksome, but it serves as a wholesome discipline
and training; serves to strengthen and harden
them for the endurance of further trials and
heavier.

And according to the law of this our life,
these will come;—still, with the way to escape,
that we may be able to bear them;—still, in
due proportion to the strength which is given
to us, and the help which will not be withheld.
But come they will. There will be times
when the cross is more heavy, and we more
ready to faint under it; but HE will not fail
those who follow HIM; HE who called upon
us to take up our crosses, and bear them after
HIM, called us to nothing short of His own
Brotherhood; from His Cross, and from HIM,
virtue will go forth, to make ours also instruments of strength and healing.

Thus to all who seek to endure in the
strength and through the grace of GOD, small
trials and great are but the lower and the
upper rounds of that ladder which is set up
upon the earth while its top reaches to heaven.
And even in the time present, the growing
severity of discipline is itself to the eye of faith

an evidence of growth in grace, an assurance of abundance of help; "seeing that HE will not suffer us to be tempted above that we are able."[5] But to those who will not hearken to the rod, and HIM who hath appointed it, such dispensations speak with another voice. For the heavier sorrows will not be withheld, because the lighter are not received according to our FATHER's will. And when they come, they will come in very different guise. If they do not train for good, they will punish for evil; and all their bitterness will be without relief, without end: it will be without hope, without faith, without GOD.

If then we have hitherto run with the footmen only, and yet have been weary, how pressing is the need to take heed betimes, and lift up the hands which hang down, and strengthen the feeble knees[6]; to rouse ourselves from dreams of peace and security; to look beyond the limits of our own isolated sanctuary; to join our yearnings with those of all that is subjected to vanity; to recognise our own part in the groaning and travailing of creation[7].

5 1 Cor. x. 13. 6 Hebrews xii. 12. 7 Rom. viii. 20-22.

It may be, that our race with the footmen
is only over, that our contention with horses
may begin. It may be, that the breaking up
of that peace in which our land has had rest
for forty years, portends a breaking up of
the ancient foundations, a removal of the ancient landmarks, and a sore judgment upon
us, who, through having been undisturbed
from our youth, have settled upon our lees[8].
Oh, may HE who by so many ministries
conscious and unconscious, so many workmen
willing and unwilling, is now stirring us,
and teaching us a sterner lesson of the reality of life, purify, refine, strengthen us by
the workings of His providence; and nerve
us for the work of our obedience and the trial
of our faith.

For, assuredly, there is a hard work, a hard
trial before us,—before the Church—before
the nation—before the University—before
every individual of those who are knit together in each one of those bodies. And
while we draw breath in the stillness which
yet oppresses our atmosphere, it will be well
if we use that pause to attune our own spirits

[8] Zephaniah i. 12 ; Jerem. xlviii. 11.

to the awful harmony of GOD's dispensations;
to "remember them that are in bonds, as bound
with them; and them which suffer adversity,
as being ourselves also in the body."[9]

And, especially well will it be, if we seek
diligently to know how our own part is to be
performed. For a part we have to perform,
even here;—always, in guarding and tending those who are to go forth from hence to
the various ministries of Church and State;
grafting them with principles fruitful of good;
not unchristianizing secular life, but imbuing
it with the element of a life that is higher;
disciplining zeal to duty; enlightening patriotism and hallowing it. And now, above all
times, we have a work, in lifting up our
hands, like the Hebrew lawgiver in Rephi-
dim[10], on the mount where we sit apart from
the strife of peoples; praying for ourselves,
our sons, our country;—yea, even for our
enemies, that the Prince of Peace may over-
rule the sharp arbitrement of war to hasten
the coming of His kingdom.

And while our duty and our work as GOD's
fellow-labourers become more and more clear.

---

9 Hebr. xiii. 3.   10 Exod. xvii. 11.

as we devote ourselves with more and more singleness of heart to the little things which we are permitted to do in His service, we shall unlearn at the same time our miserable jealousies and petty ambitions, and the justling and bustling of our earthly rivalries; we shall see the smallness of what we are tempted to think our own interests; the vastness of those which we are permitted to serve if we put our own aside; the difference between the rewards which we perhaps have been seeking and those with which our LORD crowns His servants. — "Thou didst say, Woe is me now! for the LORD hath added grief to my sorrow; I fainted in my sighing, and I find no rest. Thus shalt thou say unto him, The LORD saith thus; Behold, that which I have built will I break down, and that which I have planted I will pluck up, even this whole land. And seekest thou great things for thyself? Seek them not!"[11]

And we shall recognise all the more the community of our bonds with those who are bound, as our individual anxieties, our corporate difficulties and grievances come surg-

[11] Jerem. xlv. 3, 4, 5.

ing in upon us, eddies of the great flood whose roaring waves are working distress and perplexity to the nations. For are not all these so many additional remembrancers that we are bound with our brethren, yea are members with them, and must suffer together; so many additional warnings that our faith still needs to be further proved, our obedience still needs to be confirmed and made more fruitful; so many additional pledges, that as our day is, so our strength shall be? Provided that we can look up and watch and pray and work; blessing GOD even for the narrowness of the way, whereby HE would keep us from wandering; blessing HIM for the very weight of the cross upon our shoulder, whereby HE would steady our undisciplined steps; blessing HIM for the holy footprints before us, which mark the straight path for our feeble feet; blessing HIM for every added trial and danger and difficulty, which HE permits us to accept as the earnest of added comfort, and strength and grace sufficient to make us more than conquerors.

Only let us believe, through the Saviour helping our unbelief, that if we work in faith,

GOD is working for us, though it may be behind the cloud; that if we faint not in running with the footmen, HE will nerve us when we have to contend with horses; and that, although it is only in part that we can know and prophesy the future even of the things which concern us most nearly and deeply, yet there is one thing which we can speak, for we know it assuredly; that the End is in His hand; and that if we follow the light which HE vouchsafes, all our trials, all our struggles, all our perplexities will be overruled to bring us ever nearer to its heavenly Fount. "It shall come to pass in that day, that the light shall not be clear, nor dark: but it shall be one day which shall be known to the LORD, not day, nor night: but it shall come to pass, THAT AT EVENING TIME IT SHALL BE LIGHT."[12]

[12] Zechariah xiv. 6, 7.

SERMON II.

CHRIST RISEN.

Preached on Easter Day, 1857.

St. Luke xxiv. 26.

Ought not CHRIST to have suffered these things, and to enter into His glory?

THIS is the same prophecy which is traceable, as if struggling to work its own fulfilment from generation to generation, from the words which comforted our first Parents in their fall, until the day when all was fulfilled in HIM who alone could fulfil it, the Son of Man, who came down from Heaven. Age after age, within the sphere in which it pleased GOD to work, the two characteristics of His blessed purpose,—the partial triumph and the eventual defeat of the Powers of evil, —reappear. But the time is not yet. There is an indication of the end, but dashed with failure. There are the elements of sorrow and

of joy, but sorrow to one and joy to another.
There are fulfilments of prophecy, but so unsatisfactory and imperfect, as to shew that
they are but shadows of some great reality
which is behind them in the march of time.
And perhaps, among the evidences which confirm our Christian faith, there are few more
powerful than that which is afforded by a
world strewn with the wrecks of premature at-
tempts at restoration, amidst which the faithful
though baffled instincts of humanity maintain
their indomitable struggle after the promise.
"The children are come to the birth :"[1] and if,
age after age, "there is not strength to bring
forth," still even this suggests the comforting
oracle, "Shall I bring to the birth, and not
cause to bring forth?" Even this bids the
prisoners of hope look forward to the fore-
ordained time when "she which travaileth
shall have brought forth"; and "out of Bethlehem Ephratah HE shall come, whose goings
forth have been from of old, from everlasting."
In the blood of Abel and the gift of Seth ;
in the reward of Enoch's faith ; in that
twofold character of the flood, which makes

[1] Isaiah xxxvii. 3 ; lxvi. 9. Micah v. 2, 3.

Christian Baptism its antitype[2]; in the sacrifice of Isaac and his redemption ; in the life of Joseph ; in the whole pilgrimage of Israel from Canaan to Egypt, from Egypt to Shiloh and Zion; in the Kingdom under David the abundant shedder of blood, and Solomon the man of rest and peace ;[3] in the chequered fortunes of their most godly descendants ; in the persons of the Prophets, their missions, their deliverances, their sufferings;—all speaks of the certainty of a future for which the time is not come: all forecasts that struggle between the Powers of good and evil, in which there shall be One suffering and triumphant ; One in whom death shall be swallowed up of life ; One whose travail shall work an abiding deliverance and redemption for the exiled family of Heaven.

But even if these and the like shadows of the truth which was to come, and if the more articulate testimony of Psalmists and Prophets, suffice to shew us that in CHRIST all these fruitless

[2] 1 St. Peter iii. 21, ὕδατος, ὃ καὶ ἡμᾶς ἀντίτυπον νῦν σώζει βάπτισμα :—very inadequately translated, "the like figure whereunto even baptism doth also now save us."

[3] 1 Chron. xxii. 8, 9.

yearnings and baffled efforts of human nature
were at length to attain their end; yet who are
we, that we should wonder at the sadness of the
bereaved disciples in their communications as
they walked on the way to Emmaus? With
the Bible—New Testament as well as Old—in
our hands; rejoicing in the light of the Holy
Spirit sent down from Heaven to confirm the
Apostolic testimony of these things, it is
indeed hard to put ourselves in the position
of these orphans, and make all the allowance
which their despondency may claim. But it
is our duty to attempt it, and to place
ourselves, in thought, by their side from a
somewhat earlier period of their discipleship.
Their attachment to their Lord had been
tried indeed and not found wanting throughout the course of His ministry. It had been
sustained by love: but it had also been sustained by hope; and it was not for them con-
sciously to detect how much that was earthly
had blended itself with that hope. It is, however, to be noted, that this hope, whatever
its character might be, had rapidly risen and
brightened during one short period. It is
true indeed that their Lord had begun to

depress and modify their expectations by
dwelling on His approaching death. But
outward influences had been at work to an
extent not known before, to stimulate their
belief in the near advent of the glory and the
blessing so long hoped for, so long delayed,
so often, as it seemed, withdrawn from the
race of Abraham when on the point of its fulfilment. The raising of Lazarus had very
much changed the outward position, if we may
so speak, of JESUS CHRIST. There were
now abundant indications that a crisis was
approaching. There were fair grounds for
those who had adhered to the Prophet of
Nazareth in His humility, to expect that they
should stand beside Him in His glory. Jerusalem was moved. All the concourse of
Jews and devout proselytes, whom that Passover had congregated in the Holy City, had
become alive to the mighty works and lofty
claims of JESUS the Prophet of Nazareth
of Galilee[4]. Surely the hour had come.
Surely the Hope of Israel, the Desire of all
Nations, was here recognised; HE had but to
declare Himself, and take possession of His

4 St. Matth. xxi. 8—11.

father David's throne! Never before had the fulfilment of the promise seemed so nigh; never yet had hope been so stimulated. And after all, was this so, only to be dashed down again like the castle-building of a child? Was this, only that to the long roll of shipwrecks should be added the highest aspirations, and therefore the direst disappointment that had ever stirred the heart of man? What wonder, if the tempter was busy at their ear, mocking their day-dreams, and whispering the subtle doubt, whether, after all, mankind were not to be for ever the sport of juggling fiends; were not to have the cup of blessing brought to the very lip, only that it should be shattered again and again, for ever?

And now, with these thoughts in our minds, and having realized the change which had come over the Disciples' feelings between the Palm Sunday and the Passover, we may in some degree understand their state of mind; we may sympathize with their afflictions; we may feel the reproaches of their consciences; we may perceive the terrors of man begin-ning to assume proportions which had been impossible in their LORD's presence. Mournful therefore as was the scepticism of the Apostles when the messages of joy reached them on this Easter morning; sad as were the communings of the Two on the way to Emmaus; obstinate as to us the incredulity of St. Thomas may seem; all these were the manifestations of one common and natural feeling, the sense of bereavement, which *will* not be comforted, because its loved ones are not; which *cannot* be comforted, so long as it cannot believe that they *are.*

To such penitents and mourners without hope, their risen LORD appeared, breathing peace and bringing Heaven with His presence; with no rebuke on His lips, but such as their own consciences must draw from His tender solicitude to reassure their failing faith. But still, even *then*, we read that the impulse was the same. As before for sorrow, so now they believed not for joy[5]; until by proof after proof, effort after effort, HE overcame their doubts; and "then were the disciples glad, when they saw the LORD."[6]

It will not be difficult to see the important

---

[5] St. Luke xxiv. 41.   [6] St. John xx. 20.

purpose which this natural misgiving of the Apostles was made to serve, when we come to consider the position which the preaching of the Resurrection holds in all those discourses by which the first thousands were added to the Church. Recognising this prominence of the doctrine, we cannot but be struck by the fact, that it was *forced* upon them. Looking upon them as witnesses, whose testimony was so important that this was the very qualification specially indicated for the Apostolate[7], we find them, even though it be in their own case, reluctant witnesses. So important was it " for the more confirmation of the faith," that they should have been permitted to doubt of the Resurrection of their LORD[8].

And the use made of the Resurrection of JESUS CHRIST in the teaching of the Apostles afterwards, is in another way also connected with the discourse of the risen Saviour which has supplied us with a text.—"O fools, and slow of heart to believe all that the Prophets have spoken : *Ought* not CHRIST to have suffered these things, and to enter into His glory ? And beginning at Moses and all the Prophets, HE

7 Acts i. 22.   8 Collect for St. Thomas's Day.

expounded unto them in all the Scriptures the things concerning Himself."[9] There are here two things most worthy of our attention :—first, the appeal to Moses and the Prophets in connection with the divine fact of the Resurrection ; and second, the counsel and purpose of GOD, so far as we may infer them from His revelation through His servants the Apostles, which thus required the Captain of our salvation to be made perfect through suffering,... to bring many sons to glory.[10] The first must be illustrated from the Acts of the Apostles : the second from their Epistles. Yet the limits which are prescribed to our present meditations, forbid us to enter into the full examination of this last division of the subject, or to do more than to suggest lines of inquiry and thought,—objects to be set before the mind in perusing portions of Holy Writ afresh,—indications of spots where deeper search may be made in full confidence that no one will return empty from his labour in such a mine.

The appeal to the prophecies of the Old Testament is, of course, prominent in the

[9] St. Luke xxiv. 25, 26. [10] Heb. ii. 10.

preaching of the Apostles to the Jews. And there is a consistency, an uniformity in the mode of the appeal, which suggests to us how mysteriously through the minds and mouths of various ministers in diverse manners one Spirit guided the teaching; for St. Peter[10], who shared the high communings of our risen Lord's forty days' sojourn, and St. Paul[11], who received his doctrine from the same Saviour after His ascension, unite in clothing the same argument in almost the same language, to shew that the hope which in David had reached only a shadowy and shortlived fulfilment, was perfectly accomplished in his Antitype.

In Jerusalem, then, we have these promises urged[12] : and the Apostles are the witnesses that they have been performed. And combined with this there is a reference to the Ascension (which meets us still more emphatically, but in a slightly different connection, in the Epistles) as the immediate source of the outpouring of that Holy Spirit, Whose testimony is the decisive confirmation of all other. But this is not all : for on one of the earliest occasions recorded, (that of the miracle at the

10 Acts iii. 24, sqq. 11 xiii. 35, sqq. 12 Acts xiii. 33 ; v. 30.

Beautiful Gate of the Temple,) we have a chord already struck, once again to sound in this same book—but which rings through all the Epistles afterwards; the teaching of our resurrection, in and through that of CHRIST; "they preached through JESUS the resurrection from the dead."[13]

In the tenth chapter of the Acts[14], we arrive at a new point of view in the discourse of St. Peter to the Gentile Cornelius and his friends. In this the fact of our Redeemer's Resurrection is indeed strongly asserted, on the personal authority of the speaker and his brother Apostles, "which did eat and drink with HIM after HE rose from the dead." But as the argument is addressed to Gentiles, not to Jews, it is here connected (precisely as we find it connected by St. Paul at Athens[15], in the only other discourse distinctly addressed to heathens which alludes to it at all) with GOD's purpose to judge the world by HIM whom HE had raised. And if the Prophets are appealed to, it is not to prepare the way for a belief in the fact, but to shew that they associated the

[13] Acts iv. 2, ἐν τῷ Ἰησοῦ τὴν ἀνάστασιν τὴν ἐκ νεκρῶν; cf. xxvi. 7, 8, 23.

[14] Acts x. 39–43.   [15] Acts xvii. 31.

belief on the Messiah with the remission of sins[16].

Coming next to the preaching of St. Paul at the Pisidian Antioch[17], we shall see that, Jews though his hearers were, he does not treat them as guilty, nay, not even as cognisant, of the awful doings which had desecrated their holy city. But here the adoption of the historical style carries us strangely back to the day when the last words of Stephen cut his judges to the heart, and the young man of Benjamin (who in this chapter does not forget his royal tribesman and namesake) was consenting to his death[18]! We hear of the Prophets, we hear of David, in the same quotation, with the same interpretation with which St. Peter has already made us familiar; and we learn that in this JESUS is the fulfilment of all which had seemed a failing prophecy in the human destiny of David.

Lastly, the same Apostle is found in the synagogue of Thessalonica, "reasoning out of the Scriptures, opening and alleging (almost in the very words of our glorified LORD Himself on the way to Emmaus), that CHRIST must

16 Acts x. 43.　17 Acts xiii.　18 Acts viii. 1; xiii. 21.

needs have suffered,[19] and risen again from the dead; and that this JESUS, whom I preach unto you, is the CHRIST." So much emphasis is there in the words in which he asserts over and over again[20], that the hope of the resurrection of the dead is the hope of Israel,— that hope for which he is called in question and accused, for which he is bound with chains;—that same hope of the promise of GOD made unto the Fathers, unto which the twelve tribes instantly serving GOD day and night hope to come." So close is the bond which joins the Resurrection of CHRIST with the general resurrection, whether in the view of St. Peter at the Temple Gate, or in St. Paul's when he addresses King Agrippa, " Why should it be thought a thing incredible with you, that GOD should raise the dead ?" So plain is the meaning which cool unbiassed heathens attached to the words of St. Paul's teaching; whether it be Festus[21], speaking

---

[19] Acts xvii. 3 ; ὅτι τὸν Χριστὸν ἔδει παθεῖν, καὶ ἀναστῆναι ἐκ νεκρῶν :—compare St. Luke xxiv. 26, οὐχὶ ταῦτα ἔδει παθεῖν τὸν Χριστὸν καὶ εἰσελθεῖν εἰς τὴν δόξαν αὐτοῦ ;

[20] Acts xxiii. 6 ; xxiv. 15, 21 ; xxvi. 7.

[21] Acts xxv. 19; xxvi. 24.

of "one JESUS, which was dead, whom Paul affirmed to be alive," and deeming him a madman for his pains; or whether it be the Athenians[22], who held him "to be a setter forth of strange gods, because he preached unto them JESUS and the resurrection."

Proceeding to the Apostolic Epistles, we find the words of the text almost reproduced by St. Peter, where he tells how diligently the Prophets " searched what or what manner of time the Spirit of CHRIST which was in them did signify, when it testified beforehand the sufferings of CHRIST, and the glory that should follow."[23]   But here we are on very different ground. Addressing Christian converts, there was but little need that the Apostles should dwell on the demonstration of the fact, or even its connection with prophecy. And accordingly, with the one exception of the xvth chapter of the 1st Epistle to the Corinthians,—an exception momentous indeed, but solitary, and

22 Acts xvii. 18 ; ὅτι τὸν Ἰησοῦν καὶ τὴν ἀνάστασιν εὐηγγελί- ζετο.—This must mean the doctrine of the Resurrection generally, not the mere fact of CHRIST'S Resurrection.
23 1 St. Peter i. 11.

accounted for by the rise of actual false teaching in their Church,—we meet with no more of this. Nor is it so much the actual triumph of that Easter morning, as our LORD's abiding glory in the state into which HE then re-entered, that is naturally suggested to the writers, as the subject on which the Christians' minds must rest. Easter day was indeed a high day : but "the Easter day in every week"[24] which hallowed the whole course of Christian life, was an embodiment of the belief that it is HE Who *is risen* from the dead, rather than the event of His rising, that must be the object of their thoughts. And this will help to shew how the Resurrection and the Ascension appear linked together, as forming parts of one whole. "Now that HE ascended, what is it but that HE also descended first into the lower parts of the earth ? HE that descended is the same also that ascended up far above all heavens, that HE might fill all things."[25] "It is CHRIST that died, yea rather, that is risen again, Who is even at the right hand of GOD."[26] The germ of this thought has been found al-

[24] Christian Year ; Easter. [25] Ephes. iv. 9, 10.
[26] Rom. viii. 34 ; cf. Heb. x. 12 ; 1 St Pet. iii. 21 ; Col. iii. 1.

ready, in the very commencement of the Acts of the Apostles, with reference to the gift of the Holy Spirit at Pentecost. *Here* it is connected with the continual outpouring of the same Spirit throughout the whole duration of the Mediatorial Kingdom.

In various Epistles, indeed, the Resurrection of CHRIST is mentioned as one of the glories of the FATHER or the SON, one of the titles of their honour and praise in all the Churches of the Saints. "HE that raised up JESUS from the dead," is one of the most familiar paraphrases of the FATHER's name[27]. Again, of the SON we are taught that " HE hath abolished death, and brought life and immortality to light through the Gospel ;"[28] and that " to this end HE both died, and rose, and revived, that HE might be Lord both of the dead and living."[29] Again, as in the Acts St. Paul applies the words, " Thou art my Son, this day have I begotten Thee,"[30] to this event, so he writes to the Romans "concerning JESUS CHRIST our

---

[27] See Rom. viii. 11 ; x. 9 ; 1 Cor. vi. 14 ; Gal. i. 1 ; Eph. i. 20 ; 1 Thess. i. 10 ; Heb. xiii. 20 ; 1 St. Pet. i. 21.
[28] 2 Tim. i. 10.   [29] Rom. xiv. 9, (note the various reading.)
[30] Psalm ii. 7 ; Acts xiii. 33.

LORD, which was made of the seed of David according to the flesh ; and declared to be the SON of GOD with power, according to the SPIRIT of holiness, by the resurrection from the dead."[31] In this passage (it may be remarked in passing) there is a singular proof of the identity recognised between CHRIST'S Resurrection and that of all of whom HE became the first fruits. The same thought again suggests itself to the Apostle in writing to the Colossians, where he speaks of CHRIST as "the firstborn of all creation, by Whom were all things created...by HIM and for HIM...Who is the beginning, the firstborn from the dead; that in all things HE might have the preeminence."[32]

We are reminded, moreover, by St. Peter[33], "how HE was put to death in the flesh, but quickened by the Spirit," in words where the antithesis seems to lie between the human nature which made it possible that HE should die, and the Divine nature, "the quickening Spirit," which made it "impossible that HE should be holden of" death; so that the thought is akin to that which is contained

31 Rom. i. 3, 4 ; see Sermon X. note 9.
32 Coloss. i. 15—18. 33 1 St. Peter iii. 18.

in the words, "though HE was crucified through weakness, yet HE liveth by the power of GOD," with which St. Paul[34] parallels the working, in his own human weakness, of the strength which God giveth.

But these quotations do not set forth the uses for which the writers of the Epistles are wont to appeal to the Resurrection of our LORD. With them, it is not so much a fact to be established, or a doctrine to be believed;—why should it be, when they were writing to the Churches on whom the risen and ascended Saviour had poured out the unction of the Comforter?—not so much a fact to be established or a doctrine to be believed, as it is *the* fact, on which the relation of the Believers to their LORD depended, and *the* doctrine, from which their practical duties flowed. It is, that as HE died for our sins, so HE rose for our justification. It is, that as we were reconciled by His death, so we are saved by His life. It is, that HE died for us, that we should live together with Him[35]. The beginning, middle,

34 2 Cor. xiii. 4; compare 1 Cor. xv. 45.
35 Rom. iv. 24, sq.; v. 10; 1 Thess. v. 10.

and end of the Christian life alike consist in what the Christian derives from CHRIST's Resurrection. It is the *beginning;* for is it not said, " Baptism doth save us ... by the Resurrection of JESUS CHRIST, Who is gone into Heaven, and is at the right hand of GOD ;"[36] and, "Ye are buried with HIM in baptism, wherein also ye are risen with HIM through the faith of the operation of GOD, who hath raised HIM from the dead. And you, being dead in your sins...hath GOD quickened together with HIM ;"[37] and, "if the SPIRIT of HIM that raised up JESUS from the dead dwell in you, HE that raised up CHRIST from the dead shall also quicken your mortal bodies by His SPIRIT that dwelleth in you ;"[38] and by St. Peter again, " Blessed be the GOD and Father of our LORD JESUS CHRIST, which according to His abundant mercy hath begotten us again unto a lively hope by the resurrection of JESUS CHRIST from the dead ?"[39]

It is *the middle:* for "therefore we are buried with HIM by baptism into death: that like as CHRIST was raised up from the dead by the

---

[36] 1 St. Pet. iii. 21.   [37] Col. ii. 12, 13.
[38] Rom. viii. 11.   [39] 1 St. Peter i. 3.

glory of the Father, even so we also should walk in newness of life...In that HE died, HE died unto sin once: but in that HE liveth, HE liveth unto GOD. Likewise reckon ye also yourselves to be dead indeed unto sin, but alive unto GOD through JESUS CHRIST."[40] Thus the Apostle describes himself as "always bearing about in the body the dying of the LORD JESUS, that the life also of JESUS might be made manifest in his body."[41] Thus the constraint of the love of CHRIST is this, "that HE died for all, that they which live should not henceforth live unto themselves, but unto HIM which died for them, and rose again."[42] "If ye then be risen with CHRIST, seek those things which are above, where CHRIST sitteth on the right hand of GOD. Set your affection on things above, not on things on the earth. For ye are dead, and your life is hid with CHRIST in GOD. When CHRIST, Who is our life, shall appear, then shall ye also appear with HIM in glory."[43]

For, lastly, herein is also *the end* of the Christian's course; according to the aspira-

40 Rom. vi. 4–11.　　　41 2 Cor. iv. 10–14.
42 2 Cor. 5. 15.　　　43 Col. iii. 1, sqq.

tions of the Apostle for himself, "that I may know HIM, and the power of His Resurrection, and the fellowship of His sufferings, being made conformable unto His death ; if by any means I might attain unto the resurrection of the dead ;"[44] according to his doctrine to the Corinthians, "GOD hath both raised up the LORD, and will also raise up us by His own power ;"[45] and to the Thessalonians, "If we believe that JESUS died and rose again, even so them also which sleep in JESUS will GOD bring with HIM."[46]

What need then, with the curious fool, to ask *how* are the dead raised up, and with what body do they come?[47] Enough, that we have the assurance of this day, that neither is our faith vain, nor are they which have fallen asleep in CHRIST perished; for "CHRIST *is* risen from the dead, and become the first-fruits of them that slept ;...for in HIM shall all be made alive,—every man in his own order; CHRIST the first fruits; afterward they that are CHRIST's at His coming !"

44 Philipp. iii. 10.　　45 1 Cor. vi. 14.　　46 1 Thess. iv. 14.
47 1 Cor. xv. 35, 36; ibid. 17, 18, 20, 22, 23.

SERMON III.

THE CHRISTIAN RISEN IN CHRIST.

Preached on Easter-Day, 1856.

COLOSSIANS iii. 1.

If ye then be risen with CHRIST, seek those things which are above.

SORROW hath endured for a night: and now the morning of joy has dawned,—the day of days, the beginning of the new Creation after that Sabbath in the Tomb, in which old things had their consummation and were done away. By suffering and sorrow, through life and in death, all that the serpent could effect to bruise the heel of the SON of Man has been accomplished: and now his own head has been bruised, his hour is past, his power, the power of darkness, has an end. CHRIST is risen. He has risen indeed! In becoming the firstborn from the dead, HE has become by a new title the firstborn of every creature—of all creation[1].

HE is risen, and that, not alone. In the resurrection of the Very GOD and Very Man, GOD has brought Man with HIM. His Resurrection is ours, through the reality of that human nature which HE has taken for ever. And hence, if HE is the first fruits, we are the harvest; if HE is the firstborn, it is among many brethren. Great is the significance of that Scripture which tells us that " many bodies of the saints which slept arose, and came out of the graves after His resurrection."[2]

It is only after the historic truth of the fact, as such, has been demonstrated, that the Resurrection of our Blessed LORD can be used or applied for doctrine, for instruction, for edification, for comfort. Afterwards, indeed, we may generalize, we may idealize. But all our trains of thought and speculation are futile to ourselves and to our race, unless doctrine presupposes fact. And see what interests are at stake. HE rose, (we learn it

[1] Col. i. 15.   [2] St. Matt. xxvii. 52, 53.

from Scripture) for our justification[3]. That
His rising, therefore, should be certain, is no
less than a matter of life and death,—the
second death, the life everlasting! And this
view of the question was from the beginning
adopted by the Apostles of the LORD. From
the beginning, that SPIRIT which guided them
(even before the full outpouring of His fiery
baptism) had taught them that this was to
be the foundation of their preaching. The
crucifixion, indeed, was sufficiently notorious.
Enemies there were enough, to prove that
that oblation had been duly offered, even
while they stumbled or scoffed at it. But it
was for this that the number of the Apostolic
College was to be filled up, ere the Dispensation of the Third Person of the Holy Trinity
began, that of those who "had companied with
them all the time that the LORD JESUS went
in and out among them,...one should be ordained to be a witness with them of His
Resurrection."[4] It was this which St. Peter
preached to the first Gentile congregation in
the house of Cornelius, that GOD had raised
up CHRIST "and shewed HIM openly; not to

3 Rom. iv. 25.　　　　4 Acts i. 22.

all the people, but unto witnesses chosen before of GOD."[5]   And when St. Paul would declare to his Corinthian disciples the Gospel by which they were saved, he proclaimed indeed briefly "how that CHRIST died for our sins according to the Scriptures, and that HE was buried;" but passed on to teach at length, and with much speciality of detail, how, after HE rose the third day according to the Scriptures, one witness or group of witnesses after another had beheld HIM, from Cephas to Saul, from the Twelve to the five hundred brethren at once[6].

On such foundation of evidence was the great and cardinal truth established.   And being so established, it becomes the source of consequences and results doctrinal and practical, in which our relation to our risen Saviour at once involves us and our eternal interests; —but which would be nugatory and null, unless the objective truth of the facts were first recognised.

The teaching of the Apostles is, that, inasmuch as CHRIST is risen, we are also risen. We are risen with HIM; nay we are also risen

5 Acts x. 40, 41.   6 1 Cor. xv. 3—8.

in HIM; raised, as His members; and thus risen from the death in which we lay while we were alive to sin: so that now, having died unto sin, and having been buried with CHRIST, (for he that is dead is free from sin, owes no more under the penalty of that ancient bond,) we are alive unto GOD[7]. All the blessings which we enjoy, flow from our union with our Saviour JESUS CHRIST. In HIM it is that we are made partakers of every good gift here, as well as heirs of the kingdom and the glory hereafter. In HIM it is that we have the least as well as the greatest of those blessings, of which HE has made our nature once more capable, by uniting it to His own;—yea, of blessings in heavenly places far transcending aught of which our nature ever could have been capable, save by its consecration and glorification in Himself.

Thus HE rose for our justification, even as HE died for our sins. HE rose, not merely, though most truly, because the Resurrection was an evidence that the work of Redemption was complete, and that the death which had swallowed up Humanity was itself finally

7 Rom. vi. 4—11.

swallowed up in victory. HE rose, not merely "because we were justified,"—because when the Redemption had been once completed, nothing else remained to be done; but HE rose for our justification, as a distinct and substantive part of His work for His fallen creatures. As for our sins HE was delivered, so for our justification HE was raised again.

It is especially in contemplating the union which, so to speak, identifies us with our LORD and Saviour both in His death and His resurrection, that we shall become conscious of the nearness with which they are linked together in importance as well as in fact. We follow HIM in death;—for to the Christian, death is no longer a subjection to him which had the power of death; but it is to follow the LORD whither HE has gone before, and to be with HIM more nearly than in what we on this side of the grave call life. And in like manner we follow HIM in rising again. His one righteousness is upon us all, not merely unto justification, but, in the emphatic words of Holy Writ, "unto justification *of life*."[8] The language of

<hr>

[8] Rom. v. 18.

St. Paul is not, "If CHRIST be not raised, ye are uncertain touching the Redemption;" but it is, "If CHRIST be not raised, your faith is vain; ye are yet in your sins."[9] You have not regained that, of which your sins stript you : you have no way opened out of that grave of His in which you are buried, if the stone has not been rolled away from it. Weigh well that most notable paragraph : see by what a process of almost formal logic he works out his conclusions. "If HE rose from the dead, how say some among you that there is no Resurrection ? But, if there be no Resurrection, then is CHRIST not risen : and if CHRIST be not risen, then preaching is vain,.. faith is vain....If the dead rise not, then is CHRIST not raised:—and if CHRIST be not raised, your faith is vain; ye are yet in your sins ; and they which are fallen asleep in CHRIST are perished.....But now *is* CHRIST risen!" and what a gush of blessed consequences flow from that verity! "As in Adam all die, even so in CHRIST shall all be made alive." This is the argument of our own faith ; this is our prevailing consolation on

<hr>

9 1 Cor. xv. 17.

behalf of those for whom we are tempted to sorrow selfishly ; as if any thing short of our own falling away could separate us from those which sleep in JESUS. This makes our Easter Day the Festival, primarily indeed of our LORD, as HE rose in His own personality ; but also of His whole Church and Body,—of all those who have died with HIM to live again, —of all who, whether in their warfare here, or having entered into their rest, are living to HIM and in HIM.

And these things are an allegory,—in the same sense in which the facts of Abraham's history become an allegory in the teaching of St. Paul [10],—full of deep and spiritual meaning : but which would have been no meaning whatsoever, had not the plain truth of the facts been first established. Thus these things, as soon as their objective truth is realized,—but not before,—become an allegory pregnant with practical teaching, warning, encouragement for our guidance. The lesson of our rising to holiness of life is deduced from our *having* risen with CHRIST ; and it is enforced from our having yet to rise after the

[10] Gal. iv. 24.

likeness of His Resurrection. And we are
referred to the record of His sojourn upon
earth after HE rose from the dead, as a pattern by which to shape our own Christian
life " in the world," but "not of the world,"[11]
having the sphere of our duties on earth, but
our citizenship and conversation in Heaven.
This is to be the example of the change which
is wrought in our position, and must be
wrought in our hearts, through our oneness
with HIM Who in the days of His flesh dwelt
amongst His creatures as in a tabernacle[12];
but Who now, since and by virtue of His
Resurrection and Ascension, dwells in us in
a way infinitely transcending His local and
bodily presence with His disciples when HE
as yet went in and out amongst them.

We are not to understand St. Paul as ac-
knowledging the least shade of uncertainty,
with reference to this application of CHRIST'S
resurrection, in the words of the text. He had
not so learned CHRIST, neither did he so preach
HIM. His Gospel had already in the pre-
ceding chapter been stated without an " if."

11 St. John xvii. 11, 14 ; Philipp. iii. 20.
12 'Εσκήνωσεν ἐν ἡμῖν, St. John i. 14.

"As ye have received CHRIST JESUS the LORD, so walk ye in HIM." " Ye are complete in HIM, Which is the Head of all principality and power : in Whom also ye are circumcised with the circumcision made without hands, in putting off the body of the sins of the flesh by the circumcision of CHRIST : buried with HIM in Baptism, wherein also ye are risen with HIM, through the faith of the operation of GOD, Who hath raised HIM from the dead. And you, being dead in your sins and the uncircumcision of your flesh, hath HE (the FATHER) quickened together with HIM (CHRIST), having forgiven you all trespasses" [13].

Under the old Covenant, the children of those who had been once baptized,—whether of the Fathers who had been " baptized unto Moses in the cloud and in the sea," [14] or of those who from time to time submitted to that ordinance on becoming proselytes,—were counted as baptized in their forefathers' baptism, but received in their own persons the seal of circumcision. Conversely, the Colossians are here taught that they who are baptized into CHRIST and made one with HIM;

[13] Coloss. ii. 6, 10–13.   [14] 1 Cor. x. 2.

E 2

become thereby partakers of His, the true circumcision,—that inheritance of Abraham's seed which is His, and thereby, thanks be to GOD, becomes theirs.

And therefore the Apostle says to us, as he said to the Christians of Colossae, with no doubtful meaning, " If ye be," as indeed ye are, " risen with CHRIST, seek those things which are above." And to us in like manner, in the unity of the same hope, in the communion of the same blessings, he speaks in other passages of kindred meaning ; such as, " Blessed be the GOD and FATHER of our LORD JESUS CHRIST, Who hath blessed us with all spiritual blessings in heavenly places in CHRIST, ... even as HE raised HIM from the dead, and set HIM at His own right hand in the Heavenly places"..." GOD hath quickened us together in CHRIST, ... and hath raised us up together, and made us sit together in Heavenly places in CHRIST JESUS."[15] This is the " Heavenly calling," in virtue of their " partaking" of which, he addresses the Hebrews as " holy brethren :" this is the " Heavenly

---

[15] Eph. i. 3, 20 ; ii. 6.

gift," whereof he reminds them that they had " tasted," being made " partakers of the HOLY GHOST."[16]

Our great object then, " if we be risen with CHRIST" and in HIM, must be to trace His steps, that we may follow HIM and be with HIM. And as soon as we begin to do this, from the time of His rising again, we find ourselves at once placed in a different world.— HE is indeed still upon the earth ; but no longer as before ; no longer as if it were His home. HE is among His disciples, to comfort their sorrow, to strengthen their faith, to enlighten their spirits ; but not " to go in and out among them ;" not, even with *them*, to be united in the old bond of brotherhood, " as he that serveth."—HE comes, they see not whence ; HE passes away, they know not how :—a little while, and they see HIM ; and again a little while, and they see HIM not.—HE " appears to them ;" and that, " in another form," so that their eyes are holden, and they know HIM not in this transfiguration ;—only, their hearts burn within them when HE talketh by

[16] Hebr. iii. 1 ; vi. 4.

the way."[17]   Freed from the bondage of the
elements of this world, and walking at large
amidst material obstacles, as though they were
not[18], in the truth and identity of that Body
which had been nailed to the Cross, His presence carries Heaven with HIM whithersoever
HE moves ; and His speech is " of the things
pertaining to the Kingdom of GOD."[19]—Before
His death HE had shewn HIMSELF, as upon
the earth, and rising from it to teach us how
to rise.—After His Resurrection HE rather
reveals HIMSELF as stooping from Heaven,—
plunging (if we may so speak without irre-
verence) into a grosser element than that of
His own existence ; and not without effort
resisting the tendency to re-ascend on high ;
—as lingering a while, hovering, like the bird
over her nestlings, till HE has wrought His
Holy and Blessed work in the hearts of His
chosen : so that when HE finally ascends from
Mount Olivet, we view it less as a rising
from the earth, than as a severing of some

[17] Acts i. 21 ; St. Luke xxii. 27 ; St. Mark xvi. 12.
[18] St. Luke xxiv. 16, 32.
[19] St. John xx. 19, 26 ; Acts i. 3.

bond which had detained HIM in its atmosphere.

And what is this stooping and condescension meant to effect? What is the attraction powerful enough to arrest His heavenward course, making Heaven and Earth kiss each other while HE thus seems to waver between them? His work of Redemption is finished; and the victory over him that had the power of death is complete. His Resurrection is manifest; and the witnesses, chosen before of GOD, are prepared to bear their testimony. Yet still HE lingers.—Not, surely, without an object:—not from mere human sympathy with those whom HE has already taught that it is expedient that HE should go, that the Comforter may come to them. The object was, we may believe, twofold,—twofold, yet one. First, to prepare the redeemed Believers for that kingdom of Heaven upon earth which was even then ready to be revealed, and was to be inaugurated "not many days thence" by the visible outpouring of the HOLY SPIRIT to crown the Sacrament of Baptism which in the meantime HE instituted. And next, to mould their spirits, individually, for the Kingdom which was to come, by the spiritual power and virtue of that His mysterious communion with them.

And this latter object it was, which was present to the Apostle's thoughts when he wrote the Exhortation, that we should seek those things which are above, *because* we are risen with Christ.—If we are indeed heirs of that glory into which He has re-entered to prepare a place for us, it is ours, while we still remain on earth, to set before us for a pattern Jesus Christ; and Him, not only humbled, not only crucified, not only buried; —but Him, risen from the dead; Him in His glorified nature; Him, only lingering upon earth to do His work and to fulfil His mission, but no longer, even in His human nature, of the earth, earthy. This is our privilege: but it is, besides, our duty.—It is the needful step on our road from earth to Heaven. We are upon the earth: but we are inheritors of the kingdom of Heaven; destined for it; in training for it. Heirs we are; but we shall never enter upon the perfect fruition of our heritage, unless, under the guidance of the Holy Spirit of God, we go on thus in our

preparation. For there is an essential dis-
agreement, issuing in a perpetual conflict, between this world and the next, between the
kingdom of darkness and that of light: so
that, if we are conformed to this world, which
passes away, leaving no other monument of
its existence than the foundations of eternal
happiness or misery which have been laid in it,
we are unfitted, and (whenever we may be
taken hence) we shall be unfit for the enjoy-
ment of the inheritance and the kingdom
which are provided for us.

Provided, they are. The place is found:
the banquet is made ready: the inheritance
is there: the way is cast up, and our feet
are placed in it. HE has done His part
in preparing, and inviting, and summon-
ing; in teaching, in warning, in threaten-
ing. But HE does not (may we not say
that according to His wisdom, justice and
mercy HE cannot?) make mere machines
of us. And therefore HE does not bring us
into the fruition of His own presence, without
that conquest and utter destruction of the
power of the Prince of this world within us,
which HE begins here by the first gift of spi-

ritual life, and ever, day by day, helps on by further gifts according to our use of that which He has given before : nay, helps on, daily and hourly, in unwearied mercy and unexhausted love, even while all is wasted, despised and mocked ; when nothing but the depth of our spiritual misery remains to draw towards us the overflowings of His compassion ;—even up to that very last hour, when its further indulgence would confound good and evil, right and wrong.

We may not fix a time or set a limit for this operation of God's saving grace in Christ. He can see, even in the last hour of a sinner's dying agony, whether the heart is really changed or no. He sees the end with the beginning,—ay, sees that which would have been, though it is not ; and calls the things that are not, as though they were. And therefore, even on the sinner's death-bed, if there be repentance, we are permitted, yea, we are commanded to hope, though it may be hard to say where despair ends and hope begins ! But this is sure, that either in health or sickness, either in life or at death, that momentous change of heart must be effected; the germ which is planted within us in Baptism, must have expanded into active, energetic life within,—must have overcome the corruption which is in the world through lust, yea, which *is* even in the regenerate, warring against the law of the SPIRIT. Unless, before we die *from* this world, we have already died *to* the things of this world, so that, preparatory to our rising again with CHRIST, we have risen to newness of heart and life in CHRIST, it is useless, Oh, how far worse than useless! for us to rest upon our Christian privileges, and to claim the heritage which has been prepared for us.

GOD has indeed prepared it for us, and has been preparing *us* for *it*, in CHRIST.— And HE has striven and is striving, by the SPIRIT of His SON, against the natural corruption of each one of us, to make His gift effectual.

But Paradise was not for the evil Spirit; and the hell of that Spirit's own nature was but stirred within him when he entered there. Much less is the place of the Holy One's own presence in Heaven for such as would carry thither the spirit of this world. It is not that the mercy of GOD is limited, or that HE would not have all men to be saved. What good thing can HE withhold, Who hath not withheld His own dearly beloved SON? But HE gave HIM, to bring us towards Heaven. HE has bridged over the great gulf between it and us: HE has set the ladder up on earth, whose top reaches to Heaven. It is for us to look forwards, to look upwards. It is for us to fix our eyes, our thoughts, our hearts on the things which are to be revealed in their season. It is for us to set our affection on things above, not on things on the earth;—to set our affection *there* with a devotion so intense as to set us wholly in motion, body and soul and spirit, to climb thither.

Widely different indeed are the feelings, is the behaviour of too many who call themselves Christians. How is it, brethren, with *us*? When we look back on the past so as to be able to form an estimate of it, do we not often feel in ourselves that the greatest of our exertions has only been to lay one hand, perhaps to plant one foot, on the lowest step of the ladder of Beth-El? And how is this? Is it not, because we have not lifted up our hearts?

Our heads are turned backwards; our eyes
are cast downwards; because our hearts are
like those of the Israelites in the wilderness,
already at the first effort and trial turning
back again to the fleshpots of Egypt[20], the
pleasures of sense, the temptations of the
world.   Alas, for those who have so soon forgotten the warning, "No man having put his
hand to the plough, and looking back, is fit
for the Kingdom of GOD."[21]   "Fit for it!"
How can *he* be fit, who does not even desire
it ? How can *he* be fit, whose affection is set on
things on the earth ; and who would fain live
again to the world, after he has once died to
it ;—to live a living death ; in corruption
here, the *life* which stirs and creeps in a de-
caying corpse ; in torment hereafter, the *death*
where the worm dieth not.

But you are called upon to remember that
you are not only dead, but risen again ; risen
again with CHRIST, and having your life dead
to the world only to be hidden with HIM
in GOD.   Your hand, your foot is on the ladder, and that not of yourselves ; for HE has
placed them there.   Turn not then ; look not

[20] Exod. xvi. 3.   [21] St. Luke ix. 62.

back! Lay aside every weight, every sin which besets you, every load of thick clay which would cumber you. Lift up your hearts; yea, lift them up unto the LORD! Lift them up, that they may be there, even where your exceeding great treasure is! Lift your voices up, to call upon the LORD for help, and to praise His name with holy songs, in faithful anticipation of the heavenly hymn, "Alleluia, the LORD GOD omnipotent reign-eth!"[22]—Lift up the hands which hang down, and the feeble knees, though the climb be long and steep. Lift up your eyes, to see the angels ascending and descending on their blessed errands of obedience and love, to mi-nister to you and all the heirs of salvation. Lift them up with the glance of faith, till they pierce the mists and clouds that veil your heavenward course; till they behold HIM Who has gone before to prepare a place for you, and Who now looks down from the throne of His Father's glory, as HE looked on His first martyr, to help your weary steps with the right hand of His power; to melt away the load of your sins with the sunlight

[22] Revel. xix. 6.

of His countenance ; and, when earth and
the things of earth shall pass away, to receive you into those everlasting habitations,
where HE Himself sitteth at the right hand
of the FATHER.

SERMON IV.

THE SIN AGAINST THE HOLY GHOST.

Preached on Whitsunday, 1855.

St. Matt. xii. 31, 32.

I say unto you, All manner of sin and blasphemy shall be forgiven unto men: but the blasphemy against the HOLY GHOST shall not be forgiven unto men. And whosoever speaketh a word against the Son of Man, it shall be forgiven him: but whosoever speaketh against the HOLY GHOST, it shall not be forgiven him, neither in this world, neither in the world to come.

THESE words sound so awfully, that many have shrunk from the vague terror of their possible meaning; and so mysteriously, that many others have lost themselves in unfruitful speculations upon the object of them. Yet, surely, both have erred, and both must suffer loss. For they are the words of JESUS CHRIST; spoken for the warning of those who surrounded HIM at the time; written afterwards under the inspiration of the HOLY SPIRIT; thrice written by three several Evangelists[1], at a time when the generation which heard them spoken was vanishing away,—for all succeeding ages of the Church.

It becomes us, then, to approach their consideration with awe; yet still, to approach, and to search into the depths of their meaning; but as those who look for a blessing upon their enquiry only in proportion to the humility with which it is conducted; as feeling that it may prove to be no matter of abstract speculation, but a question of life and death, of Heaven and Hell.

It is true that the words were originally addressed to the Jewish gainsayers in the days of our LORD's ministry; and that, until HE returns again, we expect no such collision between the Powers of Heaven and Hell, no such demonstration of the Spirit of Good and of the Spirit of Evil, as was then produced by the presence of " GOD manifest in the flesh" to redeem the world from the power of the Enemy.

But why is it, that there is preserved to us

---

[1] St. Matt. xii. 31, 32 ; St. Mark iii. 28–30 ; St. Luke xii. 10.

F

the record of these battlings with the Evil One, and these reasonings with his children? And why, of the small volume of our Blessed LORD's sayings and doings, is so much taken up with that which never can be literally repeated? Is it not because those things which cannot be repeated in the letter, are yet repeated continually? The same searchings of heart go on : the same combat is renewed : the same SPIRIT of GOD is met by the same Spirit of blasphemy, day by day, even to the end of the world. As men change their fashions, but not their nature; so through all vicissitudes of time and varied trappings of circumstance, mankind are ever acting afresh the same tragedy which has been a spectacle to angels from the beginning.

Let us put away, then, all coward unwillingness to enquire into the meaning of that which our SAVIOUR spoke, and which His SPIRIT has recorded for our learning and instruction. But let us also put away, by His help, all vain curiosity; and, especially, all intrusiveness of enquiry into the destiny of those to whom the words were spoken; except so far as the examination of our own position makes it necessary to attend to theirs. It is not because this sentence was spoken to the Jews, that we are to occupy ourselves with it. It is because, if the sentence had not in some solemn way applied to our own position, it would not have been there, where it stands, for us to occupy ourselves with.

When the Pharisees and Scribes declared that our LORD cast out an unclean Spirit by the help of Beelzebub the prince of the Devils, HE pointed out the irrational nature of their assertion, that the Supreme and Central Power of Evil, that very Spirit in whom consists the unity and body politic (so to speak) of the kingdom of Darkness, could without self-annihilation divide himself and make his members go to buffets. And then HE turned upon the blasphemers, and spoke, whether in warning or in judgment, the words which have been read to you. These have been thought by some to refer to a passage in the Book of Leviticus[2], where we read that " whosoever curseth *his GOD* shall bear his sin ; and he that blasphemeth *the name of the*

[2] Ch. xxiv. 15, 16 ; v. Nitzsch, Christliche Lehre, 143, note.

LORD, he shall surely be put to death, and all the congregation shall certainly stone him :"— where it has been supposed, that there is a distinction between the merely *punishable* nature of the one offence and the *unpardonable* character of the other, corresponding with the distinction between the more general expression " his GOD" (אֱלֹהָיו) and " the name of JEHOVAH," the awful, almost unutterable name in which was the hope and the fear of the children of Israel. At all events, those who were conversant with this portion of the Law, would be prepared to receive and appreciate the difference here made between all other sin and blasphemy, even that which is spoken against the SON of Man, and the sin against the HOLY SPIRIT. Again, it has been plausibly argued[3], that "sin" and "blasphemy" are the distinctive expressions for all sins against our neighbour and against GOD respectively. We need not, indeed, maintain this: although it may be admitted that whereas sins against the second table reach their completion in act, it is not always so with sins against the first. Evil words, among men, may grow to evil

---

3 By Olshausen, Bibl. Comment., in loco.

deeds : but reversely, against GOD, it is disobedience which culminates in blasphemy. But the force of the expressions " blasphemy,"—" whosoever speaketh a word against the SON of Man, . . against the HOLY GHOST," requires to be considered : and the whole tenor of the narrative gives us an unbroken clue to the right interpretation. The sin of the Pharisees which gave rise to the rebuke, was a sin of the tongue ; and there was a manifest reluctance among them to recognise the same duties and responsibility as attaching to their words, which they professed to acknowledge in their actions. CHRIST therefore shews what fearful sins the tongue may commit. And then (which is still more important) HE shews how this comes to be so ; because the words are the fruit of that tree which is rooted in the heart, the most direct proofs of its corruption. Blasphemy, then, is not severed from all other sins against GOD ; but it is indicated as the natural outpouring of the heart which is possessed by the most malignant Spirit of Evil ; as being, of all modes of sin, the most significant, from its infallible connexion with the inner man. It is the flash which tells what is taking place in the chamber of the mine.

Those words therefore of the Pharisees which drew from the Blessed JESUS such a denunciation, must have contained a very terrible sin, and indicated the presence and the possession of a grievous spirit of blasphemy. And we can scarcely avoid the question, however willingly we would leave it untouched, Of which character was their blasphemy? Was it, or was it not, the sin which never can be forgiven, either in this world or in the world to come?

And in approaching the answer to this question, it is necessary to consider their position. They were not Gentiles, but children of Israel. They were not of the ten rebellious tribes, who seemed to be already cast off; but of that loyal and faithful seed, to which light arose out of darkness, and redemption out of captivity. They were not as the common multitude among their brethren, " which knew not the law;" but of that influential class which claimed to be the teachers of babes, and counted their humbler brethren accursed for their ignorance's sake[4]. .They were not of those to whom the word of the LORD had not come. They had the oracles of the Prophets,—nay, they had the personal revelation of the Living WORD Who had spoken by all these ; they had watched His goings, listened to His teaching, seen the miracles of His mercy,—even His triumphs over evil Spirits, and the deliverance of *their* captives from bondage. Every one of these specialities implied additional insight into GOD's dealings with men, and involved an additional privilege of His giving.

Now, it will scarcely be asserted that Gentiles, *as such*,—those who had never had the knowledge of GOD imparted to them,—could in any correct sense be said to blaspheme HIM. Such persons might be ignorant, degraded and superstitious : they might be grovelling in spiritual darkness and moral uncleanness ; —but *blasphemers* of a GOD of whom they had never heard, they could not be. It is in exact proportion to the knowledge of GOD which men have received, that they can blaspheme HIM.

The Jews were a people of glorious privi-

<hr>

4 St. John vii. 49.

leges ; and on that very account they could blaspheme GOD in a sense in which the Gentiles could not. But this is not all. The same argument shews that each generation among them, to whom new revelations of the essence and the will of GOD were made, could thus sin more awfully than their predecessors. All the Prophets of the Old Testament contributed to swell the amount of their responsibility : John the Baptist yet more :—but the coming of the SON of Man most of all. The Very Light was then come into the world. Would they,—and particularly would the masters in Israel,—come to the light ? Or would they hug themselves in their darkness, while yet they said that they saw ?

They made their choice ; and we know what a fearful choice it was. They avowed it in blasphemy undeniable ; but against whom ?—Against GOD and HIS SON, the SON of Man.

Was it also against the HOLY GHOST ?

Doubtless, in one sense at least, it was ; in virtue of the Personal Godhead of that HOLY SPIRIT, and His essential Unity with the FATHER and the SON. But here we must draw

a distinction ; for our Lord Himself has drawn
one ;—a distinction which would be ground-
less and unmeaning, if that doctrine were true,
according to which the Son and the Holy Ghost
are explained as mere Modes by which the
one God has communicated His will and revealed His Person to men,—as mere accom-
modations and condescensions to the imperfection of human Metaphysics, but not *Beings*,
not *Persons*, as these words are understood, I
will not say by Catholic theology, but by
common sense. Christ teaches us here that
as we may blaspheme the Son, so we may
blaspheme the Holy Ghost ; and that there
is a distinction between these sins, dependent
on the distinction between the Persons against
whom they are committed.

The Jews had evidently committed the one
sin : and from the words added by St. Mark[5],
" Because they said, He hath an unclean Spirit," it may be, indeed it has been inferred,
that they had fallen into the other ; having
by implication called the Spirit of God an unclean Spirit.

Yet, perhaps, even here the more charit-

<hr>

5 Ch. iii. 30.

able judgment may prove to be the more true. Their guilt was in proportion to their knowledge ; and this was measured by the progressive character of GOD's revelation of Himself. The Unity of the Godhead and the Person of JEHOVAH were clearly declared throughout the older Covenant. *We* can read there also undoubted revelations of the SON and of the HOLY GHOST. But it does not necessarily follow that the Jews could read this with equal clearness or certainty. In fact, we know that the great majority of them were unable to do so. There were hints, indications, promises : there were hopes held out of that which was to come : and, by the grace of GOD, these were gradually made more and more effectual, to enlighten the hearts of such as would receive them ; dawning even into actual revelations of the Dayspring from on high, to meet and reward the eagle glance and eagle wing of saintly faith. But if in ordinary cases all this fell far short of actual knowledge even of the WORD of GOD as a Divine Person, what shall we say touching a belief in the HOLY GHOST as a consubstantial and coequal Person in the ever blessed Trinity ? The revelation was gradual. The FATHER sent the SON ; but first prepared the way before HIM. And the SON, in sending from the FATHER the HOLY GHOST the Comforter, used the like preparation. " The Spirit of the LORD " is indeed frequently spoken of in the Old Testament. But who shall blame those who, while as yet the Spirit was not given, " because JESUS was not yet glorified,"[6] did not understand the words as implying more than the Operation, or the Grace of GOD ? If of any Saint of the older dispensation we might venture to say that his insight into the mystery of the Divine nature was deep, surely it would be of him, who saw the SPIRIT of GOD descending like a dove and lighting upon JESUS,—who heard the voice from Heaven saying, " This is My Beloved SON ! " And yet, what was the Baptist's preaching ? He was the Forerunner of the Messiah ; but he had no message to deliver of the Comforter. And when years had passed, and St. Paul wondered to find certain disciples at Ephesus, who knew not so much as whether there were any HOLY GHOST,—the

6 St. John vii. 39.

explanation of their ignorance was, that they had been baptized " unto *John's Baptism.*[7]"

We are permitted, then, to believe that, though the guilt of these Jews was deep, and their ignorance may have been wilful,—though they were manifestly tending to plunge into the irremediable sin,—there was still hope, still a place of repentance[8]; and that the words of CHRIST are a call to repentance ;—a last call, perhaps, and as of one hoping against hope ; but still a warning, not a peremptory condemnation. For let us remember that, when these words were uttered, the revelation even of the Second Person of the Trinity was not yet complete. Though His words were such as never man spake,—though His works were such as no man could do unless the FATHER were with him ; yet what was all that had gone before, in comparison of that which was to come ? At this time Gethsemane and Golgotha were but common words. The " tomb in a garden " was as yet

---

[7] Acts xix. 1-3.

[8] Compare St. John xvi. 2 ; and note CHRIST's prayer for them on the Cross.

an allegory of a lost Paradise, not an evidence of its Recovery. The Mount of Olives had still to receive the last print of the ascending SAVIOUR's feet. May we not, must we not believe that for many, even of those who had up to this time rejected His warnings and exhortations, the whole of these later miracles of mercy and proofs of Redemption were not in vain. Must we not confess that, as the Jews were privileged above the Gentiles, and the Jews who beheld our LORD above their forefathers,—so those who lived to witness the Passion week, the Easter morning, the forty days of the sojourn of the glorified SAVIOUR, and the Ascension up on high which crowned that period, were higher in knowledge, in privilege, and, therefore, in peril also, than any could be at the time when the words of our text were spoken by JESUS CHRIST.

And yet, when all this had occurred, the Comforter *was not yet come!* HE Who had been so awfully proclaimed, could not be revealed until JESUS was glorified. HE was yet to come, to make the revelation of the Deity complete ; to bring the believers into communion with GOD ; to give life to the Church's organization, by uniting and sanctifying the members of CHRIST in His mystical Body ; to sum up all the dispensations of Divine Providence ;—making this " the last time,"—these " the last days ;" bringing upon us " the ends of the world ;"[9] because we have to look for no further confirmation of faith, no further communication of knowledge, no further sacrifice for sin, since the Day of Pentecost has consummated the mighty work, and revealed the Godhead in Trinity, as the Creator, the Redeemer, and the Sanctifier.

And as it was not until this day that GOD vouchsafed to reveal (as fully as our imperfect capacities admit) His whole Essence and His complete work ; so the full measure of their iniquity who would not repent, was only then filled up, when the complete revelation had been made, and the final gift had been given ; —when those who had ascribed CHRIST'S miracles to Beelzebub, and had accused His disciples of stealing His body, went on to mock the utterances of the HOLY GHOST as the babblings of drunkenness. Surely we are not unwarranted in characterizing the scoff of the

9 1 St. John ii. 18 ; Hebr. i. 2 ; 1 Cor. x. 11.

day of Pentecost, " These men are full of new wine," as the key-note of the blasphemy,—as the type and embodiment of the new mystery of iniquity working in these last days with the fury of a last struggle in a time that is short. No sooner was the HOLY SPIRIT revealed to the world, than by the world HE was blasphemed. Scarcely was HE given to the Church, when within the bosom of the Church HE was sinned against. And the deaths of Ananias and Sapphira, and the curse, scarcely less awful, of Simon the sorcerer, seem to inaugurate the dispensation wherein the Sin against the HOLY GHOST became a reality, and its punishment a fact[10]. We seem at last to hear the voice of One who had gone into a far country to receive for Himself a kingdom, and had returned, saying, " Those mine enemies, which would not that I should reign over them, bring hither, and slay them before me."[11]

We have thus been led, step by step, to connect this terrible sin with the times of the Christian, rather than those of the Jewish dispensation ;—to connect it, indeed, in the

[10] Acts ii. 13 ; v. 3,9 ; viii. 20–23.   [11] St. Luke xix. 12, 27.

most literal sense, with that particular age in which the miraculous outpourings of the SPIRIT challenged the belief of the world, and stirred up the malice of the Adversary ; but, generally, with the Christian dispensation, as the period in which that HOLY SPIRIT has His work,—from the day when the SON fulfilled His parting promise, even until the day when HE shall again stand upon the earth in judgment. By the HOLY SPIRIT, in the mean season, CHRIST is present with His Church. By His inspiration the whole Body of CHRIST is informed and quickened. HE it is, who has breathed into every member of CHRIST the breath of spiritual life. If, then, there was a cumulative load of guilt on the unbelieving and rebellious among the Jews, ever growing, from the era of their first national adoption to the crowning revelation of the Day of Pentecost,—what shall we say of Christians, if they have received the grace of GOD in vain ? What, but that which JESUS CHRIST Himself said of Capernaum, of Chorazin and of Bethsaida, as compared with Tyre and Sidon and the cities of the plain ? What, but that which His Apostle has said of the angels which kept not *their* first estate,—who found no Mediator for them with the FATHER, no Sacrifice or Atonement for their sin, which had been committed in the full blaze of Heavenly light and glory? And in saying this, we are but repeating what the Apostles of CHRIST thought it necessary to say to their immediate disciples, of the awful nature of a reprobate Christian's guilt. Have we not heard of the impossibility of renewing again unto repentance those who have been made partakers of the HOLY GHOST, and then have fallen away [12]? Are we not warned that if we sin wilfully after that we have received the knowledge of the truth, there remaineth no more sacrifice for sins [13]? Are we not led to contrast, as signs of the times, the SAVIOUR's prayer for those who crucified HIM, with the recognition by His beloved Disciple of a " sin unto death," for which we are not even bidden to pray [14]?

Not without a cause, then, do we treat this as an enquiry intensely practical to Christian men,—as one in which we have no mere intellectual and speculative interest, but as deal-

---

[12] Hebr. vi. 4, 5, 6.   [13] Hebr. x. 26.
[14] St. Luke xxiii. 34 ; 1 St. John v. 16.

ing with a sin which we may commit, and a judgment that we need to shun.

But in this new phase of our subject, the same principles which have hitherto guided us, will still stand us in stead. They will make us humble and cautious in stepping onward : they will teach us that we are not to run to and fro, flinging about the reproach of the unforgiven sin as a mortal weapon of offence,—denouncing this man's or that man's transgressions, in proportion as our own temper and temptations make us more sensitive to the enormity of one form of sin or another. We have received that which is meant for a light to guide our own steps clear of danger. We must not use it as a firebrand to consume our neighbour's life and living. Wisely, indeed, has one of our Church's Articles declared that "not every deadly sin willingly committed after Baptism is sin against the HOLY GHOST, and unpardonable."[15] In this sentence we can see at once, what caution had been found necessary, lest our LORD's words should be abused to justify an uncharitable dogma-

[15] Article XVI.

tism ; and with what lively jealousy the terrors of those words have been maintained against a licentious indifference. "*Not every sin*"—though "*deadly*"—though "*wilful*"—though "*committed after Baptism*"—"is *unpardonable!*" Truly, a perilous warranty for a baptized Christian to continue in sin! Nay, do not the very necessity of the declaration, and its cautious form, rather add to our sense of the nearness of such sins to that which is unpardonable? And not without reason ; if we have been right in refusing to acquiesce in such a meagre interpretation of CHRIST's words, as would limit their application to one only generation of mankind ; if we have been right in our adoption of a standard whereby to measure the sinfulness of our own sin. Does not sin become exceeding sinful, in proportion to the knowledge of GOD's hatred of it ? Does it not approach to the unpardonable, in proportion as those who continue in it have been brought near to GOD ? If, then, any sin be irremediable, it can only be so, because it has done despite to all the mercies of GOD in CHRIST. If any sin more directly than another be committed against the HOLY

GHOST, it can only be because it is more directly than any other an outrage upon GOD's Majesty, in His fullest manifestation of Himself, and His nearest relation to His people.

Now this is, in other words, to assert that the sins of those to whom the mystery of the adorable Trinity has been made known by faith, and who have been made partakers of the privileges of Baptism, shew most likeness to this abomination. We need not rake up the embers of a controversy which once agitated the Protestants of the continent,—*whether it be the regenerate alone, or the unregenerate alone, who can really commit this definitely unpardonable sin.* Truly, questions of deepest import are here broached : but as regards our present subject, they dwindle into a criticism of words and definitions. If regeneration imply, as the Calvinists meant, the indefeasible grace of final perseverance, then indeed it is a pointless truism to say that the recipients of this gift cannot sin beyond forgiveness. But if it places us, as our own Church's Catechism teaches, in " a state of salvation," in which we have to "pray that we may continue" through a continual renewal, then the Lutherans were justified in replying that those who sin against the greatest amount of grace, approach the nearest to the sin which cannot be forgiven [16]. For he who has received the HOLY SPIRIT, is the person who, if any, can grieve the SPIRIT, can rebel against HIM, can quench His influence. He whom the indwelling of that SPIRIT has once made to be a holy Temple of the LORD, is the person who, if any, may incur destruction for having defiled that Temple [17].

But does this imply that there is any one distinct species of sin which is irremediable? It does not. Blessed be GOD and the FATHER of our LORD JESUS CHRIST, there is none. It is a faithful saying and worthy of all acceptation, that the SON of GOD came into the world to save sinners, and that His blood cleanseth from *all* sin [18]. It is not partially that the fountain of mercy has been opened.

[16] Quenstedt, quoted in Müller on Sin, 2. p. 480 (Engl. Transl.); Tholuck on Hebr. vi. 4, and Vermischte Schriften, 2. 461 sq. See Studien u. Kritiken, 1833, p. 935 sq.; 1834, p. 599 sq.; and Nitzsch, Christliche Lehre, as before.

[17] Ephes. iv. 30; 1 Thess. v. 19; 1 Cor. iii. 16, 17.

[18] 1 John i. 7.

From of old, the promise of the Gospel had been, " Though your sins be as scarlet, they shall be as white as snow."[19]

Nor is this any contradiction of what has been said above. Nay, it is not even a mystery beyond our powers to understand. For, as we believe that our relation to the HOLY GHOST makes all our sin approach so much nearer to the sin against HIM, we are led to infer that this enhancement applies to all manner of sin equally,—that no individual act, or particular description of sin in itself can claim the bad pre-eminence of that fearful title. We have to guard ourselves on both sides. On the one hand, There is no sin to which we dare, as Christians, to affix this condemnation. On the other, There is no sin of which, in Christians, we can affirm that it is secure against it. It is not ours to pry curiously into the point at which sin ceases to be pardonable. This has been reserved in mercy by HIM who is to judge us; that no sinner may make his sin unpardonable by despairing of forgiveness. It is better, surely, for us to hold to the conviction that there

<hr>

[19] Isaiah i. 18.

is no absolute line or point of division, no gulf
fixed between certain sins and certain others ;
but that (to adapt again our phraseology to
that of our Articles) to us all sin is deadly ;
but, through JESUS CHRIST, not every *deadly*
sin is *death*. As we stand in a relation to
the HOLY GHOST, the sinfulness of our sin is
relative also. And whatsoever avails most to
quench the SPIRIT within us,—whatsoever
tends most to make the grace of GOD of none
effect, and to root out our faith in HIM,
this must come nearest to the awful guilt
spoken of in the text. But this need not be,
cannot be, in all men one and the same description of sin. Rather, it resides not so
much in the actual transgression objectively,
as in the state of the sinner's mind to God-
ward, wrought by the power of sin.

It can indeed hardly be denied that there
are certain classes of sins which seem to bear
more prominently than others the mark of
sins against the HOLY GHOST, short of the
actual blasphemy. Such, it may be admitted,
are those which tend especially to direct rebellion against GOD, or to the hardening of
the sinner's heart against HIM,—τὸ ἐκ παρα-

τάξεως ἁμαρτάνειν[20]. May we not say that the former class embraces sins of pride and presumption, as being the most direct inspiration of the Evil Spirit (" ye shall be as gods"), and the nearest approximation, of which human nature is capable, to the guilt of rebellious angels? May we not include among the latter, those sins of fleshly uncleanness and lasciviousness, which, as even Heathen wisdom taught, deaden the heart and chain the very intellect to earth; but of which we, as Christians, know yet further *what* and *how* they work; because our body is the Temple of the Holy Ghost; and the Spirit of God dwelleth in us: and if any man defile the Temple of God, him shall God destroy[21].

But even to these sins we can only ascribe such a character, in so far as they appear to be specially energetic in producing an evil state of heart;—a state to which all descriptions of sin tend in their degree. Not as if these, or any sins had power to bar the efficacy of the Saviour's blood; not

[20] Constit. Apost. 2. § 23, ἐάν τις ἐκ παρατάξεως ἁμαρτάνῃ πειράζων τὸν Θεὸν ὡς μὴ ἐπεξιόντα τοῖς πονηροῖς, ὁ τοιοῦτος ἄφεσιν οὐκ ἔχει.   [21] 1 Cor. iii. 16; vi. 19.

as though they *were* the sin which cannot be forgiven ; but as being especially liable to the aggravation which makes all or any sin unpardonable. Would GOD indeed, that this thought might find its way into the hearts of some at least of those multitudes who are sunk in the sins of the flesh or of the mind, of youth or of age!—Haply, it might manifest to some a precipice of danger of which they had never dreamt. It might reveal to others the blessing of a hope that they had hitherto despised. It might whisper to the hearts and consciences of all, those words, at once gracious and awful, " *Neither do I condemn thee :—go, and sin no more.*"[22]

There seem to be two aggravations of sin, which belong especially to what St. Paul calls τὰ πνευματικὰ τῆς πονηρίας ἐν τοῖς ἐπουρανίοις[23] (I use the original words for reasons which those who compare them with our English version will appreciate) ;—Despair of forgiveness, and Hatred of HIM who can forgive. And these the ruler of the darkness of this world would fain produce in his captives, one or both of

[22] St. John viii. 11.   [23] Ephes. vi. 12.

them (for they will often be found to alternate the one with the other) ;—the hardness of heart which has become actively blasphemous ; or that more subtle form of sin which believes in an offended GOD, but has lost the power to believe in His readiness to forgive. All sin, in proportion to its hold on men, and its power to extinguish the graces of repentance and faith, tends to produce one or other of these states. Nor can it be deemed a breach of Christian charity to say that such a condition is " reprobate," and has no forgiveness to expect. Not that the LORD's hand is shortened ; not that the Blood of CHRIST has lost its healing virtue : but because such persons have lost that whereby they might lay hold on HIM ; they have lost the power to repent that they might be saved. They have rejected the assurance of GOD that " the Blood of CHRIST cleanseth from ALL sin ;" they have made GOD a liar, Who hath set forth His SON to be the propitiation for the sins of the whole world[24]. They have renounced the sacrifice which was offered for them. They have done despite to the SPIRIT of Grace which dwelt in

[24] 1 St. John i. 7 ; ii. 2.

them.   They have brought back into His
Temple seven other Spirits more wicked than
that which HE had first cast out.—" Against
this free gift, against the very grace of GOD
(says St. Augustine) doth the impenitent heart
lift its voice : and, therefore, *that* impenitence
is the blasphemy of the SPIRIT which shall
never be forgiven, neither in this world, neither in the world to come : ... for repentance
procures in this world forgiveness which shall
avail in the world to come."—And again, "How
shall *this* sin be forgiven, which hinders the
forgiveness of the rest ? All are forgiven to
those in whom is not found this which is unpardonable : but where this, which is unpardonable, is found, neither can others be forgiven ; for this is the bond which makes all
loosing impossible."[25]

Of such a case what could we say, but that
this is the sin unto death ?

[25] *S. August. Serm. ad Pop.* 71, § xii. (20), " Contra
hoc donum gratuitum, contra istam Dei gratiam loquitur
cor impoenitens.   Ipsa ergo impoenitentia est Spiritus
blasphemia quae non remittetur neque in hoc saeculo,
neque in futuro.   Contra Spiritum enim Sanctum, quo
baptizantur quorum peccata omnia dimittuntur, et quem
accepit Ecclesia," etc..... "Haec omnino impoenitentia non

But of whom *can* we say, that he is in such a case ? Surely, of none who are mourning over their sins. Nay, of none can we say it, even among those who are not yet mourning over them, so long as He Who would have all men to be saved, gives them still further time for repentance[26]. Not in vain is it written,

habet remissionem, neque in hoc saeculo, neque in futuro : quia poenitentia impetrat remissionem in hoc saeculo, quae valeat in futuro."

Ibid. xiii. (23), " Quomodo autem hoc dimittetur quod etiam remissionem impedit aliorum ? Omnia ergo dimittuntur eis in quibus hoc non est quod nunquam dimittetur : in quibus est autem, quoniam hoc nunquam dimittitur, nec alia dimittuntur ; quia omnium remissio vinculo istius impeditur."

[26] *S. Augustin. Ibid.* xiii. (22), " Sed ista impoenitentia vel cor impoenitens quamdiu quisque in hac carne vivit, non potest judicari. De nullo enim desperandum est, quamdiu patientia Dei ad poenitendum adducit, nec de hac vita rapit impium, Qui non vult mortem impii, quantum ut revertatur et vivat. Paganus est hodie : unde scis utrum sit futurus crastino Christianus ? Judaeus infidelis est hodie : quid si cras credat in Christum ? Haereticus est hodie : quid si cras sequatur Catholicam veritatem ? Schismaticus est hodie : quid si cras amplectatur Catholicam pacem ? Quid si isti, quos in quocunque genere erroris notas et tanquam desperatissimos damnas, ante quam finiant istam vitam, agant poenitentiam et inveniant veram vitam in futuro ? Proinde, fratres, etiam ad hoc vos admoneat,

"Judge nothing before the time, until the LORD come, Who both will bring to light the hidden things of darkness, and will make manifest the counsels of the hearts."[27] Is it not of deep significance, that although St. John says, " There is a sin unto death ; I do not say that he shall pray for it ;"[28] yet the SPIRIT by which he spoke did not reveal what that sin might be ; and by this expressive silence has licensed, ay, commanded us to pray for all the sins of all our brethren ? Is it not striking, that in the example which seemed to shew us the sin against the HOLY GHOST actually committed, even that Simon, who was " in the gall of bitterness and the bond of iniquity," was bidden to repent of his wickedness, and pray GOD, if perhaps the thought of his

quod ait Apostolus, Nolite ante tempus quidquam judicare. Haec enim blasphemia Spiritus cui nunquam est ulla re-missio (quam non omnem, sed quamdam intelleximus, eam-que perseverantem duritiam cordis impoenitentis vel diximus vel invenimus, vel etiam quantum existimamus, ostendimus) non potest in quoquam, ut diximus, dum in hac adhuc vita est, deprehendi."—Add also his *Retractation*. i. 19, 7, " Quoniam de quocumque pessimo in hac vita constituto non est utique desperandum ; nec pro illo imprudenter oratur, de quo non desperatur."

[27] 1 Cor. iv. 5.   [28] 1 St. John v. 16.

heart might be forgiven him.[29]   As though to teach by the most startling example, that while we *can* repent, while we *can* pray, the grace of pardon is correlative to the graces of penitence and prayer!

And if we turn to the passage already quoted from the Epistle to the Hebrews[30], which asserts the impossibility of renewing unto repentance those who have been once enlightened, and have tasted of the heavenly gift, and have been made partakers of the HOLY GHOST, and have tasted the good word of GOD, and the powers of the world to come, —and then, after all, have fallen away; we shall find the same wholesome comfort blended with its terrors, in proportion as we resolutely and faithfully embrace its doctrines in their fulness.   I will not stay to discuss the interpretation, which is to be found in Oecumenius, according to which we should translate the passage, " to renew them again unto repentance, by crucifying the SON of GOD and making HIM a public example afresh for their individual benefit;" or that other, though it be found in several of the

29 Acts viii. 22, 23.   30 Hebr. vi. 4–8.

Fathers[31] and some of the Reformers[32], which explains the words "renewing again," as meaning a *reiterated baptism*. I will not dwell on all the privileges, from the first grace in Baptism, up to the miraculous gifts in spiritual things, against which these reprobates must have sinned. I will not even dwell on the limitations, though plain and necessary, which the words of JESUS CHRIST Himself affixed to the word *impossible*, when HE had to combat the same inference of despondency arising from the same sense of overwhelming duty[33].

No! Let us not extenuate our responsibilities, our difficulties, our dangers. Let us not call the strait gate wide, or the narrow way broad. Let us realize all that has been given to us, all the powers for good that we have neglected, all the light against which we have sinned, all the influence of the HOLY SPIRIT which we have striven to make ineffectual. Let us contrast what we are, with what GOD

[31] E. g. Theodoret and Chrysostom on Ep. Hebr.; Athanasius, Epist. 4 ad Serapion. § 13 (p. 705 A); see Cramer's Catena on Hebr. vi. (p. 500, sqq.).

[32] See Hutchinson's *Image of God*, ch. 18 (p. 114, sq., Parker Society's edition.)

[33] St. Luke xviii. 27, and the parallel passages.

has commanded us, and CHRIST enabled us to
be. GOD forbid that we should salve our consciences by explaining away one jot or tittle
of that law which shall never pass. The
Gospel of CHRIST is a savour unto death as
well as unto life. It has divided mankind
into two classes, of them that are saved, and
them that perish[34]; and there is no third.
We must search which it is to us, not according to any criticism of minute portions
of the Apostle's language, but according to
the broad scope of his entire teaching. Else
the labouring conscience will refuse to be comforted; and the enquiring spirit will find neither rest for the sole of her foot, nor an olive-
branch to bring home to the ark of her refuge.

What is it then that is "impossible" for those
who have sinned against the light and grace
of GOD in the way which this Scripture describes?—" It is impossible to renew them
unto—*repentance.*" Let us well mark the
word! Let the humble and faithful, though
imperfect and inconsistent Christian mark it,
as a beacon to warn him of the possible end
of a Christian's inconsistencies. Let those
mark it, who live in hope of the future, yet

34 2 Cor. ii. 15, 16.

in carelessness for the present, counting on
some midway landing-place of repentance between a life of worldly and carnal pleasure
here, and one of heavenly holiness hereafter!
But more than all, let those mark the word,
who are overwhelmed with the true and deep
sense of their own sins and unworthiness, feeling the weight and misery of their burden,
and tempted to believe that for them renewal
and restoration are impossible. It may be that
they have lost the testimony of an approving
conscience; and that they have no longer the
comfort and joy in believing which once was
theirs. It may be, that their sins have gone
over their heads. But if any such there are
among those who hear me, I would fain say
to them, Even if this be so, have you lost the
sense of your sins?—Are you content to remain as you are? If you are tempted to think
that GOD has forgotten you, can you forget
HIM? Have you practically ceased to mourn
and bewail your sins as you would bewail them
if you felt that HE still heard you? Do you
not long to be freed from your burden?
Would you be willing to exchange your tears
and groanings and wounded spirit, for all the

light hardness of heart of those that "go down the primrose path to the everlasting fire?" O ye of little faith, why look abroad to seek for signs of that which is within you? Hath HE not *already* begun to renew you unto repentance? Is not every pang a proof that HE is still striving with you in the very way which His Apostle shews to be the test that you are not abandoned? Comfort, peace, joy,—these perhaps are not yet yours. But there is time; there is hope. And that, which in the mean season HE demands of you, is that you wrestle in prayer and watchfulness for continued renewal to the godly sorrow of repentance, without which you would be indeed lost. And behold, HE has already given you the foretaste and earnest of the blessing! Sin no more, lest a worse thing come unto you. Pray, to repent more and more deeply, until your very repentance and its imperfections be repented of: and first of all, repent of your want of faith; repent of the thought, that HE Who gave His SON to redeem you, will reject your prayers now when that SON makes them His own, and intercedes for you in Heaven. And then, believe that grace for grace will be vouch-

safed ; that every gift which you have received
and made your own, will be rewarded in you
by the Giver with fresh measures of the Spirit;
until those, who have been renewed unto repentance, are, when repentance has her perfect work, renewed time by time unto comfort.
Look for the HOLY SPIRIT first as the Sanctifier, then as the Comforter. And through
whatever dispensations the returning prodigal
be brought back to his Father's house, the
first fact, that he has become willing and able
to turn his face thitherward, is an assuring testimony that his sin has not yet severed him
from his SAVIOUR,—has not yet so grieved
the SPIRIT of GOD as that he cannot be forgiven, cannot be renewed, first to repentance, and then through faith, in due order, to
peace, to joy, to glory.

Faintly and imperceptibly the gentle dews
of mercy may fall. Barren and thirsty may
be the land, for the wickedness of them that
dwell therein: but the dews will fall, and the
springs flow, " and the brook become a river,
and the river become a sea." [33] Only, let us
remember wherein consists the difference be-

[33] Ecclesiasticus xxiv. 31.

H 2

tween the complete and perfect character of GOD'S promises, and their slack and partial fulfilment in us. HE sees the end with the beginning. Past, present and future lose their distinctions in His eternity. Where perfection is, there is no progress. But with us, progress, in its true sense, is at once our duty, and the condition of our nature. We must be content to begin at the beginning,—to let faith be the substance of the things that we hope for, the evidence of the things that as yet we see not. We must neither despair of GOD'S mercy, because it is *only* to repentance that we are called; nor doubt His promise, because the path of repentance is rugged. If we have been " dead in trespasses and sins," and if by the SPIRIT striving with us we have been quickened to consciousness once more, there must be trial, there must be agony. Even in the physical world, returning life is agony : but it is *life.* And repentance is life from the dead.

And to this conclusion have our enquiries brought us ; that we, as being heirs of the promises, living under the dispensation of the HOLY SPIRIT, with that Divine PERSON Him-

self mysteriously dwelling in our hearts, are
indeed, even through the exceeding preciousness of our mercies and in proportion to them,
in peril above others of sinning (as often as
we do sin) against the HOLY GHOST;—that
all sin is deadly;—that every act of sin is
deadly in itself, and may be deadly to us.
But this, GOD be praised, is not the whole.
For we have also learnt in what the deadli-
ness of sin resides. Not in its own sinfulness,
—as if that could make the death of CHRIST
of none effect; but in its power to deaden
the heart, to extinguish repentance, to destroy even the will to call upon GOD, to make
us doubt His mercies in CHRIST, and His
power to save us.

All other sin does indeed tend to this hopeless consummation. Yet all other sin and blasphemy shall be forgiven. All shall be forgiven,
because all may be repented of. But this shall
not be forgiven. For how shall a man repent
of his sin, while that sin is impenitence?

But to those who repent and abhor their
sins, and seek (however feebly) for forgive-
nesss; who believe in the power of JESUS
CHRIST to save them, and, believing, dare to

love HIM, how comforting, how reviving is the assurance that all these are the operations of that selfsame SPIRIT against Whom they dread to sin ; and, therefore, are the evidences of His still abiding presence, the manifestations of HIMSELF still indwelling, albeit in a polluted Temple! Though they were guilty of all sin short of thinking that any sin can cut them off from the mercies of GOD in CHRIST, yet let them believe that *this* is the bruised reed which HE will not break, this the smoking flax which HE will not quench.

Nay, though in the crisis of their struggle they seem to have that voice borne in upon their souls, which in the hour of Jerusalem's abandonment proclaimed her heavenly Guardians departing[34], let even that terror of the LORD only nerve them to pray the more earnestly in their agony. And HE Whom CHRIST has sent, will not depart, but remain " to revive the heart of the contrite ones,"[35] and "to make intercession with groanings unutterable" for those who "know not what they should pray for as they ought."[36]

[34] Μεταβαίνωμεν ἐντεῦθεν, Joseph. Bell. Jud. vi. 5, 3.
[35] Isaiah lvii. 15.   [36] Rom. viii. 26.

SERMON V.

THE BOND BETWEEN TEACHER AND DISCIPLE.

Preached on Sunday, November 6, 1853.

1 Thessalonians ii. 19, 20.

*For what is our hope, or joy, or crown of rejoicing?
Are not even ye, in the presence of our LORD
JESUS CHRIST at His coming? For ye are
our glory and our joy.*

St. PAUL is seldom satisfied with merely
urging his disciples to flee from the wrath to
come, and lay hold on the mercy of God in
Christ. This indeed is the first call,—the call
to become disciples. But he is accustomed to
lead them on by the motives of love and hope;
he sets before them the recompense of reward[1]
laid up for the good soldier and faithful servant of Christ; he invites them to that stream
of grace, ever fresh and full, which waters those
that have made the first gift effectual; he

[1] Hebrews x. 35 ; xi. 26.

points to that special corollary of blessing, whereby the work which GOD has enabled us to do, is rewarded in us by Him Whose own work it is, not ours.

Thus the Apostle, writing to the Corinthians, contrasts the Christian strife with their own Isthmian games, where all contended, to swell a single conqueror's triumph; shewing that the LORD of the festival has crowns for all, if they strive lawfully, and strive earnestly[2]. Thus, to the Philippians, he represents himself as pressing onward for a prize, which he could not feel that he had yet attained, so long as anything remained between him and the end of the course[3]. And in the last scene of all, when imminent death gave him assurance that his work was done, and that all hazard of his becoming a castaway was at an end, it is thus that he speaks forth the revelation which had nerved him for his martyrdom: "I have fought a good fight, I have finished my course, I have kept the

---

[2] 1 Cor. ix. 24, 26 : Οὐκ οἴδατε, ὅτι οἱ ἐν σταδίῳ τρέχοντες πάντες μὲν τρέχουσιν, εἰς δὲ λαμβάνει τὸ βραβεῖον ; οὕτως τρέχετε, ἵνα καταλάβητε… ἐγὼ τοίνυν οὕτω τρέχω, ὡς οὐκ ἀδήλως.

[3] Philipp. iii. 12–14.

faith : henceforth there is laid up for me a crown of righteousness, which the LORD the righteous Judge shall give me at that day : and not to me only, but unto all them also that love His appearing."[4]

Such, also, is the language of St. Peter, recognising the same reward as held out to those who have laboured with the like zeal for the flock of CHRIST,—" Feed the flock of GOD which is among you, taking the oversight thereof, not by constraint, but willingly; not for filthy lucre, but of a ready mind ;—not as lording it over the heritages, but being ensamples to the flock : and when the Chief Shepherd shall appear, ye shall receive a crown of glory that fadeth not away."[5]

Further : it is thus that St. Paul addresses the Philippians as being not only his brethren dearly beloved and longed for, but themselves his joy and crown."[6]

And finally, lest we should interpret this as

4 2 Tim. iv. 7, 8.

5 1 St. Peter v. 2–4 ; ὡς κατακυριεύοντες τῶν κλήρων. The English Version, " as being lords over [*marg.* overruling] GOD's heritage," is scarcely justified by the references to Ps. xxxiii. 12., lxxiv. 2.

6 Philipp. iv. 1.

nothing more than the evidence of his own emotions, while he thought and wrote of their love, the whole is as it were summed up and combined in the words of the text, which carry us forward to that day of the LORD's appearing, in which the Saints will receive 'their crowns; and which set before us the Apostle, placing his hope for that day in his loving and beloved disciples; seeing in them and their presence before CHRIST's throne, the very joy which was promised, the very crown which was laid up for him.

It is a common remark, that Scripture reveals but little respecting those joys which are the portion of the blessed in Heaven. "Light and music," it has been said, "contain all that we know of them definitely." Too hastily on both sides :—for on the one hand, there is a symbolical and mystical character even in the language which has suggested this very criticism. And on the other, the primary beatitude of all, that which makes Heaven what it is, is omitted.

It is true that we have need to be very carefully guarded against craving for definite notions on such a subject: for in proportion as

these images are definite, they will be earthly.
The very criticism upon our visions of Heaven
cannot soar beyond the sensuous conceptions
of earth ! And the nature of things forbids
us to know how many inlets of spiritual en-
joyment may be closed to us here, simply because as yet the body is of that flesh and blood
which cannot inherit the kingdom of Heaven.

Yet there are blessings, which we can feel
to be so pure and free from taint of earth, as
to make it at least harmless to fix our eyes on
them in contemplation. And there are here
and there glimpses given us in Holy Writ,
—rifts, as it were, in the cloud which veils
the excellent glory from our eyes,—sufficient
to encourage us to meditate on them. And
of these, one is to be found in the words which
this day's Scripture lesson[7] has suggested for
our meditation.

There is, especially, a very natural chain of
analogy beginning with that in which the
Essence of Heaven consists, the blessed presence of the FATHER, SON, and HOLY GHOST,
and the fruition of their glorious Godhead; and
carried onwards through many a golden link

[7] Second Lesson for the 6th of November, Evening.

of Church-Communion, through our fellowship with all the angels, all the saints, all the
redeemed of God. The love of God, extend-
ing outwards and shewing itself in the love of
our neighbour on earth, is the root which will
grow and expand into the full flower of this
beatific vision of the Deity, this glory and joy
in the bliss of all our brethren in Heaven.

Deep indeed is the descent from Divine
Love to human sympathy. Yet not so deep,
but that Our Father has let down His
golden chain even thus far. Here also His
compassion and His love have found the way
to unite Heaven and Earth, in the Incarnation of His beloved Son. This mystery, while
it teaches us to behold the Son of God as
the first among many brethren whom He is
bringing to glory, encourages us also to ex-
tend our hopes of Communion with His Father and Himself, till they embrace all the
company of those who are also one with Him,
and therefore, in Him, one with us. And that
which we know of the undying character of
Christian love, gives us a clue also to interpret the hints of Scripture respecting con-

scious fellowship and personal recognition among those members of CHRIST, who have helped one another in the struggles of this life, and who may be blessed to attain together to the consummation of the next. So much at least seems to be implied in the parable of Lazarus and the Rich Man[8]. CHRIST'S answer to the treacherous question of the Sadducees leaves this untouched, and, so far, tacitly admits it[9]. This is surely included (if we take the whole context into account) in that hope with which the Apostle bids the Thessalonians temper their sorrow for them that have fallen asleep[10]. This is the comfort contained in his promise, that they which are alive in the day of the LORD's coming shall not prevent (get before) them that are asleep, but that the dead in CHRIST shall rise first, and then the living shall be caught up *together with them* to meet the LORD in the air, and so shall ever be with the LORD. This is necessary, to give any force or meaning to that which is said in the Epistle to the Hebrews[11]

---

[8] St. Luke xvi. 23, sqq.   See Sermon IX.

[9] St. Luke xx. 34, sqq.   [10] 1 Thess. iv. 13, sqq.

[11] Chap. xiii. 17.

of the account which one has to give for another in the great day, and of the joy or grief
of those who must give it,—the profitableness
or the loss to those of whom it is to be given.
It is necessary, to bring out the full meaning
of the words which the Apostle uses to the
Colossians, where he describes himself and
his fellow-workers as warning every man and
teaching every man in all wisdom ; that they
may present every man perfect in CHRIST
JESUS[12].   And, to rise from the comparison
of individual phrases to more general considerations, the same conclusion necessarily results from that identity of GOD's Kingdom
here and hereafter, which the Christian Scriptures recognise, teaching us to expect that
the one shall be developed into the other,
not substituted for it :—a line of thought
strikingly illustrated by the way in which
St. Paul applies the doctrine that we are dead
and risen again with CHRIST, and our life hid
with HIM in GOD, to shew, not only that we
must set our affections on things above, where

---

[12] Coloss. i. 28, ἵνα παραστήσωμεν πάντα ἄνθρωπον τέλειον.
—See 2 Cor. iv. 14 ; xi. 2 ; Ephes. v. 27 ; and Col. i. 22 :
—also Rom. xiv. 10 (παραστησόμεθα).   See Sermon XIII.

HE sitteth at the right hand of God; but, with far more detail, that we must fulfil those very duties of brotherly love which seem at first sight most peculiarly limited to a sublunary sphere[13].

Nor can we resist the conclusion to which all else of GOD's spiritual work in our sanctification leads us, that those dispositions and graces, which from the outset of our career help us onward towards the prize,—which, as our course goes on, are heightened in intensity and purified from earthly admixtures, growing with the growth of our Christian character, strengthening with the strength of our Christian principles,—will enter with us within the veil, to receive there the full perfection of which they are capable. In some instances, indeed, they may require to be transfigured at Heaven's gate, as we know that faith and hope are glorified into sight and fruition;—but in the case of charity, not even with this modification. For charity is the greatest of these, even because its never failing character is unchangeable. In short, the whole tenor of that which is revealed to us in

---

[13] Coloss. iii. 1, sqq.   See Sermon III.

the New Testament, brings us to the conviction that the domestic and social character
of the Church of CHRIST, as GOD's Household and Kingdom, is no mere accident of its
militant estate on earth; but rather one of
its essential characteristics, such as will be
only exhibited in more perfect purity, when
the new Jerusalem is revealed from Heaven
as the city of GOD's children, the home where
they will dwell as brethren in their FATHER's
presence.

But the same considerations suggest, and
the same analogies confirm the belief, that it
is not to the mere indulgence of a sentiment
or an emotion that such glorious results are
promised. They are the rewards of the work
and labour of our love. In that day when
the LORD makes up His jewels,—in that day
when HE gives such gifts to men,—those
whom we have loved may indeed, as such,
be our joy; but only those for whom we have
laboured, will be our crown. It is not of those
whom he had known after the flesh, or with
whom he had any tie but that of his Christian ministry and apostleship, that St. Paul declared that they were his hope and joy and

crown of rejoicing in the presence of the LORD JESUS CHRIST at His coming.

Here then a glimpse is afforded us of that which may have a place among the rewards of the faithful, the prizes of CHRIST'S bounty, to those who have first received the gifts of His mercy.

And such a meditation, if pursued in a reverent and unpresuming spirit, will be neither barren nor unfruitful, but effectual to stir up to more abundant life and power the gift that is in us ; the gift, which we have received of GOD, but have too often suffered to languish, through weakness and weariness of the flesh. For it is one of the temptations which beset our weakness, to lose much of the interest in our work, when we do not immediately realize its results, and the way in which it is connected with them. Is it not a true confession, that for the most part we are less ardent and resolute in general well-doing that good may come, than in doing this or that definite good thing, that this or that definite result may follow ? We seem to need an object, if not set clearly before our bodily eyes, at least, revealed as distinctly as may be, to our *mind's* eye, to keep our spirit from sinking, our zeal from waxing cold, our convictions from becoming unpractical.

Is it too much then to assert that the vocation of the Christian ministry among ourselves, whether in the work of education here, or in the pastoral care elsewhere, would be fulfilled with more living zeal and more sustained energy, if we accustomed ourselves more to look at it in the cheering light which St. Paul's hopes supply?

Do *they* not bespeak a merciful condescension of the LORD to our weakness, in furnishing this additional spur to our flagging efforts, instead of abruptly judging our efforts when they flag? Not only were the labours of the Apostle to be rewarded by a crown; but the crown was one essentially connected with and arising from the labours themselves;—it was, partly, at least, to consist of the very presence, the very communion in bliss, of those on whom the labour had been effectually bestowed.

And this is the earnest, which should be present to our minds also, of our Christian hope and joy, heirs as we are in our humbler rank of the same privileges and duties as united Apostle and Disciple together of old, in the bond of that communion which death itself is powerless to sever.

But it must be asked, and (I fear) asked with no sanguine expectation of a cheerful answer, Do we continually look upon and think of those for whom we have to watch,— do they think upon their teachers and pastors, as those who shall be united in fellowship of joy and glory hereafter, in proportion to the mutual blessings which have redounded from the one to the other upon earth ?

If this were indeed our spirit, would it not shew itself in ways many and continual, in which the manifestation, at present, is sadly wanting ? Let us. take the subject first in its bearing on our pastoral relations. Let us refer, as St. Peter's words have already referred us, to the pattern of the chief Shepherd, and the completeness with which HE identifies Himself with those that are His ; going before, to prepare a place for them, that where HE is there they may be also ; not ashamed to call them brethren ; nay, bringing them to glory with the words, " Behold

I and the children which GOD hath given me."[14]   And then let us think, how much is often lost between those whose feelings as well as duty would draw them most closely together.   There are the poor of CHRIST'S heritage needing and thirsting for instruction in doctrine and guidance of life ; but shy of intruding on the studies or occupations of their Minister, of occupying his time, or of taking the first word in talking of the subjects which are nearest to their hearts.   And there are pastors, men of prayer and meditation, earnest in character, abounding in the richest treasures of things new and old, which befit the scribe instructed to the kingdom of GOD, —such men as the studies, the influences, the communion of a school like this, are powerful to mould,—men, who, but for one deficiency, might evangelize the world ;—longing to pour forth the emotions of their hearts as well as the stores of their intellects ; but wanting the power to doff the wrappings of conventional reserve, and to place themselves heart to heart, as well as face to face, with the immortal beings who will rise beside them

---

14 Hebr. ii. 11, 13 (Isaiah viii. 18).

in the day of the LORD. And thus, the step is not made; the ice is not broken; time after time their communings fall short of the point from which all would be sure to flow on full and clear ;—and they part, strangers as before ; nay, more estranged, because they part with a sense of recoil on both sides. But if the mischief is on both sides, judge ye on which side is the greater responsibility!

And is not the same evil at work, under a slightly modified form, even in this spot, from which the Church's and nation's teachers are from year to year issuing forth? Nay, is it not rather here that the harmful influence is imbibed? Would it be so widely felt throughout the land, were it not first felt here? For here, too, there is the same general relation between the teacher and the taught, the pastor and the disciple. They are drawn together by every impulse of love and sense of duty : but they are kept apart by the repulsion of etiquette and conventionality, by constraints of feeling and reserves of manner. Does the teacher always in such intercourse sufficiently remember that he was once him-

self a pupil? Does the pupil sufficiently feel
that his teacher may yet retain enough of
fresh feelings and youthful impulses to understand *his*? Do both sufficiently grasp and
use the fact that there is this point of con-
tact between their spirits ;—the fact, that the
points of difference and separation which thrust
themselves forward, are stamped even by this
very obtrusiveness, as being things external
and accidental ; but that the inner reality is,
that heart beats to heart in Christian love ?
Sad indeed it is that between such classes,
among such persons, we may see Christian
love hidden by a mask of coldness on the
one part and shyness on the other,—perhaps
of stern authority on one, and jealous independence on the other. And as time passes
and opportunities slip away, the younger go
forth from hence without the impression, which
might have been made for good on their duc-
tile minds at a turning point of life : the
elder go on striving, but with ineffectual efforts ; carried round and round in a cycle
of disappointment :—and the flowers drop,
one by one, from coronals which might have
bloomed in Paradise.

If we did but look on those who are entrusted to our charge, not merely in a strict
and hard way, as persons for whom we have
to give account, but as those who are the
helpers of our joy ;—if they did but look on
us, as watching, not merely *over* them, but
for them, loving them, yearning towards
them ;—if each looked on the other as his
joy and crown at the coming of the LORD
CHRIST JESUS, how different the face of the
Church of GOD would be ; how differently
would the LORD's work be done, as by those
who felt themselves no longer servants, but
friends[15].

Where then do the difficulty and the evil
reside ?

Not often, I trust and believe, in a want of
zeal and affection in those who stand in a
pastoral relation to others. Not often in any
want of amiability, or any contumacious independence on the part of the disciples. Still
more rarely, we may hope, in recklessness on
the one hand or profligacy on the other. But
commonly in the want of a mutual understanding, the want of openness in those who ought

<hr>

[15] St. John xv. 15.

to be beyond all others confidential with one another. *We want faith.* This is the secret of our shrinking. We want faith, and therefore we suspect others of a want of love. Men have not the courage to unbosom themselves, for fear of meeting with coldness or ridicule. And each watches in vain for the first tokens of that affection which he dares not be the first to offer, though he would return it with his whole heart. And they are kept apart by this false shame. Both lose what they need and crave. Both are hardened and grow suspicious. And perhaps the suspicions of both in time make themselves true ;—the openness of youth clouded with premature craft ; the influence of riper years lost in selfish cowardice. And thus pastor and flock, teacher and pupil are estranged ; a blessing is changed into a curse ; and when they have to give account, it must be done by both with grief, it must be unprofitable for both.

O for one breath—were it but one—of the Apostle's spirit, to whisper to teacher and pupil, to Clergy and Laity, of the joy and glory which they are casting away, and bartering for shame and confusion of face in the day of their account, by reason of this false shame which separates them now,—now, when each might help the other, alike by secret prayer and by mutual interchange of comfort; the one confiding their difficulties, their doubts, their temptations; the other guiding, cheering, helping along the better way, stretching out the hand to steady the wavering, or raise the fallen;—and these too, we may be well assured, receiving at least as much, in support and comfort and blessing, as they give!

O for the courage to despise the scoffing of fools; or rather and better still, to believe in the warm and healthy feelings which need but to be evoked to put all scoffing to silence and shame! Would that, for our uncircumcised lips and stammering tongue, a mouth were given us to utter the words of the Apostle which have so often kindled a fire in our hearts, " Our mouth is open unto you, our heart is enlarged. Ye are not straitened in us, but ye are straitened in your own bowels. Now for a recompence in the same, (I speak as unto my children,) be ye also enlarged."[16]

[16] 2 Corinth. vi. 11–13.

And this might yet be so, if we all realized more fully that we are bound together not for this world only ; that our accounts are to be rendered together ; and that in the next world we are doomed to be either the glory or the shame of one another. It is but a nightmare that paralyses us. We have only to move a finger, and it is at an end. But the finger is *not* moved, and the spell remains unbroken.

And yet, even while we are dreaming, the truth is present with us. Who amongst us all is there, that has ever dwelt in thought on the future kingdom of his Christian inheritance, and has not connected with it some tender memory, brightening into hope,—the image of some, who have so linked themselves on earth with his best aspirations, that in every vision of Heaven their forms must find a place ; who have been guides or fellow-pilgrims once, in such a sort as to make it felt that they have but outstript him now, to receive and welcome him at the end of his course ?

If there be any, who have never known

what it is to receive such human help, woe indeed would it be to them, were it not that HE who withholds earthly succour, can more than replace it by the nearness and the power of His own inward presence!

Again, if there are those who have not yet experienced the withdrawal of their helpers, —well indeed may they be joyous! And yet scarcely may they be accounted, in the highest sense, happy[17]. For they have not yet found their full trial, or proved their Redeemer to the uttermost. They have not yet bridged over the dark gulf, and learnt to live in the land of their own future beyond it. Speaking as of ordinary cases, and of the calm tenor of that every day life in which our lot is mercifully cast, must we not say that such persons have yet to undergo a discipline; and therefore they have yet to experience the strong confirmation of their faith, in learning the certainty and sufficiency of the grace which will be present to bear them up through the darkest hour of trial, and under the deepest consciousness of sin? They have to learn to be alone :—and they have to learn

[17] St. James v. 11.

that they are not alone, for the FATHER is with them;—not alone; for to such lonely ones is the Comforter sent.

But even those on whom this rod has been in mercy laid, and whose conversation is already within that veil which must so soon be lifted for themselves, may be reminded of a further lesson;—that it is not by musing and dreaming that the Saints have earned their rest, or have been disciplined for their glory; and that for themselves, who have not yet entered into their own rest, such sympathies, affections, yearnings, are not enough;—that if their strife is to be effectual, it must not be merely by loving, but by labouring in love. Even "the Desire of our eyes"[18] may become an idol, and prove a snare. But "the Fruit of our labour"[19] will be our joy and crown of rejoicing in the presence of our LORD JESUS CHRIST at His coming!

To this end, may HE help our unbelief; may HE increase our faith! May HE, of Whose free grace we have been adopted into a heavenly citizenship and family, grant us the further gift to seek this further crown,

[18] Ezek. xxiv. 16.   [19] Philipp. i. 22.

not as running uncertainly, not as beating the air,—but pressing forward diligently to the mark which every one who runs may attain, teacher and scholar, priest and people alike, in a race where the success of each ministers to the success of all.

SERMON VI.

THE PORTRAIT OF CHRISTIAN LOVE.

Preached on the fifth Sunday in Lent, 1854.

1 CORINTH. xiii. 1.

Though I speak with the tongues of men and of angels, and have not charity, I am become as sounding brass, or a tinkling cymbal.

THE mode in which the New Testament has been divided into chapters has been sometimes criticised ; and not without reason. For although this work of the Cardinal à S. Caro[1] seems to have been done with more deliberation than that of Robert Stephens in subdividing the chapters into verses ; yet it must be confessed that, when the chapters are divided in the wrong place, the effects are

[1] He divided the text of the Latin Vulgate into chapters, to facilitate the use of an Index or " Concordance," about the middle of the 13th century. At a later period his numbers were applied to the Greek Text. The verse-numbers appear first in the edition of the New Testament by R. Stephens, Geneva 1551. See *Guerike, historisch-kritische Einleitung in das N. T.* § 19. 2 and 3.

equally, if not even more serious. Men quote by verses, and perhaps mislead others. But they are apt to read by chapters, and thus often deceive themselves.

But if there is any chapter in the New Testament which seems to prescribe its own limits, to isolate itself and stand independently of what goes before and follows, that chapter is the thirteenth of St. Paul's first Epistle to the Corinthians. It is true that the twelfth and fourteenth seem to link themselves to the thirteenth; but the thirteenth connects itself with neither. It stands out, as each individual Psalm stands in the Psalter, rather than as a portion of the continuous work which includes it. And indeed, *a Psalm* it has been not unhappily called,—*a Psalm of Love.* Its very style is unique. In its rhythm there is music which translation can neither destroy, nor assimilate to that which stands on either side of it. And in considering its singularity, the thought may perhaps suggest itself that we have here a veritable hymn, a specimen of inspired Christian poetry, which the Apostle has adopted, and set, like a gem, in the precious metal of his Epistle.

But in that case, who is worthy to be deemed the organ of such inspiration? Perhaps St. John might be suggested,—the very Apostle of Love. But there is that in it, which separates it even from him. Steeped in that Divine Love with which his Master's bosom overflowed, St. John is ravished by the object of his affection; he is absorbed in its contemplation. Here, on the contrary, the grace displays itself differently, though no less characteristically, in its human recipient and in its practical working. It is still, indeed, the love of CHRIST; but that love working, in love to all His members, instead of resting in His contemplation. Even while we are most reminded of St. John, we have the Apostle of the Gentiles imprinting his spirit on the page;—we have St. Paul, and "the love of CHRIST constraining" him[2].

But when we have returned from these speculations, to recognise St. Paul again with a clearer and more reasonable conviction, there still remains a perplexity. The chapter gives us the impression rather of a jewel in the setting, than of a link in the

[2] 2 Corinth. v. 14.

chain of the Epistle. And though we well know how little St. Paul is accustomed to resist any digression to which a glimpse of a Divine Attribute or a Christian grace may seem to invite him; yet there is a difficulty,—a manifest difficulty, I should have said, were it not for the fact that it has been so little noticed[3],—arising from the tenor of the whole discourse in which it seems to be interpolated. In the midst of all the rebukes which the Apostle has to utter to the backsliding "saints" of Corinth, how is this chapter introduced with "Yet shew I unto you a more excellent way?" How does it introduce the sequel with, "Follow after charity, and desire spiritual gifts, but rather that ye may prophesy?"

The consideration of the question, What does the 'Psalm of Love' mean *here*, in the particular place in which it stands, may, perhaps, under God's blessing, tend to clear our understanding and heighten our appreciation,

---

3 It is suggested cursorily by Calvin on v. 4 ; " Neque mihi dubium est quin oblique perstringere voluerit Corinthios, dum antithesim illis proponat, in qua ex adverso sua vitia recognoscant."

both of the chapter itself, and of the rest of the Epistle. Perhaps it may lead us to think that the very position which has seemed to detract from its significance, has in reality enhanced it.

If we look upon this thirteenth chapter in two distinct points of view, we shall find that it bears a twofold aspect of strongly marked contrast, accordingly as we examine it by itself, in its specific details as an independent whole; or embrace it in a more comprehensive view of the whole Epistle. Viewed by itself, it is all tenderness and delicacy: but as we gradually see the connection and harmony between it and the rest of the Epistle, it produces entirely new impressions;—it breathes a spirit of sterner love. The varying effect is not unlike that of some of our old ecclesiastical buildings. We stand near them, and are dazzled by the lavish details of gorgeous beauty in separate portions of the structure. We draw back sufficiently to take in the whole at a glance, and are amazed at the new effect with which the entire mass stands out against the sky, in the simple grandeur of austere proportion.

If we keep our attention fixed on the peculiar temptations which seem most easily to have beset the Corinthian disciples, and try steadily to trace them back to that root of bitterness from which all of them may most fairly be said to have sprung, this new light will be gradually shed on the Apostle's portrait of the crowning Christian grace. We shall begin to see in it, not merely the pattern of that " more excellent way" into which he was anxious to guide them, but those especial and definite manifestations of the Christian temper, which were most unlike the prominent faults of their conduct. We have forcibly suggested to us a series of contrasts,—reaching, in most instances, even to the very details of the phraseology employed,—between all that charity is and is not, on the one hand, and, on the other, all those varied but kindred errors of temper and of practice which St. Paul had been compelled to rebuke in the Church at Corinth. And we shall observe, as we pass on, how truly he shews himself the Apostle of that MASTER, who was wont to glide into the minds of His hearers through winning parables, when He had to inculcate the most distasteful lessons ; how much not merely of wisdom, but of another grace, of which we are apt to take too little notice in the pattern of St. Paul, or of St. Paul's MASTER and ours, —how much of delicacy pouring in oil and wine into the very wounds which sincerity is compelled to inflict,—tempers his dealings with those who were, after all, his dearly-beloved and longed for, the children whom HE had begotten in CHRIST JESUS through the Gospel.

But these children were still *carnal.* And their carnality seems to have shewn itself, speaking generally, in one way. In the midst of all their privileges and opportunities, not-withstanding all the gifts which they possessed, and the guidance which they enjoyed, they were yet *selfish.* This was the canker which had eaten into the very heart of their religion. Many, indeed, were the forms in which it had appeared, according to individual characters and temptations ; in some developing itself especially in self-complacency, arrogance, and vanity; in others, with more extensive ill effects, in indifference to their brethren's welfare, sometimes even in active enmity to their persons; frequently, involving a disregard of the most ordinary moral restraints, and the plainest considerations of propriety.

Taking this as a clue, let us endeavour to follow the course of this thirteenth Chapter, observing, in connection with its contents, how the very things which should have been for the weal of the Corinthian Christians, became the occasions of their falling ;—how they contrived that the very gifts of GOD should become snares in which the devil might take them captive. They spake, indeed, with the "tongues of men ;" and in the vanity of their minds they were but as the brasen vessels which sound for very hollowness and emptiness. They had prophecy. But they used the gift so as to make it a means of disorder and indecency. They had knowledge of mysteries. But theirs was not that knowledge which culminates in the being known of GOD ; for its effect was to puff them up. They had faith, ay, faith of that kind which wrought miracles in things natural. And they used it as a plea for scandalizing their brethren, and setting themselves above the laws of GOD. Nay, when the climax is introduced of giving one's goods to the poor and one's body to the fire ;

this suggests to us a still more painful contrast; "In eating every one taketh before another his own supper,—and one is hungry, and another drunken;" shaming the brethren who have nothing, as well as despising the Church of GOD!

And then their Apostle proceeds to portray, still more feelingly and delicately, *his* ideal of Christian Love, in lines wherein Christian courtesy and fatherly partiality struggle with the austerity of his affection towards his erring children. Here indeed, if we were to set out all the parallel passages which make every word a grave rebuke of the faults which he had been already obliged to point out, our work would scarcely find an end, until half the Epistle was, as it were, hung in fragments on the separate phrases of these few verses. We can only take a few of those illustrations which offer themselves first.

Charity suffereth long, and is kind.—They went to law, brother with brother ; nay, they defrauded, and that their brethren[4].

Charity envieth not.—But he had had reason

4 Chap. vi. 1, 6, 8 ; 2 Cor. xii. 20.

to appeal to their envyings and strifes as the undeniable evidence of their being carnal[5].

Charity vaunteth not itself, is not puffed up. —It is unnecessary here to enter into any philological discussion respecting the word περπερεύεται[6]. I need only remind you of the general notion of *the display of gifts or acquirements, marred by vanity and bad taste,* which this word and its cognates always contained, to satisfy you that if one single word more than another could express a character, this very tendency *to shew off* (to use an every-day expression) was the marked Corinthian feature. And accordingly we have them designated continually, not only as "puffed up for one against another;" but as glorying in that which they had received, as though it had been of themselves, and not the bounty of another;—overweening, as those who said, We are full; we are rich; we have reigned as kings without you[7].

---

5 Chap. iii. 3.

6 The fullest illustrations of it are, as usual, to be found in the note of Wetstein. Later commentators have added little or nothing.

7 Chap. iv. 6, 7, 8, 10.

Charity doth not behave itself unseemly.—
But to them, seemliness and decency were
lightly held, in comparison with the use of
their gifts to their own glorification, even in
the House of Prayer, in the service of GOD[8].
Nay, more miserably still, they identified
themselves with " unseemliness," even beyond
the licence of Heathenism, beyond the lasciviousness of Corinth ; and blushed not (St.
Paul's language makes it too plain) to assert
a Christian liberty to fornication and incest[9].

Charity seeketh not her own.—But how they
stood on their own supposed rights, careless
of the offence they gave, and of the shipwreck
they were preparing for the faith of scrupu-
lous consciences,—how they asserted that all
things were lawful to them, whether they
tended to edification or not ;—all this we
know from the necessity of laying upon them
as a strict command, the rule that none should
seek his own, but every man his neighbour's
weal[10].

Charity is not easily provoked.—And yet

[8] Ch. xiv. 26, etc.

[9] Compare ch. v. 1, 2, 6, with vi. 12, 13.

[10] Ch. vi. 6–8; viii. 9; x. 23, 24.

among these Christians there were conten-
tions, bitterness, and strife ; party spirit, and
personal rancour[11].

Charity thinketh no evil.—But what their
"thinkings," their imputations even against
the Apostle himself, what their construction
of his simplest and most affectionate dealings
had been, we see from his incidental self-
assertions and vindications. If he was merciful, it was because he was afraid. If he
rebuked with authority, he was a braggart.
He, forsooth, was no Apostle ;—his authority
was a nullity,—he knew this,—he durst not
exercise it. He was making merchandise of
them. He was taking them with guile, cloak-
ing greediness under a show of disinterested-
ness. All kinds of imputations were thrown
out in turn. Possible or impossible, compatible
or contradictory, the evil was imputed, even
to him[12].

*Charity rejoiceth not in iniquity, but re-
joiceth in the truth.*—Their charity, however,

---

[11] Ch. i. 11 ; iii. 3 ; iv. 6 ; vi. 7, 8 ; xi. 16.

[12] Ch. iv. 3, 8, 10, sqq., 18; ix. 1 sqq., 15 sqq. ; xiv. 37,
sq.; xv. 8–11.—2 Cor. i. 17 sqq., 23, 24; iii. 1 ; iv. 2 ; v. 12 ;
vi. 11–13 ; vii. 2, 3 ; viii. 20, 21 ; x. 1, 2, 6–12 ; xi. 5 sqq.;
xii. 11, 12, 15–21 ; xiii. 3–10.

by a strange perversion, found in iniquity its element of rejoicing : for their joy and glorying had been not good, but in their very shame : it had been in their countenance and sanction of unrepented incest, when they ought rather to have mourned over the stain on their Church's purity[13]. And, as a natural result, when the truth confronted them in the fatherly but peremptory rebuke of the Apostle, there were many who only hardened themselves against the truth, and, like the Galatians at another time, counted him their enemy for having spoken it[14].

Charity, in fine, *beareth all things, believeth all things, hopeth all things, endureth all things.* —But what had they to do with such a charity as this ? Had they borne the burdens of their weaker brethren ? Had they endured the teaching of sound doctrine, or the precepts of practical holiness ? Their belief? Had it not been to disbelieve all that clashed with their own conceits or crossed their carnal inclinations ? Their hope ? Had they not set themselves to destroy the Christian's hope in

[13] Ch. v. 1, 2, 6, sqq.

[14] 2 Cor. vi. 11, 12 ; vii. 2, 3 ; x. 2 ; xi. 12 ; xii. 20, 21 : —Galat. iv. 16.

his LORD'S resurrection, and leave him of all men most miserable[15]?

What a melancholy list of backslidings does our brief study of these few, but most suggestive verses supply! And against all this, what had they to set? They were by no means wanting in self-assertion. They set their tongues, their knowledge, and their prophesyings against it all.

But what, after all, were these? The gift of tongues could only in part reverse the judgment of Babel. Prophecy was but a light shining in a dark place[16]. Partial knowledge brought out all the more clearly the affliction of total ignorance. The very gifts of healing were imperfect efforts to redress the temporal effects of Adam's fall. Gifts indeed they were of GOD, glorious effusions of the HOLY SPIRIT, precious instruments for the work of the Church :—but gifts, at the best, only remedial of existing defects and evils; and therefore, by their very presence *as gifts*, testifying to an imperfect and transitory state of things ;—gifts, which, from their very na-

---

[15] Ch. xv. 12, 19, 35, etc.　　　　[16] 2 St. Peter i. 19.

ture, could not possibly exist, *as such*, in that perfect state in which Love finds fullest scope and highest praise. When present ignorance is enlightened, and future change is impossible, then prophecy must fail; for then it would no longer have a meaning. When Infinite Knowledge is reflected upon us, and we know even as we are known of GOD, what place shall remain for the glimmer of partial knowledge which is all that we are capable of now?

Thus, we have been enabled to trace a close connection, though of a very peculiar kind, between the Apostle's exhibition of Christian love and the rebukes and remonstrances which he addresses to the Corinthians. We have, in truth, even here—however little it may at first strike us—a portrait of these erring disciples. Not, indeed, a portrait according to the ordinary mode of painting. But a new art will furnish us with a new term for its description;—that art which has taught us to speak of pictures *positive* and *negative*,—the one representing objects in their actual semblance, according to the ordinary laws of optics;—

the other equally exact, but with their lights and shadows reversed. In the foregoing chapters, we have had the likeness of the Corinthian character, with its own dark shades faithfully represented. In the thirteenth we have the picture which is its correlative— every feature bathed in light.

The interpretation which connects the whole Epistle together, being based on the circumstances of time and place which elicited it, applies most directly to the case of those to whom it was at first addressed. But the document was not only an Epistle to the Corinthians. It was a gift, as it is a legacy, to the Universal Church : and while it retains all the ancient terrors of the LORD, to persuade those who from age to age reproduce the sins of Corinth among Christians, it reveals to the Church at large that more comfortable significance, which belongs to it in its isolation. For the Church, it is a Hymn of Love and Blessing, an outpouring of the SPIRIT which animates the Body of CHRIST, and realizes the kingdom of Heaven upon earth.

Nor are we limited to the painful experi-

ment of seeking our own edification in studying the shortcomings of the Apostle's converts. We have an equally instructive and far
more comforting example, in which, making
allowance for human frailty, this ideal of the
truest Christian charity was realized;—not
intentionally shewn; not collected into one
sketch, to be read off at a single hasty glance
into the depths of the inspired writings; but,
assuredly, drawn all the more faithfully, because unconsciously, by St. Paul from his own
heart!

For here also it would be easy to recon-
struct, from the workings of the Apostle's
life, from the casual outbursts of his feelings
and yearnings in these and all his Epistles,
the very original of his Picture of Love.
But time would fail us in dealing with the
abundance of our materials. Only let us
compare the apology which they had to plead
for their selfishness, with that which the
Apostle might have pleaded, if he had been
accessible to such a temptation. If *they*
came behind in no gift[17], what words shall
we find to describe *his* gifts without dis-

[17] 1 Cor. i. 7.

paragement ? He came to them speaking wisdom in a mystery of GOD's own revealing[18], —working miracles,—speaking with tongues more than they all[19],—breathing of the airs of Paradise,—faint with the glory of the revelations *there*[20]. And how did he come ? Working with his own hands that none might be burdened[21],—dying daily, having the sentence of death continually within himself, that in all ways, by life, or by death, he might glorify GOD and edify the Church[22]. And what was his choice ? Rather in the Church to speak five words with his understanding, that others might be benefited, than ten thousand words in an unknown tongue, to the display of his own miraculous gifts[23].

The portrait, then, in no negative sense,—the character, without its melancholy irony,—is the portrait, is the character of the Apostle of the Gentiles. He it is whose followers we are invited to be, as he is the follower of our common MASTER and SAVIOUR, JESUS CHRIST.

---

[18] 1 Cor. ii. 6–13.   [19] 1 Cor. xiv. 18.   [20] 2 Cor. xii. 2–4.
[21] 1 Cor. ix. 12,15,18; 2 Cor. xi. 7–12 ; comp. Acts xviii. 1–3.
[22] 1 Cor. xv. 31 ; 2 Cor. i. 9 ; iv. 10,11.   [23] 1 Cor. xiv. 19.

What human pattern can be more instructive or more valuable to the disciples, and,
above all, to the ministers of Christ ? Filled
with that love of God, which shewed itself
in unwearied love of men, more especially of
those that were Christ's; importunate, not
unmannerly; becoming all things to all men
that by any means he might gain some,—gain
them to Christ, not to himself[24]; jealous with
a godly jealousy over the purity of the Bride
whom he had espoused to Christ. Who is
weak, and he is not weak ? Who is offended,
and he burneth not[25] ?

This union of zeal with love was, humanly
speaking, the preparation of Saul of Tarsus
for the Divine gift and commission which was
vouchsafed to him. He had not learned it from
the Pharisees with whom he had consorted.
They had indeed a zeal, even to slaying, but
not to love ; a zeal, not according to knowledge, but by a sure instinct hating that good
thing which they understood not. In them
was revived the spirit in which Jehu had served the Lord of old, and felt most at home
when the bloodiest service was required of him.

[24] 1 Cor. ix. 22.   [25] 2 Cor. xi. 2, 29.

Nor had he learnt it from the Master at whose
feet he had been brought up. Amiable, im-
partial, tolerant as he is,—Gamaliel is the
type of knowledge without zeal. Called to a
high post at the very gate of Heaven's kingdom, he leads his pupils up to it ; he beholds
them pressing in, the violent taking it by
force ; he will not resist their eagerness ; but
with mild and philosophic temper himself will
wait to see whether this thing be of GOD or
no ; afraid of fighting against GOD,—and
not forward to fight for HIM[26]. And so the
world sweeps by him on the right hand and
the left ; and while sides are chosen for good
or evil, the almost Christian Gamaliel remains
an almost Christian still ! "I would thou wert
cold or hot !" Better far and more blessed, the

[26] Acts v. 34 —39. On the legend that Gamaliel died
a Christian, see Lightfoot's Commentary on this passage ;
and compare his "*Harmony*, pt. 2, year 33." Eustratius
(ap. Phot. Bibl. § 171) quotes Chrysippus of Jerusalem
as stating that it was revealed in a vision by Gamaliel himself to one Lucianus, a presbyter there; and that *Abib*, son
of Gamaliel, and Nicodemus (τὸν νυκτερινὸν φίλον καὶ ἡμερινὸν
γεγονότα) were baptized at the same time. This revelation
was accompanied by miracles.—Eustratius is placed by
different authorities in the sixth, seventh, and even in the
eighth century.

zeal without knowledge of the blind devotee, who, even while in deepest error, loved that which as yet was not revealed to him; and hated, not that "way" which in fact he was persecuting, but a phantom for which, in his ignorance and unbelief, he mistook it. And accordingly the warmth of his heart was rewarded; and the scales fell from his eyes; and the LORD Whom he had persecuted was revealed to him; and the love of CHRIST constrained him,—of CHRIST, Who died for all, that they which live should not henceforth live unto themselves, but unto HIM Which died for them and rose again[27].

And the characteristic of this his love,—the key to all that may seem peculiar or perplexing in it,—is that it is the love of CHRIST first, and, for His sake, of those who are, or ought to be, His. Therefore it cannot flatter; it cannot fear: it can rebuke. It is a jealous Love.

Therefore it beareth all that is consistent with the love of the truth: but it rejoiceth not in iniquity. It would not be Love, either of GOD or of man, if it did!

[27] 2 Cor. v. 14, 15.

Therefore it is no love to them that are hopelessly the enemies of GOD. Love to GOD and the children of GOD is hate to them. And the Apostle, in whom it had been purged from all dross of earthly and selfish feeling, hated *them* " with a perfect hatred,"—not even, according to the Psalmist, as though they were *his* enemies[28], but—as he could not hate his own !

Having always present in himself the sentence of death,—always delivered unto death for JESUS' sake, that the life also of JESUS might be made manifest in his mortal flesh, knowing thenceforth no man after the flesh[29], and lifted far above all carnal prejudices and partialities, against such enemies as these he could contend even to the death. Self-devoted himself, so that he could even (like Moses of old) wish himself accursed and blotted out of GOD's book for the sake of his brethren[30],—those very brethren who in the mean time were seeking after his life. He could utter the dread anathema, as an oracle of GOD. But against whom ? " If any man

[28] Psalm cxxxix. 22.   [29] 2 Cor. iv. 11, 15, 16.
[30] Rom. ix. 3 ; compare Exod. xxxii. 32..

love not the LORD JESUS."[31] He could deliver unto Satan. But whom? Those whose individual sins and pollutions were searing their brethren's consciences; those whose blasphemies were even overthrowing their brethren's faith in the resurrection to come[32]!

As it was no joy to this chosen Vessel of CHRIST to give utterance to these judgments of GOD, so it is no proof that our spirit is conformed to his, if we go on our way with war-cries in our mouths, like Shimei, cursing as we go[33]. But it was his blessing and glory,— and it may be ours,—to follow after, if that we may attain to that which made it holy, which made it possible, for him to shew his love to CHRIST and to his brethren in a form so severe. Brethren, when our gifts have upon them the stamp of Paul's; when we bear, like him, the marks of the LORD JESUS[34]; when we have conquered and foregone and forgotten self as he; when we have carried our lives in our hands, and lived face to

---

[31] 1 Cor. xvi. 22.   [32] 1 Cor. v. 5; 1 Tim. i. 20.

[33] 2 Sam. xvi. 5.

[34] Galat. vi. 17, τὰ στίγματα τοῦ Κυρίου Ἰησοῦ ἐν τῷ σώματί μου βαστάζω.

face with death for the Gospel's sake, as he ;
when all the *other* fruits of love have been
exhibited in us as in him ; when every personal object, affection, idol has become dross
to us that we may win CHRIST ; when our
love to the SAVIOUR has redounded, like his,
on the whole multitude of our brethren ; when
we know that if the choice were granted us, we
should rejoice to die rather than judge them,
—*then*, indeed, we may believe that the sen-
tences of condemnation which we, after his example, utter, are GOD's,—knowing that they
are assuredly not our own.

Even to this we *may* be called. It is possible. Perhaps one in a thousand is called ;
and he must not shrink from it. But there
is another vocation to which we are called,—
not one in a thousand, but one and all. We
are all " thereunto called, that we may inherit
a blessing." And therefore, for our own sake,
for the Church's sake, for our LORD's sake, let
us at least first learn from St. Paul to walk
in that " more excellent way," in which he
walked himself with a perfect heart ; which
he shewed to his disciples at Corinth ; which
he shews to us ! For " now abideth Faith,

Hope, Charity, these three.   But the greatest of these is Charity."[35]

O Lord, who hast taught us that all our doings without charity are nothing worth; Send Thy Holy Ghost, and pour into our hearts that most excellent gift of charity, the very bond of peace and of all virtues, without which whosoever liveth is counted dead before thee: Grant this for thine only Son Jesus Christ's sake. *Amen.*

[35] 1 Cor. xiii. 13.

SERMON VII.

THE PHARISEE AND THE SADDUCEE.

Preached on Sunday, October 15, 1855.

St. Matth. xvi. 12.

Then understood they how that He bade them not beware of the leaven of bread, but of the doctrine of the Pharisees and Sadducees.

THE unholy strifes of the Pharisees and Sadducees, and their still more unholy combinations against the Lord's Christ, form so awful a subject of contemplation in the Gospel history; and their characters are so clearly typical of the two great forms of evil which are ever working, even in the Church of God; that it cannot be a profitless labour to enquire into the history and nature of systems which have borne such portentous fruit.

In such an enquiry, it is necessary to begin with the Pharisees. Indeed it is a striking testimony to their importance and influence, that we must start from the knowledge of what they were, if we would gain the knowledge of what others were among the Jews at the same time. The belief of others can only be arrived at by contrast with that of the Pharisees.

Of their distinct and recognised existence we find no mention in any of the books of the Old Testament ; although doubtless we can trace the spirit of their peculiarities,— the spirit of rigid and zealous attachment to the letter of the Law. But in times when the prevailing temptation was to fall away from GOD's law to the idolatries and impurities of Heathen neighbours, the favourable side of the character was exhibited. And yet, when we read such messages of rebuke as those of Jeremiah[1], "Trust ye not in lying words, saying, The Temple of the LORD, The Temple of the LORD, The Temple of the LORD, are these," —we feel that they must, even in that day, have been addressed to Pharisees, not unlike those of whom we read in the New Testament.

But it appears to have been about a century and a half[2] before the coming of CHRIST, that

[1] Jerem. vii. 4.

[2] In the time of the High Priest Jonathan, B.C. 159– 144.

the name of Pharisee[3] became noted, as belonging to a sect or body of men,—a school of
doctrine, a party in politics[4],—among the Jews.
And it was given to them, or assumed by
them, to denote two things ; first (which
deserves more attention than it ordinarily
receives) that they maintained with especial
zeal that partition-wall which separated GOD's
people from the nations of the world, as the
clean from the unclean, the blessed from the
cursed of creation :—second, (and flowing from
the first,) that they separated themselves from
others, even of their brethren, by the rigour
with which they applied these principles, and
the assertion of their own exclusive pretensions
to purity of faith and formal righteousness of
life[5].   They were "*Separatists,*" "*Puritans,*"
nationally and individually,—blessing themselves as Hebrews of the Hebrews ; dealing
curses round, first on the Heathen, and then

3 פְּרוּשׁ, from פָּרַשׁ, *separavit* (Ezek. xxxiv. 12): see Epiphan. Haer. i. 16, and Suid. s. voce.

4 See, for instance, Josephus Antiqq. Jud. xvii. 2, 4.

5 "A Pharisee is he that separateth himself from all uncleanness, and from all unclean meats, and from the common people, that understand not the exact order of meats."
"Baal Aruch," in Lightfoot's Harmony, on St. Luke v. 17.

on all those of their own brethren who knew not the Law, or accepted not the Pharisee's interpretation[6].

It would thus appear that they strained to the utmost extent the principles of Judaism, as a code of strict formal obligation, measuring every man's doings by the letter of the Law[7]. And their system grew to be an example of the evil tendency of such an interpretation, not of Moses' Law alone, but of any law whatsoever.

It is reasonable to suppose that their attempt was originally honest. And there was, it must be confessed, something in the character of the Mosaic Law which might encourage it. We have, at all events, the portrait of one honest Pharisee in the New Testament : and this affords us the means of estimating the favourable side of the character, even in the age of its deepest corruption. The Jew of Tarsus, brought up at the feet of Gamaliel in the straitest sect of the Law, was a Pharisee in whom the struggle after good and the hatred

6 Lightfoot, Talmudical Exercitations, on Matth. iii. 7.

7 See Josephus, Antiqq. Jud. xiii. 10, 6. ; xvii. 2, 4 ; Id. Bell. Jud. i. 5, 2.

of evil were not stifled by the errors of his teaching respecting that which was good and that which was evil. In his own system he had been bred and trained ; and he had not been able of himself to go beyond its narrow limits. Therefore his zeal was more manifest in hatred than in love. But this zeal,—hating, persecuting zeal as it was—was in his case deeply rooted in the love of GOD. True, it did not therefore justify him. But it was not unavailing. No effort, made in singleness of purpose for the honour and service of GOD, is unavailing or unblest. And the further mercy and grace of GOD were vouchsafed, to enlighten the blindness of his zeal, to purge and hallow it, that he might do GOD acceptable service in the Gospel of His SON. And Saul, the blasphemer, the persecutor, the injurious, obtained mercy; because the evil that he had done was done through ignorance and erroneous belief[8]. And he was chosen to be the instrument of the real good that he had ignorantly sought after,—to become Paul the Apostle of the Gentiles.

Such fruit could come of the stock of Phari-

[8] 1 Tim. i. 12, 13.

saism,—crabbed as it was, cankered as it had become,—when it was grafted upon with the graft from Heaven. But at the time of our LORD's Advent, the canker had indeed spread fearfully. Evil had grown upon evil, even where the original had been good. For instance; it was surely good that they should strive after the perfect fulfilment of the law of GOD; and *that*, all the more earnestly, as others seemed to grow lax and careless of the Commandments. But this was poisoned when they claimed the title of Righteous beyond others, separate from their brethren as these were separate from the Heathen;—thus in their presumption bringing on themselves the very curse of the Prophet, where he denounces the iniquity of those who said, "Stand by thyself, come not near to me; for I am holier than thou."[9]

It was surely good that they should place their delight in the Law of the LORD, and meditate therein day and night. But they turned even this into an occasion of evil, when they used their knowledge, not for the good of their less favoured brethren, but to triumph

9 Isaiah lxv. 5.

over and insult them with such speeches as, " This people who knoweth not the law are cursed."[10]

Good, again, we know it was, that they should be continually in prayer to GOD; that they should give alms of such things as they had; that they should fast and deny themselves. But their fasts were not the fasts which GOD had chosen; their alms were not given to HIM; and their very prayer turned to abomination in His sight: because they fasted and gave alms to be seen of men, and made long prayers for a pretence[11].

But our LORD brought heavier charges against them than even these. And let us observe how they seem to have arrived, step by step, at that wickedness, which made them, under cover of zeal for GOD, the murderers of His SON. Their first profession was that of precise legal righteousness. They had aimed at this by a minute and painful study of all the rules and details of the Law. And this led them to merge all other thoughts and enquiries in the petty diligence which they bestowed upon the rules of outward conduct.

[10] St. John vii. 49.   [11] St. Matt. vi. 1–5; xxiii. 14.

And as these rules were innumerable, relating to all matters of detail, they seem to have had no clear perception of any one thing, as being more or less important than another. To the original Pharisee, every thing that was *written* was of equal consequence,—mint, anise, cummin,—judgment, mercy, and truth. But the necessary result was, that minds which studied the law in this way, however honestly, became absorbed in those things which were of least importance. They could not grasp the principles, or take in the spirit of the Law-giver. They might be honest; but they must be pettifoggers in the Law.

But what an opening was given, and what a temptation was held out, to dishonesty! If we know that the letter killeth, while the SPIRIT giveth life; and remember what St. Paul says of the Law of Moses, in contrast with "the ministration of the SPIRIT" in the Gospel[12]; we shall see how there might be the greatest semblance of strictness in out-ward things, while the plain meaning of the Law itself was neglected, or even violated.

Accordingly, the next step in advance was

[12] 2 Cor. iii. 6–9.

to multiply forms, and make further rules which were not in the Law, by way (as they said) of making a hedge round it[13]. A short and easy step, perhaps, for persons who had rigidly confined their attention to matters of outward rule and detail. Perhaps those who made it thought it so natural as to need no special consideration. Yet in this was contained the direct contradictory of their fundamental principle. They had held every detail of the Law, as a matter of life and death. Why? Plainly, as believing that every detail came from GOD, and was to be looked upon as His command. His Holiness and Majesty were communicated to every syllable of His Word: and therefore it was a religious duty to count the letters; it was a pious work to find mysteries in the mode of writing them. In language to which our Blessed LORD gave a worthier and more spiritual meaning[14], not a jot or a tittle should pass away.

In this was shewn their sense of the presence of the Spirit of GOD in His Word;—

[13] "Pirke Aboth," in Lightfoot's Harmony, on St. Matth. iii. 7, St. Luke v. 17. See also Josephus, Antiqq. Jud. xiii. 10, 6.   [14] St. Matth. v. 18.

a great truth, however imperfectly apprehended. But how are we to reconcile this
with the invention of new rules, which were
to be of equal authority and sanctity ?—
We certainly cannot : neither, it appears,
could they. And it would seem that the
legend of the unwritten precepts, communicated by Moses to the Seventy, and from
them handed down from generation to generation, was invented or adopted to meet
the difficulty [15]. These were the " traditions," by which our LORD accused them of
making the Law of GOD of none effect [16].
Grounded in falsehood, suggested by a carnal
temptation, it would have been strange indeed if these " commandments of men" which
they " taught for doctrines," had long remained
in accordance with the written Word of GOD.
Having first neglected the spirit of Scripture
in their devotion to the letter, they went on
to nullify the written letter itself through
their own precepts. Teaching things over
and above and besides GOD's Law, they also
taught that their own precepts were the more

[15] See Lightfoot's Harmony on St. Matth. iii. 7, St. Luke
v. 17.   [16] St. Matth. xv. 3–9.

important. According to their own saying, the Scripture was "salt," but the traditions of the Elders " spices ;" the Scripture was " water," but the teaching of the Rabbis " wine."[17] Evading the plainest laws of GOD first, they were soon emboldened to contradict them. Not content with making the law of none effect, they proceeded to such breaches of it as that for which CHRIST Himself denounced them, wherein they violated the fifth Commandment in the very letter, and virtually said, " Thou shalt not honour thy father or thy mother."

And these perversions reached their climax, as was to be expected, in the persecution of the MESSIAH. To shed His blood was an object for which all scruples, all principles were openly disregarded. With this object in view, we find the religious Zealots banded with the unbelieving Sadducees ; we find the political Patriots more Romish than the Roman Go-

---

[17] Lewis, Origines Hebraeae, bk. 2, ch. 20. The gloss, that water and salt are necessaries of life, while wine and spices are only luxuries, is an apologetic refinement of very modern times.

vernor, taunting him with want of zeal for their heathen master's interests[18].

But their attention to the letter and neglect of the spirit of the Commandments wrought in yet another way. It necessarily directed all their thoughts to the outward part of acts and ordinances, even when these were acts of duty, ordinances of piety. Every thing was directed to the outside (so to speak) of the duty,—the doings, the sayings, the appearance. Whether intentionally or not, the whole religion of the Pharisee, as such, might be seen of men as well as God. Close at hand, then, was the temptation to do their works,— works which might otherwise have perhaps been acceptable to God—for that less worthy purpose. Hence the widened phylacteries, the greetings in the markets, the uppermost seats, the prayers in the corners of the streets, the almsgiving by sound of trumpet, the ostentatious washings, the cleansings of the outside of the cup and platter. Hence the uncharitable comparisons of themselves with others, as " even " with " this Publican " in the Para-

---

18 St. Matth. xvi. 1 ; St. Luke xxiii. 2 ; St. John xix. 12.

ble.[19]   Hence the self-glorification, even in GOD's House, on forms of godliness and acts of common duty.

And, verily, they had their reward! As they acted to be seen of men, of men their reward was received.   They had it, in the reverence of their brethren, in their worldly reputation, in the advancement of their interests, in the authority of their words[20].   They had it, as our LORD intimates, in full, and had no more to expect[21];—no reward from GOD for that which was not done for His sake;—no reward from HIM that seeth in secret, for that which they did with parade and ostentation.

But this leads (and again by no difficult steps) to the worst part of their character, as described by JESUS CHRIST.   They lived to be seen of men.   When their sect was in its corruption, therefore, they found nothing in their principles to deter them from any secret indulgence or vice, which could be cloaked un-

---

[19] St. Luke xviii. 11.

[20] Ὥστε καὶ κατὰ βασιλέως τι λέγοντες καὶ κατὰ ἀρχιερέως πιστεύεσθαι : Josephus, Antiqq. Jud. xiii. 10, 5., 15, 5.   He compares them to the Stoics, Joseph. Vita 2.

[21] ἀπέχουσι, St. Matth. vi. 2, etc.

der an outside show of rigour and austerity.
What is the word with which the LORD continually brands them? " *Hypocrites;* " " Woe
unto you, Hypocrites !" And while you recognise the awful nature of this sin in itself, think
of its aggravation, in those who claimed to be
preachers and patterns of GOD's will, interpreters of His Law, teachers of His babes, guides
of His people[22]. Their whole position as a body,
depended on their claim to know and to practise, above others, the will and word of GOD.
And yet what do we hear, or rather, what do
we *not* hear, of their doings, from CHRIST's
lips ? Professing to keep the key of heaven,
they neither went in themselves, nor suffered
them that were entering. Making long prayers
for a pretence, they devoured widows' houses.
Full of professions of purity, so that a neglect
of washing the hands was a scandal to them,
they were within full of extortion and excess.
Abusing the Mosaic permission of divorce for
the indulgence of lust[23],—yea, unable to cast

---

[22] See Romans ii. 17, sqq.

[23] Note the grossness of the sins with which they are
taxed, St. Matth. xv. 18–20 ; xvi. 4 ; xix. 3, sqq. ; xxiii.
1–33 ; St. Luke xi. 39–44 ; and especially the juxta-posi-

a stone at the woman taken in adultery, because their own consciences convicted them;
distinguishing between one oath and another,
to give licence to falsehood; distorting " Thou
shalt love thy neighbour" into " Thou shalt
hate thine enemy"[24]; mocking GOD and man
by an unreal dedication of their goods, that
they might call it a duty to withhold help
even from father or mother[25]; can we wonder that such sinners resisted the teaching
and rejected the person of the MESSIAH? Can
we wonder at the burning words of His rebukes against those who in such a manner
made men abhor the very worship and service of the LORD?

And *this* made their cup run over. They
acknowledged His miracles and ascribed them

tion of vv. 15–17, and 18, in St. Luke xvi; and Rom. ii.
21–23.

[24] St. Matth. v. 34–36, 44.

[25] St. Matth. xv. 5, sqq., on which Lightfoot remarks, "This
form of speech did neither argue that he who thus spake,
devoted his goods to sacred uses, nor obliged him (according to the doctrine of the scribes) to devote them; but only
restrained him by an obligation from that thing, for the
denying of which he used such a form... He was not at all
bound by these words to dedicate his estate to sacred uses;
but not to help his father he was inviolably bound."

to Beelzebub. They saw that all men were going after HIM; and could not deny the evidence which had produced such an effect. But their hearts were as the heart of Pharaoh, hardened by the very manifestation of the finger of GOD. Early in the Ministry of JESUS CHRIST, they had taken counsel to destroy HIM [26]; and this design never ceased; though, until His hour was come, they were holden from murder. These were they who plotted to put Lazarus also to death, because his resurrection had brought many to believe on CHRIST[27]. These were they who eagerly gave money to betray JESUS;—who made " One of the Twelve" (how solemn and mournful is the way in which those words return again and again in the inspired narrative of CHRIST's Passion)—made One of the Twelve twofold more the child of hell than themselves; and who then, as the true brood of the old Serpent, scoffed at his remorse with " What is that to us? see thou to that;" and sat calmly down to discuss what might lawfully be done with money that was the price of blood. These were they who suborned false wit-

[26] St. Mark iii. 6.　　　[27] St. John xi. 53; xii. 10, 11.

nesses against the LORD, who accused HIM of one crime, and procured His condemnation for another[28].

On them it came to fill up the measure of their fathers who had slain the prophets, by slaying HIM to whom all the prophets bore witness, even the LORD, whom they professed to delight in !

Is it possible to find a more hopeless character than this ?

Unfortunately, it is possible, even in a class which may appear less actively malignant in wickedness. We are incidentally told in the Acts of the Apostles, that " the Sadducees say that there is no resurrection, neither angel, nor spirit ;" while " the Pharisees confess both."[29] And this negative statement is, in fact, all that we ascertain from the Bible of the theology of Sadduceeism. The chief point, the denial of the resurrection of the dead, is heard of in that part of the Gospels, which tells of their attempt to involve our LORD in a

[28] St. Matth. xxvii. 3-7 ; compare St. Luke xxii. 70, 71, with xxiii. 2, etc.

[29] Acts xxiii. 8.

difficulty on that subject[30]. The disbelief of
the existence of disembodied spirits belongs
to the same error: for if the spirits of the
departed ceased to exist, there could be no
resurrection, although there might be a new
creation of a new race of beings in the likeness of the old[31].

Striking as the contrast must appear between the original principles and the ultimate
development of Pharisaism, this is even more
singular in the case of the Sadducees. Whether we adopt the account which refers their
origin to the teaching of Antigonus of Socho[32],
and the misunderstanding of his pupil Sadok;
or whether we interpret their name as signify-
ing *Righteous*[33], and suppose that they adopted
it as an assertion that, while others obeyed
from fear of punishment and hope of reward,
they alone were righteous for righteousness'
sake; their tenets apparently originated in a

[30] St. Matth. xxii. 23–32.

[31] See Lightfoot, Exercitations on Acts xxiii. 8.

[32] " Be not as servants that serve their master, because
of receiving a reward," (Lightfoot, Harmony, as before).

[33] צַדִּיק ; hence צְדוּכִי.   Compare Epiphan. Haer. I. 14,
who refers their origin to the Samaritans.

reaction from those of the Pharisees. In politics, they found a party asserting independence and justifying rebellion on the principles of austere Judaism : and because they shrank from this extreme, they seem to have renounced all feelings of patriotism ; and to have lapsed into a habit of indifference to the public weal, careless who interfered with their nation, provided that their private ease and creature comforts were spared[34]. In religion, they found a multitude of dogmas, rules, and traditions, overlaying, nay, contradicting their Scriptures. They recoiled from these, and retired upon the assertion of the exclusive authority of the Scriptures, and their simplicity[35]. It would appear that there were three stages in this process :—first, to reject all that had been added to the written Word :—then, to include in the same rejection every thing which they did not see expressed there in so many distinct words, however clearly it might be inferred from that which was written :—

[34] As Josephus (Vita 2) compares the Pharisees to the *Stoics*, the name of *Epicureans* was frequently given to the Sadducees ; cf. Tertullian. de Resurr. Carnis 2.

[35] See Joseph. Antiqq. Jud. xiii. 10, 6.

lastly, to simplify the Bible (as they thought) still more, by disparaging the later books of it in comparison with the actual Law of Moses.

Let us take these in order.

The Sadducees rejected all that the Pharisees had added,—all those human traditions and inventions which had been imposed upon the people, not as of human, but as of Divine authority, as articles of faith, or duties necessary to the fulfilment of GOD's will. For this, at least, we can find no fault with them : for this is what we recognise continually in the teaching of JESUS CHRIST. And we must suppose that they heard HIM gladly, when HE rebuked the Pharisees for making the Word of GOD of none effect through their traditions.

But they proceeded to reject every thing which they did not find set down in express words in their Bible[36]. And this is a very plausible rule, because it may seem to follow naturally from the former. To us it is especially plausible, because it seems, at first sight, so nearly the same with the rule which guided our Reformers, and guides our Church, in

36 See Lightfoot's Sermon on Acts xxiii. 8.

protesting against Rome. But it is just so nearly the same, without being the same, as to deceive. The Sadducees measured the Word of GOD, each for himself, by his own ignorance, his own unbelief, his own want of spiritual discernment. Each believed as little as he chose. And this was not unfruitful of consequences. For instance; they professed to believe in the Law:—but nevertheless they maintained that there was no resurrection, neither angel nor spirit[37].

And this led directly to the last stage.

The books of the Old Testament, which follow the Pentateuch, were written from time to time, as the SPIRIT of GOD moved holy men, to reveal His will more fully, and to prepare His people for the future revelation of the MESSIAH. Consequently, they contain many things relating to GOD and to His plans for our Redemption, more plainly stated than in the earlier books. Every prophecy is an additional revelation : every preparation of the Jews for their SAVIOUR, is something added, something more clearly told than Moses had

37 And yet see such passages as Gen. xxxii. 1 ; Deut. xxxiii. 2 !

told it. It pleased GOD to mature His merciful plans by an orderly and steady growth, until the fulness of time came, and HE sent forth His SON. But this accumulated treasure of revelation the Sadducees refused to accept. Their process was to strip away all that had been added, not merely by the Pharisees, but by GOD's servants the prophets from generation to generation. It is very commonly thought that they actually rejected all the books of the Old Testament except the Pentateuch,—casting them away as additions overlaying or corrupting the simplicity of the Law[38]. On this point, perhaps, the evidence is not decisive. But the most lenient interpreters of their conduct agree that they treated the later portions of the Jewish Scriptures as less valuable and less authoritative than the earlier. Evidently, they did not believe in them as being, in the same sense with the Books of Moses, the Word of GOD.

[38] This is stated by Tertullian, de Praescr. Haer. 45, and by many after him :—but see the summary in Winer's Real-Wörterbuch, s. v. *Sadducäer ;* compare Lightfoot's Sermon, " The Great Assize ;" and his Exercitations on St. John iv. 25.

In connection with this disparagement of one portion of GOD's Word, and meagre interpretation of the other, we have to consider their attempt to justify by the authority of their Lawgiver a sneer at the doctrine of the resurrection[39]. Very remarkable and characteristic is the question which they put to CHRIST, "tempting HIM." But still more remarkable, and full of matter for meditation, is His answer. HE does not go beyond that Pentateuch which had furnished their objection, and which was certainly the foundation of the little belief that they had; but he produces from it an evidence of the continued life of those whom the world calls *dead*, and, consequently, of a future state of existence. But what kind of evidence? Not contained in any direct words of Holy Writ; but precisely that which they rejected as inadmissible,—an inference, an argument drawn from what is incidentally said in a passage which treats of another subject. If we had been ignorant of the words of JESUS CHRIST, how often might we not have read, "I am the GOD of Abraham, of Isaac, and of Jacob," with-

39 St. Matth. xxii. 23–32.

out noticing that these words taught us any thing respecting the life of our own souls after death! And yet how plainly do they contain this doctrine, when read in the light of Christ's explanation ;—" As touching the resurrection of the dead, have ye not read that which was spoken unto you by God, saying, I am the God of Abraham, and the God of Isaac, and the God of Jacob? God is not the God of the dead, but of the living : for all live unto Him." [40] Some have thought it strange, that Jesus Christ should have chosen a passage of Scripture for their confutation, which at first seems to have so little connection with the subject ; and that He should have fixed on them the severe rebuke, " Ye do err, not knowing the Scriptures," because they had failed to find the doctrine in a passage, where indeed it lay, but lay, as it were, hidden. But was not this the Divine Wisdom, which would not answer their quibbling objection, without striking at the root from which all their error sprung? To me it seems, that the chief lesson of all is contained in this very choice of the passage of Scripture, and of the argu-

40 St. Matth. xxii. 32 : St. Luke xx. 38, adds the last words.

ment, to expose them. It goes far beyond
the actual question which they had asked,
and shews that their denial of every doctrine
which was not directly and in so many words
set down in the Scripture, was a denial of
the deepest meaning of Scripture itself. It
shews, that we must not suppose that we have
attained to all that GOD would have us know
and believe to our souls' health, by such a
superficial study of the Bible as may acquaint
us with its simple statements in matters of
fact. It shews that we are to accept the doctrines which are fairly drawn from it, and to
believe these also as part of the revelation;
and that we are thus to believe many things
which perhaps might not at first suggest
themselves to us in the course of our reading: that is, we are to believe them, when
they are pointed out, and we see that they
follow as sure conclusions from that which is
actually to be read in various parts of the
Bible. It shews, in short, that we are not to
take the Bible into our hands as being irre-
sponsible judges of what we must believe and
what we may neglect; but that we are to
study it in humility, remembering that it is

God's Word, and therefore is the Truth itself; —that, being His Word, it has a depth and extent of meaning which no *man's* word can have;—that it is His Word, and therefore that the deepest and fullest meaning is likely also to be the truest. It bids us remember also that His Word is to be spiritually discerned; and therefore that the real depth of its meaning is to be sought by prayer to the same Holy Spirit Who inspired it, and by all the helps which (in these days when the so-called miraculous gifts of the Holy Ghost are no longer poured out upon the Church) are given through meditation, and study, and the voice of the teacher, and the writings of those holy men of former days, whose knowledge of things scriptural and insight into things spiritual has made their teaching the Household-Book of Christ's Church.

We may learn, in short, from these words of the Saviour, our duty to accept as scriptural not only such Articles of Faith as are read in express words in the Bible, but also such as (in the phraseology of our own Formularies) "may be proved thereby." We may learn this, on the one hand, as certainly, as on the other we may learn from His denunciations of the Pharisees, that "whatsoever is not read therein nor may be proved thereby, is not to be required of any man that it should be believed as an Article of the Faith, or be thought requisite or necessary to salvation."[41] The one is our vindication against the pretensions of any particular Church to have every thing which she may devise and teach, accepted and received. The other is the warrant of the Church Catholic in all its branches, as witness and keeper of Holy Writ, to draw from Holy Scripture the doctrines which are contained therein and may be proved thereby, and to teach them, as our LORD Himself taught them, with authority.

When, from this consideration of tenets and principles we turn to their concrete embodiment in the sect with which our LORD had to deal, we are indeed tempted to ask, Did Sadduceeism really contain so much within it? For we are apt to esteem the Sadducees not so much a religious sect, in any real sense of the phrase, as a mere party of men without reli-

[41] Article VI.

N

gion, who, believing in nothing that could raise them to godliness or virtue,—in no spiritual influences, no life after death, no heaven or hell,—had no care but to live in such enjoyments as the world and the flesh afforded them, saying, " Let us eat and drink, for to morrow we die."[42]   Such, undoubtedly, is the result of their tenets, as delineated in the history of the New Testament.   They were a party of no great number, but recruited chiefly from the wealthy and influential classes ;[43]— acceptable to the powers that were, through the same compliance which they were ready to shew to the powers that might be on the morrow;—even gaining a share in the government ;—sometimes (strange as it may seem) in possession of the High Priesthood and chief power in the Sanhedrim ;[44]—the " men of the world, who have their portion in this life ; whose belly is filled with hidden treasure."[45]

And therefore, awful as the guilt of the Pharisees was, and treacherous as is their ex-

---

[42] 1 Cor. xv. 32 ;—but the words are older, Isai. xxii. 13.

[43] Τοὺς εὐπόρους μόνον πειθόντων, τὸ δὲ δημοτικὸν οὐχ ἑπόμενον αὐτοῖς ἐχόντων : Joseph. Antiqq. Jud. xiii. 10, 6.

[44] Acts iv. 1 ; v. 17. .   [45] Psalm xvii. 14.

ample; sad as is the judgment which must be passed on them in comparison with the Publicans whom they despised, and the multitude whom they cursed; there was more hope for them than for the Sadducees. With all the Pharisee's errors and pride and sin, his heart preserved, his mouth professed a faith. But this—even in its lowest and most corrupt form—was wholly wanting in the Sadducee. There was nothing left to appeal to in his inward nature. His was not disease, but death! A brutish life was leading him down with an undisturbed conscience to a hopeless end. His god was his belly. Beyond the appetites which had enthralled him, he would retain no knowledge, he had no aspirations. And therefore we need not wonder, that while we find the Pharisee and the Publican, Saul and Matthew, brought within the kingdom of CHRIST, and even into the number of the Apostles, the New Testament does not record so much as one Sadducee who became a Christian.

And now, brethren, it were an easy thing to dismiss the subject by saying, *This* is the portrait of a Romanist, and *that* of a Rationalist; and by thanking God that we in our Church are not as they! Ay, it is an easy thing to construe warnings to ourselves into judgments upon our neighbours, and to think the very thoughts, to adopt the very words of the Pharisee whom we condemn! Truly, the lengthened robe and the broad phylacteries fit well, and have a comely show! But let us judge *this* rather, that there are few hearts in which the Pharisee does not strive for the uppermost seat; few which the Sadducee does not strive to drag down to unbelief or to sensuality. It is in his own heart that each one of us is to beware of their leaven. Those whom our Blessed LORD warned against it in the text, were His own favoured and familiar Twelve! And the warning is not given, that we may point to instances where special sins, for which we, perhaps, have no taste, have developed themselves; but that we may recognise for ourselves the various shapes in which the Tempter assails us, the numberless weak points which we have hitherto left unguarded against his attacks. There was a time when our LORD was warning the Jews of the certainty of judgment upon sinners; and they forthwith assented, and began to moralize upon the fate of some miserable Galileans, whose destruction had come suddenly at an instant. HE was compelled to tell of another blow, which had fallen upon the dwellers in Jerusalem, before HE could bring their thoughts home. HE was compelled to say, " Except *ye* repent, ye shall all likewise perish," before they would believe that HE spoke of them[43]!

May HE give us the grace so to lay to heart the blessings that we enjoy, and the warnings that we have received, that we may combine faith with knowledge, and zeal with charity; that we may hold the truth in righteousness; and that we may speak the truth in love!

43 St. Luke xii. 58; xiii. 5.

SERMON VIII.

THE PUBLICAN.

Preached on Sunday, November 12th, 1854.

St. Luke xviii. 13.

And the Publican, standing afar off, would not lift up so much as his eyes unto Heaven, but smote upon his breast, saying, GOD be merciful to me a sinner.

WE were lately occupied in considering the two most prominent figures in that outer circle which gathered round the person of our Blessed LORD, to spy, to scoff, or to enquire. We were studying the Pharisee and the Sadducee. But the group is not complete without the portrait of another, who mingled in the crowd with very different feelings, and bore himself there in a very different spirit, from either. Nor will the interest of the character be less; though the Publican shrank from the notoriety which the others courted. Nor will the usefulness of the sketch be less; if, at the very outset, it recalls our thoughts from wandering to our adversaries without, and bids them rest on ourselves, on our own secret sinfulness, our own need of repentance, and of forgiveness in JESUS CHRIST.

There is no need at present to investigate minutely the occupations and duties of those Publicans of whom we hear so much in the history of our LORD's life. There is no need to dwell on the contrast betweeen the estimation and position of the Equestrian *Publicani* at Rome, as we learn it from the testimony (not altogether disinterested or unsuspicious) of Cicero[1], and that of these poor provincial drudges, who did their dirty work and re-

---

[1] Adjungam, si vis, id quod tu huic obesse etiam putas, patrem *publicanum :* qui ordo quanto adjumento sit in honore, quis nescit? Flos enim Equitum Romanorum, ornamentum civitatis, firmamentum reipublicae publicanorum ordine continetur." *Cicero pro Plancio,* 9 (23); see also his oration *pro Lege Manilia,* 7 (17), etc.

plenished their coffers. Suffice it to say that
the Jewish Publicans had the collection of all
sorts of rates and taxes which the Roman government imposed. They were Excise-men ;
they were Custom-house officers ; they were
Toll-collectors. At the gates of cities, on the
shores of ferries, on roads and in market-places,
—everywhere the publicans were to be found;
men whose business, whose whole living it was
to exact money from all those who bought and
sold,—well nigh from all those who went and
came. Such a mode of living was not likely
to be popular. It never is popular, under any
circumstances. Even among those who have
a voice, through their Representatives, in deciding the matter,—and who may be thus said
to choose how they shall be taxed, and how
the money shall be spent,—it is, no doubt,
unsatisfactory to pay taxes and unpopular to
ask for them. But there was much besides,
which aggravated this feeling of dissatisfac-
tion among the Jews. Other nations, smarting
under the capricious exactions of their former
needy or greedy masters, might have at least
acquiesced in the system of Roman Finance ;
might perhaps have hailed the administration

of an upright individual ; and even erected statues, as we read in the case of Vespasian's ancestor[2], τῷ καλῶς τελωνήσαντι. But for many generations the children of Israel had no taxes, except for GOD's service. It is difficult indeed to accept the " Non erit vectigal pendens ex filiis Israel," which Tertullian quotes[3], as an accurate version of any passage in the book of Deuteronomy. But the fact was so. We do indeed read of a " tribute," in connexion with the name of Adoram or Adoniram, under David and Solomon[4]; but it is explained (in the first book of Kings) as a tribute of service, a levy of men for the works which the king was carrying on ;—and this, as is expressly stated, not levied on the children of Israel, but on the remainder of the Canaanites which dwelt among them in the land[5]. It is true that the petition of the people to Rehoboam, and the stoning of Adoram which followed its

2 " Sabinus..., publicum quadragesimae in Asia egit : manebant imagines a civitatibus ei positae sub hoc titulo, ΚΑΛΩΣ ΤΕΛΩΝΗΣΑΝΤΙ." Sueton. Vespas. i. 5.

3 Tertullian. de Pudicitia, § 9; conjectured to refer to Deut. xxiii. 19.

4 2 Sam. xx. 24., 1 Kings iv. 6 ; iv. 14.

5 1 Kings ix. 15, 20, 21, 22.

rejection[6], make it probable that in this particular the people had suffered more directly in the later portion of Solomon's reign;—true, that on special and urgent occasions the kings sometimes exacted subsidies ; as Menahem levied fifty shekels of silver of each of the mighty men of wealth, to replace the thousand talents which he had given to Pul, king of Assyria, as the price of peace[7]. Indeed it had been one of the prophetic warnings of Samuel, when the people said, "Nay, but we will have a king over us," that the king would take the tenths of their produce and their cattle[8]. But still they had little experience of taxation, while as yet they were an independent people.

In their minds it was indissolubly connected with the humbling thought of their subjection to a foreign, that is, a heathen power. And it was above all things galling, to feel that they were taxed for the benefit of the Gentile. It continually reminded them, and that in the most vexatious way, of their lost independence. We know how morbidly sensitive they were,

6 1 Kings xii. 4, 18.　　　7 2 Kings xv. 19, 20.
8 1 Sam. viii. 15–17.

whenever they suspected that an allusion was made to their loss of liberty. Thus, when our LORD spoke to them of the freedom which the truth might confer, they mistook His meaning, and answered, in the folly of their pride, "We be Abraham's seed, and were never in bondage to any man."[9] As if their fathers had never wept by the waters of Babylon! As if the very coin with which they bought and sold, did not bear Caesar's image and superscription!

Dwelling, as they habitually dwelt, upon their hereditary privileges as children of Abraham, as the people of GOD; having their minds full of the prophecies that the Gentiles should come to their light, and kings to the brightness of their shining,— that the sons of strangers should build up their walls, and their kings should minister unto them[10]; they had neither eyes to see, nor minds to understand, how this could be fulfilled in a spiritual sense,—fulfilled by any other Israel than the "Israel after the flesh." Hence their national subjection to the Romans was more than a humiliation of arrogance. It was, in many

9 St. John viii. 33.　　10 Isaiah lx. 3, 10.

and serious respects, a stumblingblock to faith.

This being their view of their heathen masters and the machinery of their government, we may easily conceive the added bitterness of hatred which it engendered against any of their own brethren, who should make themselves the instruments of these masters. And such were the Publicans of whom we read. If it had been an open enemy, they could have borne it ; if it had been their adversary, they would have hid themselves from him : —but what, when it was their companion, their brother ? With such an one they could not walk in the house of God as friends ![11]

Add to all this, the fact that the taxes which they were compelled to pay were not merely collected for the public treasury. They were farmed. A profit was made upon them. Wealthy corporations at Rome rented the taxes of whole provinces ; and gained what advantage they might by employing others under them in like manner, to levy the tolls, customs, or tribute of single districts. It was the worldly interest of those who collected the

[11] Psalm lv. 12, 13, 14; compare St. Luke xviii. 11.

money on the spot, to be extortioners. All that they could exact beyond that which was their due, was so much actual gain to themselves.

And, to say the truth, they seem to have been not unjustly accused of extortion and fraud. There were few opportunities of redress for the subjects of a remote province. The risk therefore was small, the temptation great. Treated as enemies and outcasts, they were goaded on to use their brethren unkindly. Two strong passions combined to urge them. They had it in their power to enrich themselves, and, in so doing, to revenge themselves. And, notoriously, they *did* enrich themselves[12]. So, when they sought the Baptism of John, and said to him "What shall *we* do?" the one precept which he thought needful, as a sufficient test of their sincerity and repentance, was, "Exact no more than that which is appointed you."[13]

We must take into account their temptations, and their provocations. We must take into account the influence of an ill name in making those who are compelled to bear it, act so as to justify it in the end. And we must

[12] St. Luke xix. 2, 8.   [13] St. Luke iii. 12, 13.

remember that these Publicans had the worst names which their countrymen (curious as they were in nicknames) could bestow. You know how the words "Publicans and sinners" go together in the Gospel. One can scarcely pronounce the one word without the other rising to one's lips. And they are used together in the inspired narrative itself in such a manner as to recognise the general correctness of the proverbial phrase. For it is not only that the Jews are represented as asking why our Blessed LORD ate and drank with such people: but the words "It came to pass, as JESUS sat at meat in the house, behold, many publicans and sinners came and sat down with HIM," are those of the Evangelist himself; —and what Evangelist? Matthew the Publican![14] Nay, his Divine Master Himself says, "If thy brother neglect to hear the Church, let him be unto thee as an heathen man and a publican;"—and, "If ye love them which love you, what reward have ye? do not even the publicans the same?" What, indeed, are the terms of His most merciful declaration towards them?—"Verily I say unto you, That the pub-

[14] St. Matth. ix. 10, 11.

licans and the harlots go into the kingdom of GOD before you. For John came unto you in the way of righteousness, and ye believed him not : but the publicans and the harlots believed him."[15]—Therefore the Jews would not so much as eat or drink with those of their brethren who were Publicans. In their writings they classed them with highway-robbers and murderers. In their courts of law they would not admit their testimony; for it was lawful for a publican to swear falsely. In matters of religion they treated them as excommunicate and cast out of the synagogue. A promise made to a publican was not held to be binding. Their very money was not to be accepted ; because the presumption was that it had been stolen[16].

What greater or more striking contrast could there be, than that which existed between the Pharisee and the Publican ? The one high in reputation among his brethren,— the other despised and abhorred of them ; the one avoiding the Heathen as a pollution,—

[15] St. Matth. xviii. 17 ; v. 46, 47 ; xxi. 31, 32.

[16] Lightfoot, Exercitations on St. Matth. xviii. 19 ; Lewis, Origines Hebraeae, bk. 2. ch. 26 ; Winer, Real-Wörterbuch, s. v. *Zoll, Zöllner.*

the other making his wealth by dealing with them and for them; the one trying to evade even the recognition of the foreign master,— the other lending himself to the exaction of his taxes; the one paying tithes of all that he gained[17], and fasting twice in the week,— the other making his livelihood by forbidden gains and petty frauds; the one thanking GOD that he was not as other men, extortioners, unjust, adulterers, or even (to sum up all evil characters in one) this Publican,—the other not daring so much as to lift up his eyes to Heaven, but smiting upon his breast, and crying, "GOD be merciful to me a sinner!" And, no doubt, he was a sinner, not only in that sense in which all are convicted of sin before GOD, but, in many respects, beyond others. Placed in such temptations, engaged in such traffic, driven like a leper from all other society to herd with outcasts like himself,—it is hard to think that any but those who were already degraded would undertake the occupation; harder still to think that any one could exercise it without being degraded further. It has been already remarked, that we

17 Πάντα ὅσα κτῶμαι,—not κέκτημαι.

had at all events the portrait of one *honest* Pharisee represented to us in the New Testament. Perhaps, it would be rash to assert as much of a Publican. And yet there is *that* to be said, which more than makes up the difference. It is to be said,—for CHRIST Himself has said it,—that the Publican returned home from the Temple justified rather than the Pharisee ; that the Publican went into the kingdom of GOD before the Pharisee.

He had, in fact, one great advantage over the Pharisee as regarded the future salvation, in the very disadvantages under which he was placed in this life. He could never blind himself to his own lowness and meanness, or to the need of becoming something very different from that which he was, before he could be rescued from degradation. There was no treacherous defence which he could set up between himself and the rebukes of his conscience,—no staff of a bruised reed for him to lean upon, which could even for a moment prop the hand which it pierced,—no praise and reverence of men,—no outward works of formal righteousness,—nothing whereof to glory, whether before GOD or before man. He was a sinner, and he knew it; he was an outcast, and he knew it: he knew too well that he could not save himself. Nay, the Pharisee, unconscious as he was, and unwilling, had he been conscious, was his chief benefactor. The Pharisee was the continual teacher of the lesson, which was to make him meet to receive the grace of God: the Pharisee took abundant care that the Publican should not split upon the rock of his own spiritual shipwreck. The Pharisee inculcated upon him the lessons, which he found too hard to learn himself, of his sinfulness, his humiliation, his helplessness and need of a Saviour. Thus even the evil was in God's hands made to work for good; and thus he who stood at the door of God's kingdom, was made to serve God by bringing in others, though he himself remained without.

Another advantage was, that the Publican's sins and wretchedness were such as no hypocrisy could cloak. He might, indeed, go on living, as unhappily so many do, without God in the world. But whenever his conscience was roused, he could not haggle with it, or try, as it were, to strike a balance between

the two sides of his account. There was nothing for him but repentance, restitution, and
a cry for mercy. His spiritual disease revealed
itself, as plainly as the bodily ailments of the
blind, the lame, or the leper ; and, like these,
drove him to seek the Physician. " For there
were many," we are told, "and they followed
HIM." And to such was the Great Physician
sent. "They that are whole have no need of
the physician, but they that are sick. I came
not to call the righteous, but sinners to repentance."[18]

And thus he came to Zacchaeus, not for the
merit of his good works ; not because he had
striven, even up to the light which he had
possessed, to serve GOD acceptably in his
calling ; but because he was one of the lost
sheep of the house of Israel ; because he was
lost, and knew and felt the misery of being
lost. Zacchaeus longed to be found again,—
longed to see, if it were no more, the Prophet
whose teaching offered a glimpse of hope to
those who had no other. And his longings
took an active shape. They overcame the symbolical obstacle of his short stature. They lifted

[18] St. Mark ii. 15–17.

him above the multitude which crowded round
JESUS with lower or mixed motives. And no
sooner was this effected, than the SAVIOUR
whom he longed to see, met him, as HE meets
all, half-way,—nay, at their very doors, if they
will but open to let HIM come in, and sup with
them, and they with HIM. And the wealthy
Publican made what offering he could, in alms,
and confession, and fourfold restitution of ill-
gotten gear; and that day salvation came to
his house![19]

And thus HE came to a man named Matthew, sitting at the receipt of custom by the
side of the lake of Gennesaret,—and said to
him, " Follow me!" A strange and startling
call indeed! A call, the more severe and
searching, from the time and place at which
it was given. He was at the receipt of custom,—engaged in his lucrative business, as the
moneychanger at his desk, the shopman at
his counter, the tollman at his gate. When
this business was most pressing, and its temptations most overwhelming, CHRIST called him
to forsake all and follow HIM[20]. But HE
knew the hearts of men, and HE knew whom

[19] St. Luke xix. 2–10.   [20] St. Matth. ix. 9.

HE had chosen ;—and Matthew arose and followed HIM ; and entered into the kingdom of Heaven, ay, the Apostleship itself, while as yet the future Apostle of the Gentiles was learning the lesson of persecution in the schools of the Pharisees.

And if we are tempted to wonder, as thoughtless men may, at the measure of mercy meted to those who, because they are among men more disreputable, seem sinners beyond others, let us take with us one or two contributions towards the solution of the difficulty, and the discovery of the moral. Let us look at our respectable man, the man of creditable worldly behaviour, the man who reaps the golden opinions of the world. Is he the man who rules his conduct by a heavenly standard ? No :— his rule of life and principles of action are indeed above those of the world, but not different from them. They are above them, or there would be nothing to admire ; but not different from them, or the world would not bestow the admiration. He must be such a one as the world can at least appreciate, and will approve ; not a slave, but at least a friend to the world; and therefore no implacable enemy to its Prince. And of such it was that our LORD spoke so awfully, "Ye are they which justify yourselves before men; but GOD knoweth your hearts: for that which is highly esteemed among men is abomination in the sight of GOD."[21]

This is one consideration. Another, and one still more serious, is suggested by the question,—which each amongst us must answer from the Bible and its echo in our consciences,—How is it that we have any hopes of Heaven at all? And when we have from the heart confessed that it is in that Eternal Love alone, through which the Blessed SON offered Himself a sacrifice for sin,—then comes the further questioning, What moved HIM to this; and for whom did HE die? It was His Divine compassion on those who had gone astray and had no helper, that brought HIM down from His FATHER's glory, to suffer and to die for us. It was to save sinners, to blot out sin, to redeem the captives of Satan, to recover that which was lost, to give sight to the mentally blind and healing to the sick in spirit,

---

[21] St. Luke xvi. 15.

that HE shed His most precious blood.   HE
gave Himself not for the callous or the self-
righteous, but for those who have neither hope
nor help except in HIM.

We may be in the sight of men what the Pharisees were amongst their admiring brethren :
but we have not to do with men, but with
GOD ; and before His face we must come,
" even as this Publican," or else we have not
JESUS CHRIST for our Saviour.   We must
come, not pleading our merits, but confessing
our sins ; calling on HIM to help us, not because we have earned His help, but because
we have earned none, and need all : not thanking GOD that we are unlike the rest of the
world; but thanking and praising HIM for the
faithful saying that CHRIST JESUS came into
the world to save sinners [22].

There is indeed a difference in the tone which
the message of GOD in CHRIST takes, accordingly as it is first, or it may be once for all,
addressed to those who have never before
heard of their SAVIOUR,—or as it is delivered day by day to those whom GOD has
mercifully taken into covenant in His SON,

[22] 1 Tim. i. 15.

and to whom the gift of the Spirit has already been vouchsafed.

Where His Church has been planted of old, and has struck root, and stretched out its branches and boughs from one sea even to the other, His ministers are under a strict necessity of calling on those who hear them to remember what they have received,—to remember the end for which it was given,—to remember that there is an account which they will have to render of their privileges in the day of the LORD hereafter. This then is the turn which our thoughts take in applying the doctrine of judgment to come,—" Hold that fast which thou hast."[23]

It was different when the Apostle of the uncircumcision went among the Gentiles of old ; —it is different when the Missionary has to deal with simple heathens now. Judgment to come is indeed still to be preached. But as to the times of ignorance, these " GOD has winked at."[24] The Gospel is an invitation to something new,—a call to those who have as yet enjoyed no such blessing, to repent of their former conversation, to believe that the king-

---

[23] Revel. iii. 11.　　　[24] Acts xvii. 30.

dom of Heaven has come nigh unto them, to receive the Gospel and to be baptized. That washing is at once the sign and the pledge of all things becoming new,—of cleansing, of illuminating, of inspiring. Thenceforth we have something committed to us,—something to keep, not for ourselves, but for GOD.

And therefore we cannot be as simple heathens. I do not mean to say that *they* have nothing to account for, in that sense of right and wrong and shame, which speaks, with however strange and stammering tongue, of GOD within them ;—nothing in the continual bounty of the CREATOR in outward things, which has never left them without a witness of HIM. We must not presume to speculate on the judgment which will be theirs. Let us think of our own. Let us pray that these poor heathens, whom we pity so deeply, may not condemn us, when they rise in judgment with us. Let us remember that, whatever their judgment is, ours will be different, ours will be more strict ; our condemnation, if after all we are condemned, will be more awful ; because all has been done for us in vain,—because we have rejected so great salvation.

The heathen are as those who have never had a talent entrusted to them, in comparison with us. And therefore we cannot be even as they. God would have us, and tries to make us, far better. We may, by yielding to the adversary, make ourselves far worse. But as they, we cannot be. We have a gift of which they know nothing. We have an account to render, which will not be demanded of them.

And the sense of this responsibility may, no doubt, bring with it a temptation even to despair, when we think of what has been done for us, what we are, and what is required of us. And this is a feeling which may grow, even by the honest simple preaching of the Gospel itself. For the Gospel is a savour of death, we know, as well as a savour of life [25]. And we, who have been placed in the way of salvation (σωζόμενοι), we who have been "brought into a state of salvation," we have sinned even against the mercy of God. We are publicans amid the people of the Lord! Children of His adoption and of His kingdom, we

---

[25] Χριστοῦ εὐωδία ἐσμὲν τῷ Θεῷ ἐν τοῖς σωζομένοις καὶ ἐν τοῖς ἀπολλυμένοις· οἷς μέν, ὀσμὴ θανάτου εἰς θάνατον· οἷς δέ, ὀσμὴ ζωῆς εἰς ζωήν. 2 Cor. ii. 15, 16.

have sold ourselves to do the work of His enemy, the Prince of this world.

But does the work of CHRIST for us stop here? Has HE come down from Heaven to add to our condemnation? Has HE died on the Cross to make us die eternally? Has HE risen from the dead to leave us in the tomb of spiritual corruption and death? Save us, LORD, from the hopeless blasphemy of such a creed as this! The talent was given to the unprofitable servant, as well as to the others, to profit withal. The SPIRIT has been given to every one of us to profit withal[26]. Had it not been for his kindness, that Lord in the parable might have let his servants alone. Had it not been for the mercy which rejoiceth over judgment, our LORD might have passed by and left us alone in our corruption. But GOD *was* merciful, and therefore HE gave His SON to die for us. GOD *is* merciful, and therefore HE worketh day by day, by His SPIRIT living in us, to make us live everlastingly.

And according to this mercy JESUS CHRIST died to save sinners. Not for an example of

[26] 1 Cor. xii. 7.

holiness. He lived to give us that. But an example of holiness would only have been a standard of condemnation to those who could not be holy. This is the very shortcoming of the Law. But He died *to save sinners.* This is our answer to the Tempter's whispers of despair. *This* is His name; even the Lord of Hosts, our Redeemer, our Saviour! This is His work of love, that He over Whom death was powerless, submitted *to die!* These are they for whom He died,—*sinners;* those whose sins had brought them under the power of death, without means of salvation in any other. What brought Him down from Heaven? what moved Him to take our nature, and to die our death? Even this, our sins. For whom did He come? Not for the righteous, but for sinners! For whom did He die? " Scarcely for a righteous man will one die. ... But God commendeth His love toward us, in that, while we were yet sinners, Christ died for us."[27]

These are the " comfortable words" of Holy Writ! Comfortable to all; but, most of all, to those who stand most in need of comfort,—

[27] St. Matth. ix. 13, Rom. v. 7, 8.

to those who know their sins, and feel how far these have removed them from GOD; who know, above all, how much they have aggravated their sins, in making CHRIST'S work of none effect to them, and renewing their covenant with death and hell, after they have been once redeemed from destruction. "GOD be merciful to me a sinner!"—It is in this very confession of weakness and powerlessness that their defence against the Evil One consists. In weakness is their strength—the strength of GOD—made perfect[28], when every other defence is beaten down. "CHRIST died for sinners; *therefore* HE died for *me!*"

Hatred of sin is indeed, so far as we can venture to describe the Godhead, one of His first attributes, even a portion of His very essence. But no less so is His love for the creatures, even the sinful creatures, of His hand. His hatred of sin is no hatred of them, but of that which oppresses and destroys them. It is hatred of that which has stolen them away from the outstretched arms of His love. True it is, that GOD is our Judge, and must judge right. HE must

[28] 2 Cor. xii. 9.

avenge Himself on the Powers of Evil to the uttermost, were it only for the sake of those creatures of His, whom the Powers of Evil are making their prey. But HE would save *them.* Behold the proofs of His will to save them from the Evil One! " Why will ye die ?.. turn yourselves and live ye,"[29] are His words in the Old Testament: and in the New Testament we have the very advent, the life, the death of JESUS CHRIST, to re-assure our faith. Where is doubt, after *that?* " HE that spared not His own SON, but delivered HIM up for us all, how shall HE not with HIM also freely give us all things ?"[30]

But then comes upon us the qualm of con-science, and truly a very terrible one ;—un-happily, one which we have but too much ground for feeling ; that against all this we have sinned ; that, in all this light of know-ledge and warmth of love, we have rebelled and fallen away.

But, O man, is thy sin greater than the mercy of GOD ? Is thy guilt such as the Blood of CHRIST cannot wash out ? That

29 Ezek. xviii. 31, 32.　　30 Rom. viii. 32.

Blood cleanseth us from *all* sin[31]. There is indeed one unhappy way of making the love and the grace of GOD of none effect. If we will not believe in them,—if we will not believe in GOD's mercy and CHRIST's redemption, then indeed they will be to us as if they were not; and HE must say to us in the last day, " I never knew you!" But in the mean season this is sure,— " CHRIST JESUS came into the world to save sinners."[32] O that those who are sunk in trespasses and sins would think of the love that they are rejecting, love stronger than death, higher than heaven, deeper than hell! HE is the life itself; and for this end HE came into the world *and died!* In power all-sufficient; for it is HE, the very and eternal SON of GOD. In will all enduring; for HE *died.* In mercy infinite; for it was to save sinners; to destroy sin in us; to destroy the power of sin over us; to destroy the punishment of sin for ever, for those who will believe the mercy of GOD in HIM; to destroy sin itself from GOD's world which it pollutes. Let none ask *whose* sins HE died

[31] 1 St. John i. 7.   [32] 1 Timothy i. 15.

to blot out. Yours,—mine,—His disciples',
—His murderers';—the sins of the whole
world, would the whole world only believe
it, and turn to HIM with the same grief for
sin, and hatred of it, which HE felt in the
Garden and upon the Cross. HE is the propitiation for the sins of the whole world.
Though we dare not so much as lift our
eyes to Heaven, yet, if we smite upon our
breasts, and say, " GOD be merciful to us
sinners," why should we think that HE who
received the publicans will refuse to receive
us. Are we enemies too great? Are we
sinners too miserable? We,—for whom HE
died!

This alone can stand between us and the
Evil One. But, blessed be GOD, whatever
temptation comes, this is enough. Though
we say of our sins all that sorrow and despondency can prompt, all that we can say is
in effect but this, that we are of those, whom
HE came into the world and died to save.
Whatever doubts arise, this answers them;
wherever is our weak point, this covers it
with His strength.—" If I climb up into
Heaven, Thou art there: if I go down to

Hell, Thou art there also : if I take the wings
of the morning, and remain in the uttermost
parts of the sea, even there also shall Thy
hand lead me, and Thy right hand shall
hold me."[33]

33 Psalm cxxxix. 7, 8, 9.

SERMON IX.

THE RICH MAN AND LAZARUS.

Preached on Sunday, February 25, 1855.

St. Luke xvi. 31.

*If they hear not Moses and the Prophets, neither will
they be persuaded, though one rose from the dead.*

THE parable of the Rich Man and Lazarus,
which is wound up with these words, exhibits
one of the most awful scenes which are por-
trayed in the whole Gospel. And the words
themselves are, accordingly, among the most
solemn sayings which dropt from the lips of
HIM Who spake as never man spake.

Let us endeavour, under His blessing, to
consider, with a view to edification, first, the
circumstances of the parable, and then, the
lessons of the text.

There is this peculiarity in the whole parable, that it in some degree draws aside the
veil from that which is nowhere clearly revealed either by our LORD JESUS CHRIST or by

the SPIRIT of the FATHER Whom HE has sent. It affords a glimpse into the otherwise unseen world ;—that world which exists, we know, as surely as our own ; that world in which we all have so profound an interest ; into which we desire so eagerly to look ; and concerning which, nevertheless, the knowledge which is permitted to us is so " dark," in a parable, as by a glass. It is not, strictly speaking, the world *to come,* to which our attention is called : for the brethren of the Rich Man are spoken of as still alive in their father's house ; —in a position to be warned ; with the prospect of repentance ; not without hope of salvation. It is the world which is existing, as it were, side by side with our own ; the mysterious state, into which our brethren are passing, hour by hour ; into which in a few short hours or days we must pass one by one, to await the coming of the LORD and the resurrection of the body.

It is very true that the whole narrative is but a " parable," the history of something which never literally occurred. But after all, a parable, as CHRIST used the term, is not a mere fable. It is the description of something which

might have happened,—of something which is
true to nature. In the Old Testament, indeed,
we read how the trees went forth to anoint a
king over them, or how the thistle that was
in Lebanon sent to the cedar[1] : but it is not
so in our LORD's teaching. HE does not tell
us of birds or beasts speaking and reasoning ; but of birds that feed or roost, and
sheep that follow the shepherd or stray from
the fold ; not, it may be granted, always of
things which had happened, but at least of
such things as were wont to happen. We
need not insist on every particular being ex-
actly told. But the scene as described must
communicate a true impression. Else the
most important part of the lesson would be
wanting. For instance, we may grant that
the parable of the sower and the seed may
not have described any thing which our SA-
VIOUR and His Disciples were looking upon
while HE spake of them. But, granting that
this was not so, (and yet it is far more probable that, in fact, it was so,) still, there was
at least the sowing, a thing which happened
frequently ; there was the probability of the

---

[1] Judges ix. 8–15 ; 2 Kings xiv. 9.

seed falling on the very paths which they had been traversing ; there was the certainty that whatever did so fall, would be devoured by the fowls of the air.

And indeed, although the Rich Man and Lazarus in the present parable are Characters, not Individuals ; yet there is a peculiarity in the use of proper names in a parable, which is not without its importance. That of *Abraham* might, perhaps be allowed to pass without remark, as historical and sacred. But the adoption (and, as it appeared afterwards, the prophetic adoption) of the name of *Lazarus* from the region of every-day life, creates an expectation of conformity, even more strict than usual, to matters of fact. How much this has actually been felt, is shewn in many strange ways ;—such as the common custom, even in this country and to this day, of individualizing the third character also, by speaking of " *Dives* and Lazarus ;"—such as the ordinary dedication to " St. Lazarus" of the hospitals and so-called Lazar-houses founded for the benefit of those who might suffer after the description of the beggar's sufferings ;— and as in the impudent tradition of Jerusalem, which identifies the site of " the Rich Man's house," among the sacred localities of the Gospel history. Even aberrations like these must tend to confirm the impression, that though the rich man and the pauper, of whom we read, may never have actually existed, they are at least represented in circumstances in which human beings may be placed, circumstances in the main real,—ay, and practically important to those who meditate upon the parable.

Hence we may derive from the parable a certain amount of knowledge,—not clear indeed, nor such as we can safely endeavour to make more clear than it is;—but a certain amount of knowledge we may derive, intended for our practical use, concerning that state which awaits us all in the interval between death and the final judgment. We know not, neither dare we ask, what are the particular characteristics of that abode in which Lazarus was comforted. But we find that it admitted of being described in a phrase well known and currently used among the Jews,—" to be in the bosom of Abraham."

And we ourselves are enabled to form an idea of it sufficiently clear for practical purposes, from what we read of the disciple who lay on our LORD's own bosom. This, we cannot but remember, was the privileged place of him whom JESUS loved, at His last Supper upon earth. And we may also remember that which JESUS CHRIST says of the persons who shall sit down with Abraham and Isaac and Jacob, at the heavenly feast in the kingdom of GOD[2]. Again, we are in no condition to form any distinct notions of the sufferings of the Rich Man after he had gone to his own place. But we are clearly told that they were sufferings of intense agony, sufferings such as to be imaged to our minds by the expression of "torments," ay, of "fire." Moreover, we have a distinct and solemn assertion, put into the mouth of the Patriarch Abraham, the friend of GOD, that between these two abodes of the departed, whatever may be the mutual knowledge of their occupants, there is no communication ;—that in death there is no place for repentance ; no way out, to escape from the

[2] St. John xiii. 23 ; St. Matth. viii. 11 : compare 2 Sam. xii. 3.

tormentors and the prison-house ; no way in, for those who would even enter on an errand of mercy. The angels of GOD, who minister to the heirs of salvation upon earth, must fold their wings. The souls of the righteous, who even in their own unspeakable rest are touched with angelic compassion, (what deeper compassion can we conceive, than theirs for the sinners who may have done evil to them on earth?) are debarred from acting out their impulse of love. " There is a great gulf fixed." It is no intermediate place of purgatorial fire, where the intercessions of angels in Heaven, or saints in Paradise, or fellow-sinners upon earth, can avail to fill up aught which the Atonement of JESUS CHRIST has left undone, or His Mediation is insufficient to do. *Here* is our trial and *now*, while it is called to-day. When the tree is fallen, as it falls, so it must lie ;—when it is hewn down, it is also cast into the fire[3].

And it would seem that this judgment had come upon the Rich Man, not only suddenly, but soon. For although his age is not actually specified, yet if we take together what

[3] Eccles. xi. 3 ; St. Matth. iii. 10.

is said of his circumstances and his sins,—the sins of selfish extravagance in dress and diet, —the circumstances of one who had five brethren, apparently, still residing with their father in the home of their infancy, we may without violence to our Blessed LORD's words take him as representing a class numerous everywhere, and nowhere more so than amongst ourselves. He is the type of those who are careless, and therefore selfish in their youth ; and who, having thus neglected to turn to good account the finer feelings and warmer impulses of that season, have their hearts hardened by self-indulgence and sensuality, before they can profit by the lessons of experience ; before they learn to know the value of time, or the use of money, or the exceeding preciousness of those opportunities, which GOD in His mercy brings to our very doors, of cultivating the love of our brethren, and following the footsteps of our Redeemer. For in this, be it remembered, consists the exceeding sinfulness of his sin ;—that in his unrestrained self-indulgence he went not beyond self, thought not of the good which he might have done, heeded not the evils and sufferings which he saw unredressed; remembered not them that were in bonds, as bound with them; or them which suffered adversity, as being himself also in the body[4]. In the parable of the Unjust Steward, which seems to have been spoken, as the Evangelist places it, immediately before this, and in connection with it, we have the portrait of a man who, according to the wisdom of his generation, puts out to use the wealth which had been committed to his keeping, so that in the time of need he may reap a return from those on whom it has been bestowed. Here there is no thought or consciousness of a stewardship: but, in another point of view, Lazarus is set forth as the type of those "friends," who would have received the Rich Man, had he made them friends, into everlasting habitations. But now, the one is comforted, and the other is tormented.

It is for no deliberate cruelty, it is for no want of kindness, when the impulse can be roused, that he is arraigned and condemned: but it is for this want of sympathy,—this self-gratulation, "Aha! I am warm!"[5] without recognition of fellowship with those, who

4 Hebr. xiii. 3.   5 Isaiah xliv. 16.

" are wet with the showers of the mountains, and embrace the rock for want of a shelter ;"[6] it is for this daily luxury, while the evils of poverty and suffering are abroad.

And such are, precisely, the worst features of what is called fashionable life ; such, the characteristics of that life, which, in this place, is its counterfeit ;—as if this world was our final home ; as if its comforts were those of Abraham's bosom ; as if a great gulf were fixed already and for ever, between those who are here receiving good things and evil. Nay, are there not instances (would that I were mistaken in believing it : but I am not mistaken !) in which it is not merely Lazarus at the gate, but it is those who are nearer still, even, it may be, the " five brethren in the father's house," who are struggling and suffering, denying themselves for the sake of one ; and he, the while, for whom it is cheerfully and hopefully endured, is wasting all in sinful superfluities ?

Brethren, I leave this to your consciences ; and pass on to the closer consideration of the

[6] Job xxiv. 8.

passage. The Rich Man had found too late (as all those who refuse to be warned in time will find when it is too late) what was the end of his vain apparel, his pampered appetite, his gross and selfish misuse of all the good things which GOD had lent him to make eternal friends withal. Too late for himself; yet not (he thought) too late for his brethren. They were still alive : they might yet be warned, so that they should not come to the same place of torment. For the man's feelings, when he could be made to feel, were not utterly bad. Even his selfishness was not so deeply rooted, but that it ceased, when the life which had engendered it was at an end. And this is one of the most impressive suggestions of the parable,—that his sin had brought hopeless punishment upon this unhappy man, without having rooted out his kindly feelings of affection towards his brethren. He still cherished these : they even went down with him into his place of torment. And yet we often hear men assume, both for themselves and others, that the existence of such feelings is an evidence that they are not reprobate. It is the commonest thing in the world (as every one who has had any experience in the ministry can testify), while a person is notoriously and confessedly neglecting every duty to GOD and man, openly wasting life and substance in riotous living,—to hear it pleaded (on the strength of a sort of jovial temperament which endears him to those whose tastes predispose them to yield to the like temptations) that "he has a good heart,—that he is a good companion." Such was this Rich Man, my brethren! He had been what was called "a good companion." He had shewn "a good heart," as the world uses the words. For revelry is a social, or at least a gregarious vice. But there he was, in torment! And all the effect of his social qualifications and affections, had been to draw his brethren down towards his own hopeless misery! As the Evil One had ensnared him, it was now his misery (as it must be that of all who follow the Tempter in such things) that he had ensnared them and led them astray. This is the end of what is called "the good heart," "the good fellowship" of debauchery! It adds a pang to the very agonies of Hell!

Fain would he now undo all his doings. And he proposes what seems the most likely way to bring his brethren to their senses. No doubt, if he could have gone to warn them himself, all glowing with the flame of his torment, this would have been his proposal. But this was hopeless now. Lazarus, however, was in another condition ; and Abraham might send *him*. What can be more natural, than this recurrence to the old state of things, the thought that he might command the services of the beggar who had so long lain at his gate! Ay, Lazarus might be the messenger of warning; Lazarus might testify. There was still this chance ; and although they had slighted all other warnings, it could not be that they would slight this. " Nay, father Abraham, but if one went unto them from the dead, they will repent !"

There spoke human nature! Who is there, that has not felt the same, among all who have learnt how hard it is to strive against the temptations of the world of sight and sense in the faith of the things that are not seen ? Who has not craved for something which should act more strongly on his

heart and imagination, some demonstration of
things spiritual, which should make it impossible (so to speak) for him ever to sin again?
It is this feeling which has clothed itself in so
many dreams and visions and fancied revelations of the spiritual world. It is this, which
has prompted the manufacture, and (with a
large portion of mankind) secured the belief,
of so many fabled apparitions. And whatever
be the superstructure, the foundation at least
is true. Man has a consciousness that his
weakness and corruption need a miracle to
remedy them. He has moreover a consciousness that his salvation is no unworthy object
of a miracle. And surely, it is no lying spirit
which has suggested this. Surely to this the
stable of Bethlehem, the sepulchre of Joseph
bear their testimony! GOD's mercy has met
the want : but His wisdom has not chosen to
satisfy the craving. Man fixes his heart on
something that has not been vouchsafed :—
he would fain dictate the miracle which shall
convert him. And this is not the miracle
which GOD permits us to expect. Rather,
HE peremptorily teaches us our mistake in
desiring it ; and shews us plainly its worth-

lessness if it were vouchsafed. " If they hear not Moses and the Prophets, neither will they be persuaded, though one rose from the dead." The same temper, which resists any sufficient evidence, will only harden itself the more against that which is overwhelming. Strange, indeed, it seems beforehand, that this should be so ;—contrary, no doubt, to our expectations. But it is the saying of Him Who knew what was in man. And it is, accordingly, confirmed by all experience. Take the life's history of Him Who spoke the words. Follow throughout His ministry Him " of Whom Moses in the Law, and the Prophets did speak." Look at those who knew best (as far as learned knowledge could go) the Scriptures of the Old Testament ; and see what was the effect upon them of all that He did and all that He said. Each cumulative evidence, each additional miracle, did but harden their hearts the more. The very light of the proof blinded them. " What sign shewest Thou? What dost Thou work ?" were the questions which followed immediately on His feeding the five thousand. That He should shew a sign *from heaven,* was the demand of the Pharisees and Sadducees ; as if all that had been, all that could be wrought on earth had been exhausted in vain[6]. The miracles were not, could not be, denied. But they could be blasphemed : and accordingly they were ascribed to Beelzebub. And so these miserable men went on ; until the very miracle which had been denied to the Rich Man in our parable, was performed for them ; and one did come from the dead, even one named Lazarus. They knew this, they saw it, they confessed it. But what was the result? It was only too sad a fulfilment of the warning that had gone before. "What do we?" they said, "for this man doeth many miracles. If we let him thus alone, all men will believe on him ;"—confessing, that no evidence, no miracles either could or should make *them* believe !—And the practical end was this : "then from that day forth they took counsel to put JESUS to death." Nay, yet more ; "the chief priests consulted that they might put Lazarus also to death : because that by reason of him many of the Jews went away

---

[6] St. John vi. 30 ; St. Matth. xvi. 1.

and believed on Jesus[7]." They heard not, they would not listen to Moses and the Prophets : and therefore they were not persuaded, when one rose from the dead!

And when they had succeeded in their device for putting the Christ Himself to death ; and when, in a far more awful and more glorious sense than ever had been conceived of before, One had risen from the dead,—now no more to return to the grave or to see corruption ; what was the end even of that, but a still further hardening of hearts, perjury and blasphemy? The firmer the evidence was, —the harder the rock which met all their assaults, so much the further did they recoil and rebound into unbelief. Like the magicians of Pharaoh in confessing the finger of God against which they had contended,—unlike them, in going on with their resistance while they confessed it.

But we need not dwell on the case of these sinners against their own souls. Let us view the parable in relation to ourselves ; and, if I

[7] St. John xi. 47, 48, 53 ; and xii. 10, 11.

mistake not, we shall find that GOD not unfrequently vouchsafes to us something much more like the Rich Man's petition in the parable, than we perhaps have been in the habit of believing ;—and yet, in the great majority of cases, with no better result than was prophesied in the SAVIOUR's words, and fulfilled in His life and death.

It is true that we have not messengers of GOD, of the number of those whom we have known or heard of in this life, sent back to us from the grave with a revelation of the realities of that unseen existence to which they have passed and we are passing. But how many instances there are, in which even within himself a man is conscious of such a message conveyed to him. Take the case of any one who meets with a dangerous accident,—thrown from a horse,—upset in a boat,—crushed in a railway carriage ; and who lingers between life and death for an uncertain time, while perhaps others his fellow-sufferers may have sunk ; but is at length, by GOD's mercy, restored to his strength again. Or take the case of one who is laid on the bed of sickness, stricken and smitten down, till his bodily energies and his soul's powers are broken, and nothing haunts his eyes but death, and those realities after death, of which he has been accustomed to think so little. And then think of such an one, when the hour of danger is past, his mind tranquillized and his powers collected anew, and he himself able deliberately to retrace all the dreamlike impressions of the hour of suffering and danger. What are all the feelings of such a time, what all the recollections of the sickness, what all the horrors in the prospect of an unreconciled death, but so many messengers from the dead whence he has been in a manner raised up, testifying and warning, that he may not come (I had almost said *come again*) to the place of torment? At such a time, on the verge of life and death, conscience is busy;—then, unhappily, most busy, (like the rich man's on whom we have been meditating,) when it seems to be altogether too late; calling up the forms of the past, picturing afresh forgotten, unrepented sins; sounding in the dying sinner's ear the prelude of the dreadful jubilee of fiends over a lost soul.

On restoration from such a state,—when he

has felt what a blessing one drop of cold water
to cool his tongue would be, what ought to be
the effect of that life again from the dead which
he feels his restoration to be? Say rather, what
is the effect? Is it to resist a sin, or to renounce
a luxury? Is it to remember those who have
been suffering in the flesh while he has been
pampering it? Is it to prove his sympathy,
not merely by conventional offerings but in
the full Christian meaning of the word, with
the sick and afflicted, with Lazarus, wherever
he is to be found, be it in your camps and
hospitals, or be it in the lanes and courts of
your own plague-stricken city[8]? Is this the
result? Would GOD that it more frequently
were so! Would GOD that this holy season
might plead with you effectually, thus to follow
your SAVIOUR while HE bears our griefs and
carries our sorrows. But oh! how seldom is
the heart lastingly changed, even by such a
glimpse as this of the world behind the grave!
A sharp fit of remorse, it may be, there is. A
period somewhat longer, perhaps, of doubt and
halting between conscience and temptation,
one's wishes and one's fears! A short attempt

9 February, 1855.

to serve two masters, sinning to the Evil One and repenting to GOD. And then a deep and (too often) a final plunge into the abyss ; "the dog turned to his own vomit again, and the sow that was washed to her wallowing in the mire."[9]

And is not the reason manifest ? Because we have more than Moses and the Prophets ; because we have not only the writings of Apostles and Evangelists, the works and words of JESUS CHRIST ; but we have the Very WORD of GOD, revealed in our nature, crucified for our sins, raised again for our justification, ascended into Heaven to be our Intercessor with the Father ;—because we have the SPIRIT of the FATHER and the SON, the HOLY GHOST given to dwell within us, to be the Spirit of adoption whereby we cry "Abba, Father,"—" *our* Father which art in Heaven ;" —because we have the water of life and the bread of Heaven, even the Flesh and Blood which giveth life unto the world ;—because we have the fellowship of the FATHER, SON, and HOLY GHOST here, the earnest of the full fruition of the Divine glory hereafter.

9 2 St. Peter ii. 22.

If we hear not these ; if we are deaf, and blind, and stony-hearted to such messages and messengers of love ; what avails it to disquiet them that are at rest, to bring them up[10] ? Surely, neither shall we be persuaded, though one rose from the dead !

[10] 1 Sam. xxviii. 15.

SERMON X.

THE REVELATION OF IMMORTALITY.

Preached on Sunday, May 6th, 1855.

ISAIAH xxxviii. 18, 19.

The grave cannot praise THEE; death cannot cele-
brate THEE: they that go down into the pit cannot
hope for THY truth. The living, the living, he shall
praise THEE, as I do this day.

IN these words of the thanksgiving of Hezekiah, there is an undertone of melancholy, an
echo, as it were, out of the void of man's un-
satisfied heart, even in the midst of the mercy
for which he is glorifying GOD.   And such is
no rare characteristic of the outpourings of
Hebrew poetry and devotion.   Rahel is ever
weeping for her children.   Notwithstanding
the voice of promise that they shall come
again, she refuses to be comforted, because
they are not!   Again and again does the

harp of the Psalmist fling forth the same fitful strains of gloomy foreboding, as if it were already hanging on the trees by the waters of Babylon. We have them in this morning's Psalms[1], "What profit is there in my blood, when I go down to the pit? Shall the dust give thanks unto THEE, or shall it declare Thy truth?" And so it is elsewhere in the Psalter[2], as, "In death there is no remembrance of THEE; in the grave who shall give THEE thanks?" And, "Wilt THOU shew wonders to the dead? shall the dead arise and praise THEE? shall Thy lovingkindness be declared in the grave? or Thy faithfulness in destruction? shall Thy wonders be known in the dark? and Thy righteousness in the land of forgetfulness?" And again, in words that seem to have actually suggested Hezekiah's ejaculation, "The dead praise not the LORD, neither any that go down into silence : —but we will bless the LORD from this time forth and for evermore."

We need not dissemble the difficulty which such passages suggest. It becomes us rather to meditate on them, on that account, the more

[1] xxx. 9.   [2] Ps. vi. 5; lxxxviii. 10, 11.; cxv. 17.

deeply and the more humbly. If we do so, we shall find these, as well as other portions of Holy Writ, wells of salvation. Perhaps we may not fathom their depth; but we shall draw from them waters of comfort and refreshment to our souls.

To this end, there are two points of view, in which they may be considered; one in which we are comprehended in their meaning; the other in which they are more strictly limited to the children of Israel;—one of analogy, the other of contrast, between our position and that of prophets and kings and righteous men under the older dispensation.

Let us first consider the point of contrast. No student of the Word of GOD, who soberly compares the Old with the New Testament, can doubt that various and continual glimpses of a revelation of the life after death were given to the Patriarchs and to the people of Israel. They did not put their trust in merely transitory promises. The GOD, Who admitted His faithful servants to communion with Himself, purged their eyes through faith to see the future salvation, the future SAVIOUR, the future and abiding city, the future and heavenly country.   But even while this is fully recognised, it cannot be denied that if we try to embody in words the conviction thus impressed upon our minds, the phrases in which it clothes itself will not be those of the Old Testament, but of the New.   We shall speak, not with the Saints of the Mosaic dispensation, but with HIM, Whose day Abraham rejoiced to see, and with the Apostle who proclaimed in strains so jubilant the warfare and the victories of faith.   And this consideration will in great measure prepare us to find, as further study of the Word of GOD will shew us, that the consolation was not clearly revealed to them as a nation and a Church.   Our LORD JESUS CHRIST Himself, in His answer to the Sadducees, points out to us the mode in which it was imparted to them in their Scriptures,— like a bud, to expand and unfold itself, as the eye of faith and the heart of love kept watch over it ; but yet so, that those who cared not for it should never see what precious things it enfolded.

The Jewish Covenant, moreover, with all its adjuncts, had a twofold character.   It was,

indeed, typical and transitory. But it was also
actual and substantial. This combination could
not but increase the difficulty ; as, no doubt,
this difficulty itself formed a portion of the
trial, by which the "remnant that should be
saved" were sifted and separated from the
Israel according to the flesh. As the blessing
of their Canaan was meant to foreshow the
Heaven of our future inheritance, it must
needs have within it a real element, and,
still more, must wear a distinct semblance,
of stability. Consequent on this, there was an
undeniable temptation to acquiesce in it as a
final rest, as if it were the fulfilment of their
hopes and the completion of their promises.
Again, the Law of their Covenant was an
efficient law of reward and punishment, in the
days of this life, and in the land which GOD
had given them. And this involved another
temptation. Not unnaturally, it contributed,
in exact proportion to its own seeming completeness, to obscure their notions of a future
retribution, and to lessen their expectation of
it. Hope, indeed, in their deaths they had.
But not *such* hope, as we have in ours. So
emphatic is the Scripture which teaches us

that "Jesus Christ brought life and immortality *to light*, through the Gospel."[3] He Who won them for us, revealed them also. And, until this was done, until the Dayspring from on high had flung forward its radiance into the depths of the future, it is not hard even for us to understand and realize the dreary feeling with which, in passages such as have been read to you, death is spoken of as a severance from the presence of God, and a deprivation of communion with Him, His Saints and Worshippers, in the Sanctuary—the *worldly* Sanctuary, as it is called in the Epistle to the Hebrews[4]—of their religion.

Still more :—while as yet " He that cometh," was not come, this His first Coming was the engrossing object of all their faith and hope in the future. This was their earnest expectation ; and it filled their minds and hearts, so that they could not look beyond His appearance. The expectation of His first Coming was in this respect to them, practically, what the belief of His Return is to us,—

3 2 Timothy i. 10, φωτίσαντος ζωὴν καὶ ἀφθαρσίαν.

4 Εἶχε μὲν οὖν ἡ πρώτη [σκηνὴ ?] δικαιώματα λατρείας, τό τε ἅγιον κοσμικόν. Hebr. ix. 1.

as of the event which occupies the whole scope
of spiritual vision. Now, they looked forward,
and rightly so, to this Advent, as an event
within the compass of the world's history.
As every daughter of Judah cherished some
hope, however faint, that the MESSIAH might
be born of her; so every Jew longed after
the revelation of the MESSIAH, as something
which he might survive to see. Is there
not something deeply touching, in the doubt
and despondency which crept over the minds
of St. Paul's converts at Thessalonica, when
they were tempted to complain that their
LORD delayed His coming, as they saw their
brethren sinking into the grave without having
attained (as they feared) to the completion of
His promise[5]? But their sorrow, which drew
forth such precious words of hope and comfort
from the Apostle, was but a faint shadow of
the weary sense of darkness, the loss of things
hoped for, the doubtfulness of things not seen,
which was at times permitted to cloud souls
no less faithful than Hezekiah, or than David
himself. So heavy a trial was the contemplation of death, while as yet even the tangible

5 1 Thessal. iv. 13–18.

blessings and worldly promises of the earlier Covenant interposed their veil between the eye of faith and its spiritual, its heavenly hopes!

Nay, there is still to be mentioned another burden, which weighed heavily on the souls of these our forefathers in the family of GOD, even in the hour when their faith in the eternal things of a world beyond the tomb might be fullest and clearest. There was to their anticipations, at the best, nothing but a dreary void between the hour of death and that final consummation. And they saw that ages upon ages had passed away, and that the time was not yet. Patriarchs and kings and prophets went down into the grave; and no one had as yet made them to understand that Abraham and Isaac and Jacob, ay, and all besides, were still living unto GOD! Whatever might be the morning that should dawn out of that night of darkness,—whatever the brightness of the light that should succeed that disastrous eclipse; its intermediate horrors pressed upon the chilled spirit unmitigated by revelation. *To die* was not only to lose the light of earthly life, to depart hence and be no more seen. It was also to be cut off from the light of GOD's presence, from the blessing of seeking HIM and praising His holy name. " I said, I shall not see the LORD, even the LORD, in the land of the living."[6]

But it is time to turn to that,—not whereof we have to glory, but—for which we have to glorify GOD, in His revealed mercies towards ourselves. We have our Blessed LORD's own teaching, not merely to point out the doctrine which had been implicitly contained even in such words of the Old Testament as had not before suggested it to the Jewish student[7]; but to declare *how* it shall be; to declare *what* we shall be. We have the very WORD of Life declaring Himself to us as the Resurrection and the Life; promising that he will raise us up in the last day ; proclaiming, " He that believeth in ME, though he were dead, yet shall he live." " The hour is coming in the which all that are in the graves shall hear His voice, and shall come forth."[8]

6 Isaiah xxxviii. 11.
7 St. Matth. xxii. 31, 32, etc. : see Sermon VII.
8 St. John v. 24–29., xi. 25, 26.

We have moreover the seal of confirmation set to this His teaching, in the still more blessed verity of His own Resurrection ;—and that, not merely as an isolated, external fact, from which we might gain a glimpse of hope, and argue faintly by an imperfect analogy, that we should be permitted to follow His steps ; but as virtually containing within itself our own resurrection also[9]. Of this, what can be said more plain, more cheering, or more glorious, than is said by St. Paul in that precious section of his first Epistle to the Corinthians, which lights up every Christian tomb as with the HOLY SPIRIT's tongues of fire ? CHRIST so completely took Man's nature,—so truly became Man in the fullest and most perfect sense, as the type and representative of Humanity,—that what befel Him must needs pass upon all ; as the harvest follows the first-fruits ; yea, as the impression gives back the seal. And therefore,

9 Compare, τοῦ ὁρισθέντος υἱοῦ Θεοῦ ἐν δυνάμει, κατὰ Πνεῦμα ἁγιωσύνης, ἐξ ἀναστάσεως νεκρῶν (Rom. i. 4) ; where it is the Resurrection of CHRIST Himself that is spoken of. The authorized English Version has "the resurrection *from* the dead."

if HE rose, we also rise ; and reversely, *If* we do not rise, neither can HE have risen. " But now *is* CHRIST risen from the dead, and become the first-fruits of them that slept[10]." Nay, while this is revealed as the final and perfect fulfilment of all that is most blessed and glorious in the Divine purposes of mercy and salvation, the compassion of GOD for our weakness in the mean season has provided a comfort to our souls and stay to our faith, amidst the groanings and travailings which mark our state of imperfection. We have more, far more, than the Psalmist had, even when his eye was purged to see, and his faith strengthened to apprehend the future blessing;—even when "as a Prophet" he spoke, in the hope that (through the resurrection of CHRIST) his own soul should not rest in hell, neither his flesh see corruption eternally ;—even when he proclaimed, "GOD hath delivered my soul from the place of hell ; for HE will receive me ;" or, " As for me, I will behold Thy presence in righteousness ; and when I awake up after Thy likeness, I shall be satisfied with it[11]."

[10] I Corinth. xv. 13–20.
[11] Psalm xvi. 10 ; xvii. 16 ; xlix. 15. (Prayer Book).

To us it has been revealed that even between their departure hence, and that "awaking up" of which the Psalmist spoke, the souls of the faithful are with their REDEEMER and LORD; and that this *rest* of theirs is more blessed than their lot on earth could be. So much we have had revealed to us by that Apostle, in whom the revelation wrought a cheerful, a hopeful, a faithful spirit;—cheerful in the labours of life,—hopeful in the prospect of death,—faithful in the recognition of the love and wisdom of HIM Who was with him both in life and death. "For to me to live is CHRIST, and to die is gain: ... what I shall choose I wot not: for I am in a strait betwixt two, having a desire to depart, and to be with CHRIST, which is far better: nevertheless, to abide in the flesh is more needful for you."[12] And again,—"We are always confident; knowing that whilst we are at home in the body we are absent from the LORD (for we walk by faith, not by sight): we are confident, I say, and willing rather to be absent from the body, and to be present with the LORD."[13] St. Paul here speaks in a sense in

[12] Philipp. i. 21–24.   [13] 2 Corinth. v. 6–8.

which, notwithstanding the illumination, the comfort, and the fellowship of the SPIRIT of CHRIST, we are not, in this life, present with HIM. And the characteristic of our present " absence," and the mode of our future " presence" with HIM in the intermediate state, seems to be declared and defined by the words " for we walk" (in this life) " by faith, not by sight." So that the natural suggestion (if we should not rather say the necessary inference) is, that the future presence of which the Apostle is so confident, is one in which the very sight of the SAVIOUR shall follow the dissolution of our earthly tabernacle.

But how is this ? Let us look indeed to our goings, for we are treading on holy ground. But may we not reverently believe, that it is one of the mysteries which flow from the Incarnation and the Human Nature of GOD the SON ? In one sense, even to us, the Evening which closes in with death, is but the Eve of the Morning of the resurrection. Between them, " the night cometh, when no man can work."[14] In a far other sense, when we me-

14 St. John ix. 4.

ditate on the things of the unseen world of spirits, and strive to raise our thoughts to the throne of the Eternal GOD, we must feel the incongruity of associating measures of the duration of time with the thought of HIM Who inhabiteth Eternity. And this perplexity confuses our meditations on that which lies between the hour of death and the day of judgment, when we look upon it, as we are compelled to look upon it, as an interval of time. Yet perhaps this very perplexity may throw some dim light on what we call the foreknowledge of GOD, as connected with all the questions of prophecy, predestination, and free will;—removing them out of the sphere of intellectual difficulties (such as might seem to challenge us to grapple with them), into that of spiritual mysteries, which are apprehended by faith. And in like manner it may, perhaps, throw some dim light on the language in which Holy Writ speaks of our presence with the SON in that mysterious state of Rest, without mention of the Heavenly FATHER. For we are included in time, as we are in space. But both these words are meaningless, as applied to GOD. The SON, however, in becoming man, condescended to submit Himself to the conditions of both. And thus combining the scattered hints of Holy Scripture, we may perhaps (provided that we refrain from dogmatizing on such a subject) conceive,—I do not say, *understand*, I do not say, *assert*, but *conceive*,—a mode of the SAVIOUR's presence with those hidden ones, who are awaiting the end of the world, not yet having attained to the resurrection of the dead and the glory of the FATHER Which is in Heaven ;—and this, a mode of presence which His Incarnation alone (speaking as we must speak) may have rendered possible. That they all live to the FATHER, is indeed a most comforting truth ; but yet in some degree one of uncertain signification. But of GOD the SON, our SAVIOUR JESUS CHRIST, we learn that HE is present with them even *there ;* present with them, as they are absent from the body ; present with them, even while they are shut up unto the glory which shall be revealed hereafter ;—present, it may be (according to the mysterious words of St. Peter), by that same

operation " by which also HE went and preached unto the spirits in prison ;"[15]—present with
them, even as HE spoke of Himself as present
in Heaven at the same time that HE was on
the earth, saying, " No man hath ascended up
to Heaven, but HE that came down from
Heaven, even the SON OF MAN, Which *is*
in Heaven."[16]

We have still to consider the point of analogy between the Prophet and the Psalmist
on the one hand, and the Christian on the
other. But this needs not to detain us long.
For what, after all, was their sadness, but an
intense craving after the active service of
GOD ? If we take the words of their lamen-
tation in that sense which must be the truest
and deepest, is not the thought that they contain the same which has been already quoted
from the words of their LORD, " The night
cometh, when no man can work ?" That to
which the Christian looks forward, after his
day of earthly life and labour is at an end, is
the Rest, the Sabbath of those who rest from
their own works, as GOD rested from His in

[15] 1 St. Peter iii. 19.   [16] St. John iii. 13.

the creation ; a Rest, where yet their works do follow them ; even according to the ordinance whereby (His own rest notwithstanding) " HE worketh hitherto" and continually [17].

If we then hope, when the light of this world sets upon us, thus with the Saints "to rejoice in our beds," in the communion of David's faith that we shall wake up again, but with a joy less dashed and troubled by intervening perplexity than his ; we must seek our blessing by his and Hezekiah's path. Our work, "while it is called today," is one with theirs. It is to praise and glorify the LORD : " The living, the living, he shall praise Thee, as I do this day !" This comprehends every thing. For these Saints understood that the praises of GOD consisted not in any mere lip-service, but comprised the universal business of life. This reasonable sacrifice and service was their happiness and their hope upon earth, in life. That they should be cut off from this in death, was the thought which made death bitter. And what shall avail to us the privilege

[17] Compare Hebr. iv. 3, 9, 10 ; Revel. xiv. 13 ; St. John v. 17.

which CHRIST has won for us, of living when we die, if we shall be found, notwithstanding all the measures of grace which have been lavished upon us, to have been dead to His praise and His service while we lived?

Assuredly, then, if we can truly say with the Apostle that to us "to die is gain," it ought to be, it must be, equally true that to us "to live is CHRIST." CHRIST must be our life now, if HE is to be our life when HE appears again. "*To live is CHRIST!*" Who may venture to appropriate these words, in all their awful, their glorious meaning, to himself? And yet this is what we have to do. To make them true,—to make them real; that day by day their truth and their meaning may be more and more *to us*. *To us* to live must be CHRIST, that *to us* to die may be gain! "To live is CHRIST;" to seek HIM; to lay hold on HIM; to win HIM; to be clothed in His righteousness! Nay, to be one with HIM and HE with us: to dwell in HIM and HE in us: to have our lives hidden with HIM in GOD; no longer ourselves to live, but that HE live in us: to be crucified in conformity with His death : to be risen again through the power of His Resurrection !

If these be indeed the signs that *to us* " to live is CHRIST," who shall set limits to the gain that death will be, when it has removed the one veil which distinguishes faith from sight, and makes our " presence in the body" to be " absence from the LORD!"

SERMON XI.

FORGIVENESS WITH CHASTISEMENT.

Preached in Lent, 1856.

2 SAMUEL xii. 13.

And David said unto Nathan, I have sinned against the LORD. And Nathan said unto David, The LORD also hath put away thy sin; thou shalt not die.

IT is probable that if an uninspired writer had given us the history of David's sins, he would have taken pains to trace the steps by which such a man could have been brought to such a fall. Perhaps he might have touched upon the laxity with which David had availed himself of what had been suffered, though only for the hardness of men's hearts, in the multiplication of wives and concubines. But this lesson is more strikingly set before us in the history of his son Solomon. Again, he might have dwelt on the contrast between David, while persecuted and outcast, or while actively employed against the enemies of his GOD, and the same David, when prosperity had brought with it idleness, and idleness had proved the tempter to sin.

But for the purpose with which the HOLY SPIRIT caused this history to be written, it was enough that it should merely suggest such thoughts ;—suggest them, so that we might by searching find them out, and apply the lesson to ourselves. The writer of this part of the Sacred History is guided to tell us of the sins of David (sins grievous and in their nature deadly, though committed by one who is called a man after GOD's own heart[1]) in all their bare hideousness. This peculiarity of the Bible History can scarcely be accidental. And, if we recognise it as characteristic, it is certainly not unimportant. Without one word of moralizing or application, it carries a loud warning to the consciences of men,—telling them of the extent of their nature's corruption, of the deceitfulness of their hearts, and of that deluge which may at any time burst forth to destroy all the good fruits of GOD's ordinary providence, unless His especial help and grace

---

[1] 1 Sam. xiii. 14, Acts xiii. 22.

be continually sought and used, to keep sealed
these fountains of the great deep, the abysses
of spiritual wickedness within us.

We are thus also reminded of another truth.
It is indeed most fitting that we should look up
to the "man after GOD's own heart," as to one
raised, personally, above us, as far as we are,
in our capacity of members of CHRIST, admitted to a state of privilege above even His.
But the Bible views him from another point.
And this, at the present day, it is most important to note : because by many writers the
human element in Holy Scripture is so in-
sisted on as to eclipse that which is divine ;
and the individual Prophet or Apostle is cri-
ticized with too little regard for that which
" *HE* saith *in Osee*," or " *in David*" ; the words
which " *the LORD* spake *by the mouth*" of His
Prophets ; or the reverent citation of " *THE
Scripture,*" without any recognition of the human hand which was guided to write it[2].

If the question was one of human authorities, it is not to be presumed that any would
be found to sit in judgment on the man after

---

[2] Rom. ix. 25 ; Hebr. iv. 7 ; Acts iii. 18, etc. ; Rom. iv.
3, etc.

GOD's own heart. But at the root of the matter, here as elsewhere, lies the plain truth, that the SPIRIT, and not the human writer, is the authority; and that the Word of GOD looks upon David not from below but from above.

What is the measure of the difference between one man and another, when both are referred to the standard of the MOST HIGH?—His eye indeed discerns them; for His grace has made them to differ. But, except for this grace, what is the prerogative of David over Saul, one son of Adam over another? " O my soul, thou hast said unto the LORD, Thou art my LORD: my goodness extendeth not to Thee; but to the saints that are in the earth, and to the excellent, in whom is all my delight!"[3]

But the points which I am anxious to bring before you as seasonable matter for your Lenten meditations, are the Sin of David, and his Repentance, as they were met by HIM in Whose sight he had sinned, with punishment and forgiveness; the sin chastised; the repentance effectual;—not one swallowing up the other, so that the punishment should make us doubt

3 Psalm xvi. 2, 3.

of the forgiveness, or the forgiveness make us forget the punishment; but both working harmoniously together, through the goodness and severity of GOD, to effect His eternal purpose of man's salvation.

Too little attention is commonly bestowed on the severity with which the king of Israel was actually punished for his sins. Men read or hear the chapter from which our text is taken; and they rise up with the impression that the *whole* substance of it is comprised in the words, " I have sinned against the LORD,"—" The LORD also hath put away thy sin." It is indeed true that these words contain the essence of it in one, and that a most precious sense. But it is as the tree is contained in the seed :—and the seed must live, and be shone and rained upon, and grow up, and weather the storms and trials of year after year, and generation after generation, if it is to have its place among "the cedars in the garden of GOD."[4]

The LORD read the heart of David, and knew the sincerity of his confession, the earnestness of his repentance, the reality of his faith, the depth of his love. And where these

4 Ezek. xxxi. 8.

are, there is remission of sins through the Blood of the spotless LAMB of GOD. But what came afterwards? David was punished as long as he lived, for his sins in the matter of Uriah and Uriah's wife. As long as he lived, he repented of those sins, and humbled himself under the consciousness of them.

What, therefore, is the lesson which we are to learn from the example of David? It is not that we, who in CHRIST have been brought nearer to GOD than even he was, may fall into sin, and then turn and say suddenly, " I have sinned," and reckon upon the answer, "The LORD hath taken away thy sin," and so cast all remembrance of our sin behind us, going on as if nothing had happened. But the lesson is this; that when we sin,—we who have an Advocate with the FATHER, Who is the propitiation for our sins (as St. John emphatically says in the very phrase of the Mosaic Law)[5],—we may return to GOD through repentance; and that accord-

----

5 Ἱλασμὸς περὶ τῶν ἁμαρτιῶν ἡμῶν, 1 John ii. 2 ; compare the LXX, Levit. iv. 35, ἐξιλάσεται περὶ αὐτοῦ ὁ ἱερεὺς περὶ τῆς ἁμαρτίας ; also v. 6, 10; xvi. 16, 30; xix. 22 ; Num. xxix. 11, etc.

ing to the truth and depth of our repentance, mercy will be extended to us ; and that
though we may be tried and chastised, and
may suffer bitter things, and be tempted even
to think that GOD has become our enemy, yet
in the very measure of these afflictions we shall
find our comfort, if our repentance remains
alive to remind us of the worse consummation
that we have deserved. And thus our faith
that these things come of GOD's hand, is sustained. The proof which they afford of one of
His attributes confirms our trust in another ;
according to the title which was proclaimed
before HIM of old, " The LORD, The LORD
GOD, merciful and gracious, long-suffering, and
abundant in goodness and truth, keeping
mercy for thousands, forgiving iniquity and
transgression and sin, and that will by no
means clear the guilty ; visiting the iniquity
of the fathers upon the children, and upon
the children's children, unto the third and to
the fourth generation."[6]

Men are accustomed to distinguish events
which seem special interventions of GOD, as
either judgments upon sin, or trials and

[6] Exod. xxxiv. 6, 7.

chastisements for good. And unhappily, the
distinction that they make is too often this,
—to account their neighbours' misfortunes as
judgments, and their own as trials ; as if
their neighbours had received a foretaste of
the wrath to come ; but they had themselves
established a claim to compensation for all that
they have suffered. But in truth all the visitations of GOD bear at once the characters both
of judgments and of trials. We all deserve
worse judgments than are laid upon us ; and
we are all among those whom HE would have
to repent and return to HIM when HE calls
on us so loudly. Could men, in studying
David's subsequent history, forget what the
Bible has revealed to us of his character,
they might be led, on their ordinary principles, to say that he was cast out of his LORD's
favour, and lived and died the object of His
wrath. We know indeed that it was otherwise : but we ought not therefore to shut our
eyes to the fact, that David was as much an
example of the punishment of sin as of its forgiveness. His blessing consisted in this, that
he was also an example of repentance ; and
that when he was judged, he was chastened of

the LORD, that he should not be condemned
with the world[7].

When Nathan was sent to David, he spoke
five distinct prophecies :—not only " Thou
shalt not die ;" but four others also, and these
of a very different tenor.   And all of them
were alike fulfilled.   Or rather, the prophecy
of mercy remained a matter of faith to the
end of the King's life.   Those of evil were
visibly and literally fulfilled before the eyes
of all Judah and Jerusalem ;—so that none,
even if they disbelieved the good, could refuse
to credit the evil.

These prophecies were,—

First, " Now therefore the sword shall never
depart from thine house.".

Second, " I will raise up evil against thee
out of thine own house."

Third, " I will take thy wives before thine
eyes, and give them unto thy neighbour, and
he shall lie with thy wives in the sight of this
sun. For thou didst it secretly : but I will do
this thing before all Israel, and before the sun."

Fourth, " The child that is born unto thee
shall surely die."[8]

7 1 Cor. xi. 32.   8 2 Sam. xii. 10–14.

To point out the express fulfilment of each of these prophecies in the after-life of David, is simply to give a summary of the whole history of it, as related in the remainder of the Book. For what is told us therein?

First of all, we read how the child which Bathsheba had borne to David was smitten of the LORD, and died, notwithstanding all the agony and humiliation and passionate prayers of David[9].

Second, The sword did *not* depart from his house through the whole remainder of his life. The next thing which we learn from the history is the rape of his daughter Tamar by her half-brother Amnon. This led to the murderous revenge of Absalom on Amnon[10]. Hence again grew up the disaffection, and at last the open rebellion of Absalom ; by which the father-king was driven forth once more into the wilderness, as in his youth in the days of Saul[11]. And when he was restored at last, it was to mourn more for the death of his son, than he rejoiced at the recovery of his kingdom[12]. Nay, his restoration caused a

9 2 Sam. xii. 15–18.　　　10 2 Sam. xiii.
11 2 Sam. xiv.—xviii.　　　12 2 Sam. xviii. 33—xix. 7.

quarrel between Judah and Israel, which led to another rebellion[13]. Scarcely is this appeased, when we read of three years of famine ;—sent indeed for the deed of Saul, but so timed as to fall in with the punishment of David[14]. Next in succession, we learn that the anger of the Lord was kindled against Israel ; and that David was moved to number them, and, by so doing, to bring upon them and himself the choice of God's three sore judgments, the famine, the sword, and the pestilence[15]. Nay, even to the very end is the same discipline maintained ; and in his extreme old age another darling son[16] brought sorrow upon him by rebelling against his father, and against the child of prophecy, Solomon.

This is all that the inspired history tells us of the after-life of David ; and thus the word of Nathan was fulfilled, "The sword shall never depart from thine house."

Again, take notice how this evil was raised up against David from among the members of his own house and family. And, in the *fourth* and last place, see how his own sin was literally

---

[13] 2 Sam xix. 41–43 ; xx 1-22.   [14] 2 Sam. xxi.
[15] 2 Sam. xxiv.   [16] 1 Kings i. 5, 6, etc.

visited upon himself again; when, according to the "devilish wisdom" of Ahithophel's counsel, David's wives and concubines were shamelessly abused by Absalom his son. "For he had done this thing secretly; but God did it before Israel and before the sun."[17] He had invaded the sanctuary of another's home, and afterwards shed the blood of the man whom he had injured. And therefore his own hearth was no longer sacred. Its purity and its charities were to be violated ; and instead of the mutual affection of parents and children, brethren and sisters, it was to be a scene of incestuous lewdness, unnatural strife and blood. Does this teach us that the sin from which it all flowed, is a trifle? Nay; it is one lesson the more, that "wherewithal a man sinneth by the same also shall he be punished[18]." But, above all, it is a lesson that God is never more merciful, than when He makes punishment follow hard upon sin.

It remains now to complete this last view of the subject, and it will be our consolation and our blessing to do so, by dwelling a little

17 2 Sam. xvi. 21, 22 ; comp. xii. 12   18 Wisdom xi. 16.

longer on the truth, without which the narrative would convey a totally mistaken lesson; —the truth that though David was severely punished, he was yet freely forgiven; and that his heavy chastisements were a consistent portion of that scheme of mercy, of which his forgiveness, though not earned by them, was the accomplishment.

When the Prophet's message had restored to him the hope of forgiveness, it was neither unnatural nor sinful in David to conceive the hope, that some of the lesser punishments also might be remitted, as well as the most severe. Now the first and immediately impending visitation was the death of his child. Upon the child the finger of the LORD was laid. Here was the beginning of that which had been foretold. This would be the criterion of what might be expected to follow. But there were instances, in which the LORD had been willing to grant to fervent prayer greater things than one child's life. Was it not so in the old time, in the case of Sodom and Gomorrah, when the Patriarch Abraham fainted in his prayer, before the LORD was weary of forgiving? And in later times was it not so, when the repentance of Ahab (even of Ahab!), ineffectual as it was to avert the vengeance, yet availed to stay its coming until after his own days were ended ? And when only forty days were left ere Nineveh should be overthrown, did not, even then, the repentance and the mourning of the nation preserve them for the time from the overhanging destruction ?[19] Surely, David's repentance is not to be measured by the standard of Ahab's ; surely, it is not to be thought of, as less deep and heartfelt than that of the men of Nineveh !

But these instances of GOD's willingness to suspend His judgments were yet followed by the judgments coming in all their severity at last. Here, on the contrary, where the end was mercy, GOD's will was otherwise ; and the child died. And to the astonishment of his servants David arose and put away from him the outward trappings of sorrow. He had now had, not only the severe lesson of his sin's exceeding sinfulness, but the merciful assurance that he should not die,—that the LORD had taken away his sin. And he had had another lesson besides ;—one which the whole

[19] Gen. xviii. 23-33; 1 Kings xxi. 29; Jonah iii. 5-10.

tenor of his after-life shews that he had well conned and laid to heart. We can easily understand that the forgiveness of an offender may be granted in two ways. It may be without any conditions ; or it may be, quite as truly, quite as freely, and yet not so uncon- ditionally. Taking the cases as they are dis- tinguished by our LORD Himself, we have in one parable the creditor freely forgiving his debtors who had nothing to pay; whereas in another the forgiveness implied a condition, so that it was forfeited when the debtor was himself less forgiving to another[20]. It is easy to see that to the man who is forgiven, the former mode would be the more acceptable. But it is not so certain that it would really be the better for him. GOD knows *that*, better than we do ; and according to His knowledge HE deals with us. In the present case HE had annexed a chastisement to his pardon, and declared that it should fall upon David. David had striven to have this removed from him, as the still more terrible consequences of his sin had been removed. He had striven and struggled in an agony of hope and fear :—

[20] St. Luke vii. 41–43 ; St. Matth. xviii. 23–35.

but all in vain. It pleased GOD to try him to the full, according to the Prophet's message. And the lesson, which by the grace of GOD he laid to heart, was this ;—that he was no longer as he had been before ; that he must walk the narrow road, and enter at the strait gate. The stroke which had fallen upon his child was no solitary chastisement : it was the token and earnest of a discipline which he was hereafter through his whole life to undergo. Nor did David misunderstand it. When he arose from the earth, and washed and anointed himself and changed his apparel, and came into the house of GOD and worshipped, and then came into his own house and did eat ; this very subsidence, as we may call it, into the ordinary course of daily life, indicated that he understood and accepted it. The first agony was over, and the enduring discipline was begun. A work was revealed before him, not to be fulfilled by a burst of crying and tears, but by the discharge of duties, by the endurance of evils, by the silent trial of a life of hardness ; to be borne not gloomily, but soberly ; not without comfort in the assurance of the Heavenly FATHER's love ; but neither without sadness, in the recollection of what had been, and in the consciousness of what, had it not been for that love, would have been. It was in this spirit that he bore not only the afflictions which came immediately from above,—for these always bring with them an odour of Paradise,—but also the evils which came from evil men ; as knowing that all these too were permitted by GOD, and therefore were all made to work out His purposes. Thus when Shimei followed him in his flight, cursing still as he went, the monarch rebuked the bloodthirsty zeal of the sons of Zeruiah, and said, "So let him curse, because the LORD hath said unto him, Curse David.   Who shall then say, Wherefore hast thou done so[21]?"   And in so doing he has given us the lesson, that however wicked such provocations and ill-usage may be in those who are guilty of them, yet if our conscience is awake and watching, we shall perceive that they are overruled by a Higher Power to chastise us and amend what is amiss in us.   GOD makes both evil men and evil spirits serve Him by doing His work, though they know it not, and would not do it if they knew.

[21] 2 Sam. xvi. 10.

The sin was indeed forgiven at once,—"The LORD also hath taken away thy sin,"—in consideration of the depth of repentance evinced in, "I have sinned against the LORD." But that which made the repentance and the confession so powerful to take the kingdom of Heaven by force, was this,—that it was no mere burst of momentary shame and sorrow, but a living and active abhorrence of the sin, a change of heart and soul by turning towards GOD. And the enduring condition of his pardon was, accordingly, an enduring blessing,—to keep alive the recollection of what he had done, what he had deserved, what he had felt, what he had received. "Before I was afflicted, I went astray; but now have I kept Thy word[22]!" In the time of ease and prosperity, his heart had grown unwatchful: and, as carelessness came of prosperity, so sin came of carelessness. But his trouble awakened him; and the continuance of his trouble kept him awake. It made him watch; it made him pray; it made him set the LORD always before him. And the end was that, by reason of that very trouble, "Now have I kept Thy

[22] Ps. cxix. 67.   .

word!" Again, in the same Psalm he cries out, " It is good for me that I have been afflicted ; that I might learn Thy statutes[23]." In prosperity had been the danger of forgetting them ; and how great that danger, we have seen! "In my prosperity I said, I shall never be moved...THOU didst hide Thy face, and I was troubled :—I. cried to THEE, O LORD, and unto the LORD I made supplication[24]." And the good effects of that adversity which removes the temptation, we see in numberless other passages of the Psalms ; such as, "I shall not die, but live, and declare the works of the LORD. The LORD hath chastened me sore, but HE hath not given me over unto death[25]." Words these, on which the best comment is what we read in St. Paul, " If we would judge ourselves, we should not be judged. But when we are judged, we are chastened of the LORD, that we should not be condemned with the world."[26]

The first and best thing to be wished for a sinner, is that he should judge himself. And what is this, but that, after having fallen

---

[23] Psalm cxix. 71.   [24] Psalm xxx. 6–8.
[25] Psalm cxviii. 17, 18.   [26] 1 Cor. xi. 31, 32.

under temptation, he should come to himself again, through the ordinary influences of GOD's SPIRIT,—grieved indeed by his fall, but not yet quenched through wilful and habitual sin ; that he should listen to the voice within him, which tells him the true nature of his deed ; that he should give utterance to the confession which that voice prompts him to make ; that he should acknowledge and bewail his transgressions with true and humble penitence before the FATHER in Whose sight they have been committed ? If this were our part, the Apostle tells us that "we should not be judged." CHRIST's merits would plead for us ; and our self-condemnation would for His sake be accepted. But the same temptations which have mastered us at first, are often too strong for us to resist and overcome in this way. That the ear which has once refused to hear the still small voice of GOD, should grow more and more deaf, is often both the consequence and the punishment of its refusal. It was so, even in the case of David. But, blessed be GOD, even when this first mercy fails, HE has still further means of grace in store to rouse the heart from its slumber. We have heard again from St. Paul what it is *to be judged ;*—that this also is a work of mercy, wrought for those who have neglected the former ; a work of even greater mercy, as being calculated to move those whom the former had failed to influence : a greater work, because the former was wrought by the ordinary grace of the SPIRIT moving the sinner within, though as it were imperceptibly ; whereas this is " the finger of GOD," a special work interrupting the even tenor of His dealings with us, and making His presence seen and felt externally. What then is the case, according to St. Paul, when we are judged of the LORD ? If we find that our view of this point differs from that of the Psalmist and the Apostle, it can be no shame for us to sit at their feet, and to learn their view of GOD's dealings instead of our own. The judgments of the LORD are indeed awful things. We can form no adequate conception of them. But His face is still the face of a Father ;—offended,—displeased,—above all, grieved ; but of a Father still. Too often indeed His judgments are so interpreted, as to suggest no thought but that of His anger. We not unnaturally connect the very word *judgment* with the Judgment of the last day; and this makes us think of it as something final and hopeless, bespeaking love lost and mercy exhausted. But this is not what the Psalmist found : this is not what the Apostle taught. They would not have us limit our hope to this life. And HE in Whom they trusted, would have us preserved from the final judgment, " the damnation of hell,"[27] by those judgments on this side of the grave, from which we shrink so weakly. " When we are judged, we are chastened of the LORD, that we may not be condemned with the world."[28] Heavy as are the visitations of GOD's displeasure, they are still a Father's chastisements. They shew His mercy still lingering with us ; they shew His SPIRIT still struggling with the Evil Spirit for our souls ; they shew that HE still reckons us His own; that HE has not ceased to hope for our return ; that HE cannot bear to cast us off, while

[27] ἡ κρίσις τῆς γεέννης, St. Matth. xxiii. 33.

[28] κρινόμενοι δὲ ὑπὸ τοῦ Κυρίου παιδευόμεθα, ἵνα μὴ σὺν τῷ κόσμῳ κατακριθῶμεν, 1 Corinth. xi. 32.

any means remain untried to win us back again to Himself. In one blessed word, the chastisements and judgments of GOD, terrible as they are to the sinner, are the assurance of His presence. And so long as we have His presence, there is hope. The true ground for despair would be, if we were made to believe that His presence was withdrawn; if we were made to believe that His face was wholly turned away, and that His SPIRIT had ceased to strive, ceased to warn, ceased (in the last resort) *to scare* us back from the perdition to which we were hastening.

This would in truth be a judgment of unmixed wrath and terror; for such an abandonment would be final. But such is not the course of our Heavenly FATHER's dealings with His erring children. His mercy and love cannot leave those alone to perish, whom CHRIST has died to save. And how is HE then to interfere, but with judgments? How is HE to reveal Himself, but in severity? Not that HE is changed, but *we*. Not that HE has ceased to be our Father; but that HE is then most truly so, when HE is teaching us, before it is too late, what the end and wages of sin

T

must be. This David knew and felt, when he gave vent to the penitence of his soul in the fifty-first Psalm. And from that day forward, every worldly visitation which recalled the memory of his sin, brought with it a twofold blessing. It kept his conscience tender, that his fall might be his warning; and it renewed the pledge of that final, full forgiveness, which had been promised, when the same voice that proclaimed, " Thou art the man," added also, " The LORD hath taken away thy sin ;—thou shalt not die!"

And thus, it should be our prayer that GOD of His infinite mercy would deal with us, when we omit to judge ourselves for our sins; that HE would Himself cut off the peccant limb and pluck out the offending eye, with which we ourselves have not the courage to part;— " chastening us, that we be not condemned with the world ;"—" chastening and correcting us, but not giving us over unto death ;" keeping His eye upon us, though we may quail under the severity of His glance ; laying His hand upon us, though it may seem all too heavy for us to bear; and, though we may be ready to faint under the grievous exercise of His chastisements, working the peaceable fruit of righteousness in us at the latter end.[29]

"I have gone astray like a sheep that is lost. O seek thy servant; for I do not forget Thy commandments!"[30]

[29] Hebr. xii. 11.   [30] Psalm cxix. 176.

SERMON XII.

FAITH AND HEALING.

Preached on Sunday, April 6, 1856.

ST. MARK vi. 5, 6.

*And HE could there do no mighty work, save that
HE laid His hands upon a few sick folk, and
healed them.   And HE marvelled because of their
unbelief.*

IF we compare these words with the corresponding passage in St. Matthew[1], we shall
find it written there more abruptly, " HE did
not many mighty works there, because of
their unbelief." Each Evangelist contributes
something to fill up the narrative. The one
shows us that the unbelief at which JESUS
CHRIST marvelled, was the cause that no
more mighty works were done. The other
teaches us that " HE could not do" them.
From both, we learn that the unbelief of

[1] Ch. xiii. 58.

these unhappy men was sufficient, if we may reverently speak so, to shorten the arm of the LORD, when stretched out to heal.

It is in the words of St. Mark, which thus seem to limit the power of JESUS CHRIST, that there is an apparent difficulty. And if we reflect upon these, their greater difficulty will seem to arise from their deeper meaning. At all events, it would be a miserable mistake to take refuge in the words which are more intelligible, because they seem to mean less; and to explain away the hard saying by the easy one.

It scarcely needs to be said, at the outset, that the words of the Evangelist cannot be so understood as to deny the supreme and unbounded power of the ALMIGHTY. And on that very account, there *is* a mystery in them; a mystery which, if we allow ourselves to dwell on it and play with it as a matter of abstract speculation, may perplex and bewilder us until we lose our grasp of plain truths and everyday duties. In these questions, the difficulties of detail are often greater stumblingblocks to the human intellect, than the chief mysteries of all. And if we follow the right clue in considering the less, we shall often find that they prove to be merely special instances of the greater ; as the phenomena of natural science which seem most eccentric, are resolved by more comprehensive investigation into exemplifications of some higher and more general law. The general law is, indeed, as much a mystery as was the special phenomenon. Nay, it must be, in reality, still more so. But its working on the mind is not the same. Not only, because cumulative analogies will convince, even though they may not enlighten ; but because the mind itself is attuned to a truer perception and more delicate appreciation of the harmonious result of seeming discords.

Accordingly, the mystery of this force, which is described as overruling our Blessed SAVIOUR's will to do His mighty works of mercy, is only a part of a still greater mystery, which we believe, and must believe, without questioning, and without pretending fully to explain. And in so far as we may seek any explanation of the particular case, we shall be likely to find it in a truth of which men frequently lose sight; the truth, that there is an unity and system in all the works of the Devil on the one side; and that there is also on the other an unity in that scheme for the destruction of the works of the Devil, for which our LORD JESUS CHRST was manifested. We have to recognise the common bond which unites all evil, sin, misery, death; to recognise the oneness of the life and death, the doctrine, the miracles, the sufferings, the sacrifice of our ever Blessed REDEEMER.

The destruction of the works of the Devil was, we are taught, the object of His manifestation. But we are too apt to connect this with His death alone. We dwell, indeed, if not with the glowing gratitude which is fitting, at least with full confession and recognition, on the victory achieved upon the Cross and in the tomb over him who had led us captive to death. We read and see there the power of sin and Satan overthrown, and thereby the doom of sin cancelled, and the life which we had forfeited, restored;—the sure earnest of that blessed future in which the presence of evil shall no longer be a blot on God's creation and a stumblingblock to His children. Nor are we insensible to the other evils, the suffering, the misery of this world of our trial; or forgetful of the way in which Jesus Christ, through the years of His ministry, went about doing good; how "the blind received their sight, and the lame walked; the lepers were cleansed, and the deaf heard; the dead were raised up, and the poor had the Gospel preached to them."[2] But we do not link these subjects so closely together in our thoughts as it would be our wisdom to do. We look on the life's work of Jesus Christ, perhaps as a glorious instance of Godlike compassion; perhaps also as an over-whelming proof of the truth of His mission; but yet, it may be, not as forming a necessary portion of that plan and work of our Redemption which was "finished" on the Cross.

But it was not death and the penal consequences of sin which come after death, that alone were brought into this world through the envy of the Devil. In the beginning we read that "God saw every thing that He had made; and, behold, it was very good."[3] But

[2] St. Matth. xi. 5.   [3] Genes. i. 31.

sin brought with it all evil ; and all suffering entered into this world of ours with death. All are alike the fruits of the forbidden tree. All are the gifts of him to whom our first parents sold themselves in breaking the " not grievous commandments" of their Maker. All sufferings therefore are links of that chain by which human nature has been bound through the influence of the Evil One. The slightest, no less than the most serious, ailment or derangement of bodily functions has a direct, however distant, connection with the mortality of our nature, and thereby with all which we include in the notion of death. And this is but the type of all the workings of evil in the world. All trace their origin to the fall : all are the works of the Devil. All therefore form connected portions of that mystery of evil which the Mystery of Godliness overcame.

We must not, then, allow the infinite distance between the grievousness of the evils which CHRIST relieved in His life and those which HE overcame at His death, or the infinite preciousness of the gift which HE died to give us, above those which HE scattered daily round HIM in the days of His ministry, to blind us to the oneness of the evil with which HE was struggling, and the oneness of the blessing which HE was earning for us throughout. His life and death must be looked on as one whole, —His life exhibiting a steady progress in the work which His death consummated. It was a war against the one enemy; wherein every day had its struggle, and its victory, leading towards the final decision of the great conflict, and affording an earnest of its event. It is not only when we read of sufferings strikingly typical and significant to our minds,—of blindness, of leprosy, of possession by evil Spirits,—that we are to recognise this truth. That one form of suffering suggests the association more than another, is to a certain extent accidental. But a correct appreciation of our condition will make us read the lesson in all alike. Without the crowning mercy of CHRIST'S death, indeed, all else, merciful as it was, would have been as nothing. But still the whole work of the SAVIOUR was one: the crowning mercy was a crown placed on all the mercies which had gone before.

There is a passage in Isaiah, one of the

best known of all the prophecies of the MES-
SIAH, which tells us how " He hath borne
our griefs and carried our sorrows."[4]   I need
not say how we are accustomed to understand
this.   I need not vindicate the interpretation
which refers it, generally indeed, to the sorrows which characterized the life of " the Man
of Sorrows," but, especially and emphatically,
to all that unutterable load of anguish which
HE bore for us in Gethsemane and upon
Mount Calvary. St. Peter's version of Isaiah's
words in the Epistle for this day[5], will speak
for me, where he says, " Who His own self
bare our sins in His own Body on the tree ...
by Whose stripes ye were healed."[6]   But this
is not the only application which the inspired
writers of the New Testament make of these
words of Isaiah. And when St. Matthew quotes
them, it is quite in another connection,—another, though, in that sense which is evidently the truest, the same. St. Matthew quotes
them, as fulfilled, not in our LORD's death,
but in His life ; not in what HE endured for
our sakes, but in that from which HE re-

4 Isaiah liii. 4.   5 Second Sunday after Easter.
6 1 St. Peter ii. 24 ; compare Hebr. ix. 28.

lieved us ;—" When the even was come, they brought unto HIM many that were possessed with devils : and HE cast out the Spirits with His word, and healed all that were sick : that it might be fulfilled which was spoken by Esaias the prophet, saying, ' Himself took our infirmities, and bare our sicknesses.'"[7] We cannot suppose that the Evangelist was ignorant of that deeper meaning which St. Peter and St. Paul found in the words. It is reasonable as well as reverent to believe that he recognised the meaning, deepest of all, in which both interpretations blend into one.

And the language in which JESUS CHRIST Himself was accustomed to speak, carries us onward in the same train of thought, connecting the restitution of the body with that of the spirit, and referring both to the same instrumentality of Faith. How this applies to the salvation of our souls, we see distinctly. We believe that CHRIST's sacrifice was the propitiation for the sins of the whole world[8]. Yet we admit that it will be effectual only for those who obey the call to believe in the

7 St. Matth. viii. 16, 17, Αὐτὸς τὰς ἀσθενείας ἡμῶν ἔλαβε καὶ τὰς νόσους ἐβάστασε.   8 1 St. John ii. 2.

Saviour.   We never think it any derogation
from the might or mercy of God, if we acknowledge that our sins may have power to
exclude us from the blessings which that
mercy has provided. We see that He has so
ordained His whole scheme for our Redemption, as to make our Belief its necessary condition.   Nay, we can to some extent see how
necessary it is ; as we can see how necessary
it is that the physician should be believed
and trusted, before he can do good to the
sick.   The love of God shines upon us, as
the light of the sun.   But there must be
something receptive within us to appropriate
the light ; else it is no light to us.   We need
eyes, that we may be the better for it.   He
might, indeed, if it had so pleased Him, have
given us the power of sight without eyes.
But it has not pleased Him to work so.   And
in this sense alone it might be said that He
might save us without faith.   But the answer
is the same,—that it has not pleased Him to
work so. The way in which it has pleased Him
to work, is by giving us eyes, that we may see
with them ;—by giving us faith, that we may be
saved by it. And where that faith is absent, not-

withstanding all that God has done to work it in us, we say, and say reasonably, that as it is impossible for us to please God, so it is impossible for Him to save us;—that He, Who justifies the ungodly, cannot justify the unbelieving.

We are to bear in mind then, that all these ailments, and visitations of bodily suffering, which our Blessed Lord went about healing, were as much the consequences of sin, as much the works of the Devil, as much the legacies of our first parents' fall, as was death itself. Now as regards death, the connection between the first and the second death, that of the body and that of body and soul in hell, is too evident as well as too awful to be mistaken. We cannot forget that these are both alike the result of man's temptation and fall. But what is needed is, that we should remember that it is the same with all the lesser sufferings of the world; that it was not this or that particular evil which entered into the world with sin, but *all* ill, *all* suffering, *all* sorrow; worldly trouble as truly as spiritual misery; the diseases of the body along with the sickness of the soul. A glance at the original record ought to be enough to fix this in our minds.   There, the chief attention is even directed to the outward and worldly evils. They are made signs and representatives of that which is inward and spiritual.   The curse is on the ground, as upon man: and man's burden is not death only, but, before death, labour and sorrow, suffering and sickness.   The one are the steps which lead downwards to the other. And therefore the REDEEMER and SAVIOUR had mercy upon all, took all on Himself, relieved mankind from the sting of all.   Each, in its proportion, was a part of His work: for each evil was one of those works of the Devil which HE came to destroy.

Let us beware of forgetting the honour which JESUS CHRIST has bestowed even upon these mortal bodies of ours, since HE has taken a body of our substance to Himself.   Materialism produces, by the very recoil from its grossness, an overstrained and unreal spiritualism on the other hand, which would even thrust aside the resurrection of the body from among the articles of our belief.   But in CHRIST's kingdom body and soul have each its share of glory.   Before our spirits can attain to their perfect consummation in bliss, they must await the hour in which our bodies are raised and joined to them again. Heaven itself is not open to the Saints until then : as HE to Whom it is said that they shall be like in that day, Himself took His glorified Body into Heaven, and placed it at the right hand of the FATHER on the throne of His glory. We are taught to look and wait for "the redemption of the body."[9] And the most impressive consideration, by which we are urged to watch over these earthen vessels, which the LORD has called to such honour, is this,—that HE will change them into His own image, and glorify them by His Spirit.[10]

Whatever, then, is the condition of this great salvation, must apply equally to the restitution of body and soul. And this condition is *Faith*. The same law of GOD's merciful intervention, therefore, according to which we say that it is impossible for HIM to save our souls in unbelief, has guided the Evangelist to declare of JESUS CHRIST, that HE, the SON of GOD, could do no mighty work there, where the disbelief of men was so marvellous. Nor is it only the Evangelist who declares this. By our LORD Himself we

9 Rom. viii. 23.   10 Philipp. iii. 21; 1 St. John iii. 2.

have it avowed continually, in connection with
His miracles. Such were His words to the
infirm woman, who had touched the hem of
His garment, in the strong confidence that if
she could do but so much as this, she would
be restored to health;—"Daughter, be of good
comfort; thy faith hath made thee whole."
Such, to the blind Bartimaeus,—" Go thy
way; thy faith hath made thee whole." Such,
again, when the ten lepers had been cleansed,
and only one of them (and he a " stranger," a
Samaritan) returned to give thanks to his
Divine Benefactor,—" Arise, go thy way ; thy
faith hath made thee whole."   And such, too,
were the comfortable words which HE spoke
to the woman which was a sinner, when she
wept over His feet in the Pharisee's house,"
—" Thy faith hath saved thee : go in peace."[11]

It may appear as if this last phrase, referring as it does to an act of spiritual, not bodily,
healing, is out of place in the series in which
it has been here included. But it has not been
mentioned unadvisedly : for it is this instance
which especially teaches us to connect the two

[11] St. Matth. ix. 22 ; St. Mark x. 52 ; St. Luke xvii. 19 ;
vii. 50.

classes. We must, however, go back from our English Bibles to the original, before we can estimate aright the force of the words which our SAVIOUR used. In our version they are varied, as reference is made to the soul or the body, from " Thy faith hath saved thee," to " Thy faith hath made thee whole." But in the words of CHRIST, as recorded by the Evangelists, there is no such variation. In every instance alike, His saying is, ἡ πίστις σου σέσωκέ σε. It is the same phrase in every case, conveying either the whole idea of salvation, or a portion of it, whether relating to the body, or the soul ;—but, whether in the full extent, or under this limitation, containing the self-same idea of *salvation;* and directly implying the unity of the evils to which it refers.

I cannot stay to enumerate the many instances throughout the New Testament in which the same word is used in this mixed signification[12]. But it is important to glance

[12] They are the following :—

1. The infirm woman ; ᾽Εὰν μόνον ἅψωμαι τοῦ ἱματίου αὐτοῦ, σωθήσομαι· .... Θάρσει, θύγατερ· ἡ πίστις σου σέσωκέ σε. Καὶ ἐσώθη ἡ γυνὴ ἀπὸ τῆς ὥρας ἐκείνης, St. Matth. ix. 21, 22, 23: compare St. Mark v. 28, 34 ; St. Luke viii. 48.

again at the cases which have been already mentioned, and to observe how the one meaning runs into the other. In the instances of the blind man of Jericho, and the woman who had the spirit of infirmity, the plain and direct sense is that of bodily healing. But there is a perceptible advance in what is said to the

2. Jairus' daughter ; ἵνα ἐλθὼν ἐπιθῇς αὐτῇ τὰς χεῖρας, ἵνα σωθῇ, St. Mark v. 23 ; μόνον πίστευε, καὶ σωθήσεται, St. Luke viii. 50.

3. The blind man at Jericho (Bartimaeus) ; ἡ πίστις σου σέσωκέ σε, St. Mark x. 52 ; St. Luke xviii. 42.

4. The demoniac of Gadara ; ἀπήγγειλαν ... πῶς ἐσώθη ὁ δαιμονισθείς, St. Luke viii. 36.

5. The Samaritan leper ; ἡ πίστις σου σέσωκέ σε, St. Luke xvii. 19.

6. "As many as touched ;" ἐσώζοντο, St. Mark vi. 56.

7. The cripple at the Beautiful Gate ; ἐπὶ εὐεργεσίᾳ ἀνθρώπου ἀσθενοῦς, ἐν τίνι οὗτος σέσωσται ... οὐκ ἔστιν ἐν ἄλλῳ οὐδενὶ ἡ σωτηρία· οὔτε γὰρ ὄνομά ἐστιν ἕτερον ... ἐν ᾧ δεῖ σωθῆναι ἡμᾶς, Acts iv. 9, 12.

8. The cripple of Lystra ; ἰδὼν ὅτι πίστιν ἔχει τοῦ σωθῆναι, Acts xiv. 9.

9. Lazarus ; Κύριε,. εἰ κεκοίμηται, σωθήσεται, St. John xi. 12.

10. The woman which was a sinner ; ἡ πίστις σου σέσωκέ σε· πορεύου εἰς εἰρήνην, St. Luke vii. 50.

11. Ἡ εὐχὴ τῆς πίστεως σώσει τὸν κάμνοντα, καὶ ἐγερεῖ αὐτὸν ὁ Κύριος· κἂν ἁμαρτίας ᾖ πεποιηκώς, ἀφεθήσεται αὐτῷ, St. James v. 15.

Samaritan leper ; perhaps connected with the especially symbolical character of his disease. Of their leprosy, we read that all the ten were healed alike : but he alone, of them all, was found to turn back and glorify God ; so that Christ Himself commented upon the contrast of their behaviour.   And the word of blessing pronounced over him was this, " Arise, go thy way ; thy faith hath made thee whole" (or, " hath saved thee"). We can scarcely avoid the inference that this was a blessing which went beyond the blessings of the others. And the meaning seems to be, that according to their faith it was to each ; and what each believed that he received, he did in effect receive ; —that there was a lower degree of faith, which could appreciate the outward miracle, and appropriate the worldly blessing ; and that so far they were all " saved," all made whole of their plague : but that there was a higher grace required for the due appreciation of the miracle in its fulness, its real meaning, its spiritual character ; by which, to those who received it worthily, it became as it were a sacrament of heavenly things ; and that this the Samaritan, and he alone, had manifested ; so that his surpassing faith had made him the heir of this greater salvation.

And therefore this narrative of the Samaritan leper forms a link to connect the former cases with that of the woman to whom JESUS CHRIST said (in the same words, be it remembered), " Thy faith hath saved thee."   In this instance we hear nothing of any bodily ailment or outward miracle : and yet it seems plain that the same mercy was vouchsafed, the same " virtue" went forth, the same miracle was wrought, to heal her sickness,—the spiritual sickness of sin ; and that, through the same medium, her faith.

And the inference is, not that the same words are used in different meanings ; but that in every case the same gift of healing from all the consequences of sin was there, to strike root and bear fruit according to the soil ; and that every miracle of bodily healing had its chief blessedness in that it was also a means of healing to the soul, if those on whom it was wrought would receive it.

And on the other hand, in the account of the impotent man at the pool of Bethesda, do we not seem to have a glimpse of the result of such works of mercy, if they could be appropriated without faith? To him the LORD spoke in words which suggest that his disease had been not merely a part of the inheritance of a corrupt nature, but, in some degree at least, the chastisement of actual sin;—"Behold, thou art made whole : sin no more, lest a worse thing come unto thee." It is remarkable that here the phrase is not the same as in the previous instances.[13] It could not be translated, " Thou art saved."[14] And the sequel suggests doubts as to the effect of the miracle on the soul of the recipient; for the next words are, " The man departed and told the Jews that it was JESUS, Which had made him whole. And therefore did the Jews persecute JESUS, and sought to slay HIM."

Lastly, we read in the case of the paralytic man who was let down by his friends, bed and all, through the roof of the house where the SAVIOUR was, that " when HE saw their

[13] Although St. John elsewhere uses the word σώζεσθαι when speaking of restoration from bodily sickness; e. g. xi. 12, εἰ κεκοίμηται, σωθήσεται.

[14] Not σέσωσαι, but ὑγιὴς γέγονας, St. John v. 14 : compare verses 4. 6, 9, 11, 15.

faith, HE said unto him, Man, thy sins are forgiven thee:" and that, when the Pharisees were
offended, HE rejoined, "What reason ye in
your hearts? Whether is easier, to say, Thy
sins be forgiven thee, or to say, Rise up and
walk? But that ye may know that the SON
of Man hath power on earth to forgive sins,
.... I say unto thee, Arise, and take up thy
couch, and go unto thine house." [15]   A passage of so clear and cheering import needs no
paraphrase to show, that it was the same miracle which healed the sickness and forgave the
sin, making the one the evidence of the other;
so that each of the expressions comprised both
the meanings,—"Thy sins be forgiven thee,"
comprehending "Arise and walk," as the
greater does the less; "Arise and walk" implying "Thy sins be forgiven thee," as the
sign implies the thing signified [16].

So far then is the power of these unhappy
men to paralyse the outstretched arm of our

[15] St. Luke v. 20–24.

[16] See also Acts iv. 9, ἐν τίνι οὗτος σέσωσται, compared
with 12, οὔτε γὰρ ὄνομά ἐστιν ἕτερον ὑπὸ τὸν οὐρανὸν τὸ δεδό-
μενον ἐν ἀνθρώποις, ἐν ᾧ δεῖ σωθῆναι ἡμᾶς. Here our version
has "*made whole*" in the first passage, and "*saved*" in the
second; σωτηρία, "*salvation*," having intervened in verse 11.

SAVIOUR by their unbelief, from furnishing any reason for misgivings, that in a dispensation in which faith is the condition of salvation, there would have been reason for misgiving if it had been otherwise. If we had seen the SAVIOUR of the world dispensing His mercies, without requiring the fulfilment of the condition, there would have been a temptation to think that CHRIST was removing the consequences of sin without removing the sin itself; that the punishment of sin, and not sin itself, was the curse from which we needed deliverance; that death could be destroyed, while sin continued to reign. Whereas a juster view of His work exhibits HIM struggling throughout His life with the evil which HE came upon earth to remedy; tracking it through all the ramifications of its influence; pursuing it to its remotest results, temporal as well as spiritual; day by day and hour by hour, for us men and for our salvation, living the agony of Gethsemane, and dying the death of Calvary.

It will be well, therefore, for us, if, in addition to that most emphatic lesson of the necessity of faith, both receptive and active, for our entire emancipation from the thraldom of the Evil One, which the text, in harmony with all the rest of God's Revelation in CHRIST, impresses on us, it suggests to us notions somewhat less inadequate than we have had before, of the griefs and sorrows which marred that form and visage,—of His weariness in the noontide,—of the watchings and wrestlings of those solitary nights of prayer. It will be well for us, if we are taught to feel that it was no mere allusion to the death which was to come, but a plain expression of His life's continual burden, when HE warned His hearers that no man could become His disciple without taking up his cross daily and following HIM[17].

And if these meditations bring us also to think more of the extent of the power of sin, removing in part the veil which hides its workings, and exhibiting it as a constant interruption of the good order and well-being of GOD's creation, a perpetual interference with the normal state of His creatures, instead of being, as it assumes to be, the element in which our nature works;—this also will carry our minds

[17] St. Luke ix. 23.

again to Him who has fought the fight and won the victory for us : while it will strengthen our sympathy with our brethren in all the sufferings, all the evil which may be their lot.

And above all, it will bring before us that portion of our Blessed Saviour's work, which it is our own privilege as members of His Body to share. The sacrifice of His death was "once offered ;" and there is no more sacrifice for sin. That mystery we can but adore. But the work of His life we can follow. That unremitting contest with the Powers of Evil, it is ours, after His example and in His strength, to wage. That discipline of suffering whereby He learned obedience and was made perfect, is the example which He left us, that we should follow His steps. That ministry of sympathy and charity which was His life upon earth, is our vocation and will be our blessing. To the fellowship of this, as far as active service goes, we are called always ; while, from time to time, we are brought yet nearer to Him, by the pressure of His Cross.

Feeble, indeed, is this our service, and limited the sphere of our trial. But He reckons our imperfect efforts to follow HIM, not according to the actual work, but according to the spirit which gives it reality in His sight. And whenever we are called, whether in things small or great (as things appear to us), to resist evil or to do good, this is no other, no less lofty a vocation, than to share the great warfare in which CHRIST our Head is engaged, to take our part in the overthrow of the Enemy, and the deliverance of them that are bound. We are called to share the struggle which *is*, that we may partake of the victory which shall be. For it is not His will either to suffer, or to struggle, or to triumph alone. With the cords of a man HE, the SON of Man, draws us to Himself, that HE, the SON of GOD, may make us "partakers of the Divine nature."[18] If HE went about, blending temporal mercies with spiritual, HE gives a value which never was their own to the least works of piety or charity that we do,—were they but the offering of two mites to His treasury, or one cup of cold water to His little ones. If HE did battle with the Evil One, HE gives us His strength, and clothes us with His armour to

[18] 2 St. Peter i. 4.

wrestle against principalities, against powers, against the rulers of the darkness of this world, against spiritual wickedness in high places[19]. If HE suffered for our salvation, HE also permits His disciples to know the fellowship of His sufferings, being made conformable unto His death[20]. And all this,—that we may be one with HIM and HE with us;—one in work, one in spirit, one in suffering;—that we may be one in glory, in that day when GOD shall be All in All.

O GOD, Whose Blessed SON was manifested that HE might destroy the works of the Devil, and make us the sons of GOD, and heirs of eternal life; Grant us, we beseech THEE, that, having this hope, we may purify ourselves, even as HE is pure; that, when HE shall appear again with power and great glory, we may be made like unto HIM in His eternal and glorious kingdom; where with THEE, O FATHER, and THEE, O HOLY GHOST, HE liveth and reigneth, ever one GOD, world without end. *Amen.*

[19] Ephes. vi. 12.   [20] Philipp. iii. 10 : compare Coloss. i. 24.

SERMON XIII.

WARNING AND TEACHING.

Preached on the second Sunday in Advent, 1857.

COLOSSIANS i. 28.

Warning every man, and teaching every man in all wisdom; that we may present every man perfect in CHRIST JESUS.

SUCH was St. Paul's idea of the ministry of CHRIST;—its work, to warn every man, and teach every man in all wisdom; its end, to present every man perfect in CHRIST JESUS. We can have no better authority, we can have no better example, than St. Paul. May GOD give grace to the Teachers, to labour for nothing short of this. May HE give grace to those who are taught, to bring forth no less fruit. And may His mercy be on the short-comings of us all;—for His sake, in Whom is the work of the ministry and the perfection of the Christian!

Let us take the verse piecemeal : for every word contains its lesson.   The first work is *to warn* every man.   What, then, is our warning to be ?

First, it must be the warning of the Baptist, *Repent ;*—whether it be addressed to those who have not yet received the Gospel, or to those who have received it, but have not lived according to their profession.   " Repent ye ; for the kingdom of Heaven is at hand[1]," was the preaching of John when the revelation of the Son of God was about to be made. " The time is fulfilled, and the kingdom of God is at hand ; repent ye,"[2]—was "the beginning of the Gospel of Jesus Christ the Son of God" Himself, when His preaching began.   And to this day, though His banner was set up, and his kingdom founded on earth in the days of His flesh, and of the manifestation of His Holy Spirit, still the kingdom of God is "at hand," still it is "coming"; and we pray that it may come, until it comes to all ; until the Father's name be hallowed, and His will done on earth, even as it is in Heaven.   And what hinders and delays this

---

[1] St. Matth. iii. 2.   [2] St. Mark i. 15.

consummation ? What, but our sins,—the sins of all mankind, but especially of those to whom in one sense the kingdom is already come, who have been received into it, and have bound themselves by its vows ? And therefore, as it was then, so now too, the coming of the kingdom of GOD is a reason for repentance, ever more and more earnest and deep. "*Repent ye,*" then. This is the first warning.

But there is a true repentance ; and there is a counterfeit, which would fain pass under the name. Therefore Christians must be warned, not only against the glaring hypocrisy, which puts on the show of a Christian grace to be seen of men ;—not only against that more disguised kind, which really performs a sort of mutilated and unreal service to GOD ; —but also against that most subtle and hopeless kind of all, by which men not merely succeed (it may be) in deceiving men, and try to deceive GOD, but absolutely delude themselves with the thought that their repentance is true, and that their consciences are cleansed. And therefore, as the Baptist added

another warning, so must we ; addressing
to ourselves and our brethren that which he
spoke to the Pharisees and the Sadducees.
Remember that even these were found flock-
ing to his baptism : and let that thought
make you watchful of your own hearts and
motives.   What then was his warning to that
brood of the deaf adder which stoppeth her
ears ? " Bring forth fruits worthy of repentance."[3] It is not enough, to say, I repent, and
then to go and do as you have always done.
Not enough, to walk carefully and strictly for a
while, and then to return to your old ways and
works.   Not enough, to whiten the outside of
the sepulchre, while it is full of all uncleanness
within.   Repentance is a new life, a new spirit,
a new heart.   And the new life will stir ;—
the new spirit will breathe ;—the new heart
will from its good treasure bring forth good
things.   And where there are no such fruits,
it is evident that the old canker remains.
And then the pang, the change which is professed, is either a lie or a curse.   It was a lie
in those Pharisees and Sadducees.   It was a
curse to the traitor Iscariot.   In either way, it

3 St. Luke iii. 8.

is an increase of condemnation instead of being an escape from it. *Bring forth fruits, therefore, worthy of repentance.* This is the second warning.

To the Baptist it was not permitted to go further. His mission was fulfilled in making sinners know their sins, and feel the need of having them removed. He was, literally, "The voice of one crying in the wilderness, Prepare ye the way of the LORD [4];"—no more. But there was hope in the message of preparation. Though the kingdom of Heaven had not come, it was at hand. Even then, there stood One among them Whom they knew not, Who should baptize them, not with water only, as John, but with the Holy Ghost. And thus the Baptist's preaching, blessed in this first respect, that it was a call to awaken repentance, and to elicit the fruits of repentance, was still more blessed in another; because it taught his disciples that they must look further,—beyond themselves and beyond him,—to have their burden removed from them. John was not the CHRIST : and his preaching therefore was not the Gospel,—no glad tidings of

[4] Isaiah xl. 3; St. Luke iii. 4, etc.

salvation. It was simply a preparation, though a precious and necessary preparation.

But an angel from Heaven had already outstript the message of the Baptist, on that night when the shepherds who were watching their flocks heard the good tidings of great joy,—the birth of a Saviour, even Christ the Lord. And accordingly, when Jesus commenced His preaching, He took up the strain where the voice of His minister had failed ;—"The time is fulfilled, and the kingdom of God is at hand. Repent ye, *and believe the Gospel*[5]." Here was a new warning, a new duty ;—not only to repent, but to believe ;—so to put away all insincerity from themselves, that they might put faith in another. And what was it that they were to believe ? No painful message ; no denunciation of the wrath that they had deserved ; but *the Gospel*, the glad tidings, "good tidings of great joy to all the people ;" tidings that brought down the very choir of angels from on high, as if earth were now the place where the name of God could be most fitly praised ;

5 St. Mark i. 15.

linking earth with heaven in the communion
of thanksgiving, "Glory to GOD in the highest,
and on earth peace ; good will towards men !"[6]
The belief which was required, was a belief in
the message of salvation, a belief that the
SAVIOUR had come,—HE, in and through
Whom we should be saved. This adds hope
to repentance, and produces the fruit of love.
This then was the great light to them that
sat in darkness and the shadow of death ;—
" Believe *the Gospel*, the glad tidings of salvation in JESUS CHRIST."   And this was, and is,
the third warning.

Are there any more ?

Surely, if rightly considered, these compre-
hend all.   But man is still weak, and the Evil
One strong : and whatever we might justly
argue from the full meaning of the message
of CHRIST, it was found by the Apostles, as it
is now, and will be to the end of the world,
needful to go further.   For some accept the
Gospel of CHRIST, and adulterate it ; some
glory in the grace of GOD, and turn it into a
cloak of maliciousness, or an excuse of lasciviousness.   And therefore the Apostolic writings

<hr>

[6] St. Luke ii. 14. .

X 2

are full of warning against these evils, which threatened to drown souls in the very waters of Baptism. Remember how solemnly St. Paul warns us, whether it be against breaches of the unity of the Body and the Spirit, and against false doctrine and misbelief; or whether it be against unfruitfulness in good works, which is fruitfulness in evil. Remember the spirit of the Apostolic warnings, even when most urgent and most stern. It is the urgency of friendship; the sternness of love. He admonishes as brethren; he warns with tears!

This then is the first portion of the work of Christ's ministers, "to warn every man."

But another portion immediately follows;— "teaching every man in all wisdom." In the days of our Lord's flesh the Jews had teaching and teachers in plenty,—their teachers of babes, their Scribes, their Doctors of the Law, their Rabbis, their Masters in Israel. But the teaching was naught; for they taught the wrong thing. They discarded all so-called profane learning: but they profaned the sacred lore which they professed to teach. They

rejected the treasures of Gentile wisdom ; as
if, even in that, HE who is the GOD of the
spirits of all flesh was not honoured : and they
thought that they honoured HIM by thrusting
their own inventions into His religion, and
their own commandments into His Word.

But *we* are to teach every man in all wisdom ;
—not in the wisdom of the Jewish teachers, that
made the Word of GOD of none effect by their
traditions, garnished with gross legends, and
eked out with immoral interpretations[7]. GOD
forbid ! Nor yet in the wisdom of the Greeks,
the wisdom of that world which by wisdom
knew not GOD. But in the wisdom of GOD ;—
preaching CHRIST crucified, the Power of GOD
and the Wisdom of GOD ; CHRIST, made to us
not wisdom only, but also righteousness and
sanctification and redemption[8]. This indeed
consists not in human acquirements. And yet
these are GOD's gifts, and should be consecrated.
We have to baptize the Jew and the Heathen :
we have to christianize the treasures confided
to all mankind ; bringing out of our treasure
things new and old. But all must be dedi-
cated at the altar. For it is in GOD's wisdom

<hr>

7 St. Matth. xv. 6.   8 1 Corinth. i. 21–30.

that our teaching must be established ; as it is in His power that our faith must stand. For that which we are to teach, man could not of himself discover. It is not only God's message, but His message of Himself. It is the revelation of His Person ;—of His work ; —and of His will.

Of Himself ;—that "God .. hath in these last days spoken unto us by His Son ;"—"No man hath seen God at any time : the only-begotten Son, which is in the bosom of the Father, He hath declared Him."[9] And both unite in sending the consubstantial Spirit, to be with the people of Christ, as a Comforter and Advocate.

Again, of His work ;—not of that only, which was completed in the six days of Creation, and yet still "hitherto" goes on[10], in the preservation of all things and the order in which the universe proceeds :—not of this only ; though even of this we learn what was not revealed to them of old time, how Father, Son, and Holy Ghost wrought together in the beginning ;—we learn to understand what that means, "The Spirit of God moved on

9 Hebr. l. 2 ; St. John i. 18.   10 St. John v. 17.

the face of the waters ;"—to understand the
gift, when GOD breathed into Adam's nostrils
the breath, or Spirit, of life ;—and to believe
that nothing was made in the beginning, but
by that WORD Which was with GOD and was
GOD in the beginning[11].   But more especially,
of the LORD's work in the new creation; so
that we learn to glorify the SON, not alone for
the glory which HE had with the FATHER before
the world was : but for the mercy wherewith
HE humbled Himself to become our Redeemer
from sin, our Saviour from death, our Mediator
with the FATHER, our Brother in the kingdom
of Heaven.   And again we learn to know and
glorify the HOLY SPIRIT, not only as one of
the three Persons of the One GODHEAD,—but
as HIM Who came down from Heaven to rest
upon the Church of GOD and every member
of it,—to purge our minds with His pure fire,
to enlighten our hearts with the shining of
His light,—to dwell, not among us only, but
in us, making us the spiritual temples of the
living GOD.

And thus, in the third place, we have to
learn and to teach His will,—what it is, and

<hr>

[11] Genes. i. 2; ii. 7; St. John i. 3.

how it is to be performed. And though in
the older covenant, this was revealed, both
at length, for a rule of our actions, and in
brief forms like the Decalogue, by which we
might try our hearts; yet it was left for our
Redeemer and our Revelation to show how
the Law is at once made perfect, fulfilled, and
taken away, by the full understanding of the
two great Commandments, to love the Lord
with all our hearts, and to love our neighbour
as ourselves. For what law towards God
shall we break, or what law towards men, if
we love them thus? And on the other hand,
what are all laws, with all their terrors and
their punishments, to him, whose heart thus
loves God, thus loves his neighbour? And
if we are called to love God, is it not the
Spirit that He hath given within us, Who
inspires us with that love? If we are to love
one another, is it not the same Spirit, Who
extends that love to all who are the children
of God in Christ, all who by their membership
in Him are members one of another. And thus
all Christian warning and teaching is gathered
into one; as there is one Body, one Spirit, one
Hope; one Lord, one Faith, one Baptism;

one GOD and FATHER of all, Who is above all, and through all, and in all.[12]

And now, what is the object of all this ?—" That we may present every man perfect in CHRIST JESUS."—The second Advent; the judgment-day, and our preparation to meet it. Nothing less than this, is the meaning of these words. It is clear from the whole passage, and numerous other passages wherein St. Paul uses the same phrase,[13] that our "presentation" is to GOD. Sometimes indeed, in the continual presentation of ourselves to HIM through life, as a living sacrifice, a reasonable service; but also in that final presentation before the Judgment-seat, which is to set the seal upon all. Nor in the text can we stop short of that day, so distinctly spoken of in the Epistle to the Hebrews, when those who watch for the souls of the believers must give account, profitable or unprofitable for the flock, with joy or with grief to themselves.[14]

The day, then, of our presentation is the Day of Judgment. HE to Whom every man

[12] Ephes. iv. 4–6.   [13] See above, p. 110, note.
[14] Hebr. xiii. 17.

is to be presented, is He "Who sitteth on the throne, judging right."[15]   And the object is, that every man may be presented "perfect" in that day; according to our Blessed Lord's own words, "Be ye perfect, even as your Father Which is in Heaven is perfect." The particular perfection *there* enjoined is indeed mercy; and the example of our Heavenly Father makes the application peculiarly forcible.[16]   But the precept is unlimited;—"Be ye perfect:" and the perfectness of God is at once the pattern for our imitation and our inducement to aim at it.

Now, the notion which lies at the root of all that is said of this "perfection," is that of full growth, strength and maturity, as opposed to the weakness, helplessness, waywardness of childhood.[17]   In the view which Christ's Apostles adopted from their Lord's teaching, our spiritual life has a course (except as regards the congenital seeds of decay) not unlike that of our natural life.   It begins by a

[15] Psalm ix. 4.

[16] St. Matth. v. 48 ; compare St. Luke vi. 36.

[17] Compare especially 1 Corinth. xiv. 20, μὴ παιδία γίνεσθε ταῖς φρεσίν· ἀλλὰ τῇ κακίᾳ νηπιάζετε, ταῖς δὲ φρεσὶ τέλειοι γίνεσθε.

birth. It is nourished through an infancy. It is trained through continual growth to a man-hood, even the full perfection of its nature; when the spiritual nurture has its full effect, and the spiritual stature reaches its full development. We know that there is a point in the natural life in which this is so with our bodily constitution ; and that there is a point, at which our intellect too arrives at the fullest expansion of which it has been made capable. Not that these are the same in all ; or that we can precisely, in any case, lay a finger upon the point. But as time goes on, we can form a sufficient judgment ; because our bodies and minds do not rest in the state of relative perfection which they attain. The seeds of death are in our mortal natures. Our fruits ripen : —but ripeness itself is in sublunary things only one stage of decay.

But it is otherwise in our spiritual nature. And this precept of perfection throws light upon the difference. How can we arrive at the perfection of which our Heavenly FATHER is the example ? As our earthly natures are to time, so are our spirits to eternity. The type of duty here is, "after serving one's own generation by the will of God, to fall on sleep."[18] But there the work is endless; the life is for ever; the perfection is unapproachable. As we can never arrive at the fulness of that which is set before us, we need not ask what is to happen when perfection is attained.

St. Paul sketches very clearly the history of the spiritual life within us. We are first born into CHRIST, and having received the Spirit of adoption, we are entitled and enabled to cry "Abba," "Father." We are then "babes,"— "babes in CHRIST;" spiritually alive, indeed; but still, it may be, with many of the incapacities and deficiencies of infancy; as those Corinthians were, whom the Apostle addressed not as spiritual, but as carnal, even as babes in CHRIST, and declared that he had fed them with the food of babes accordingly.[19] So too, speaking generally, though in his own person, he uses the comparison, "When I was a child, I spake as a child, I understood as a child, I thought as a child; but since I have become a man, I have put away the things of the child."[20] And elsewhere he speaks of the

[18] Acts xiii. 36.   [19] 1 Corinth. iii. 1, 2.
[20] 1 Corinth. xiii. 11.

Church in its childhood in the earlier dispensation, as the heir indeed, but under tutors
and governors,—in bondage under the elements of the world, until the fulness of the
time came, and GOD sent forth His SON.[21]
But it is in the Epistle to the Hebrews that
the parallel between the natural and spiritual
childhood, and the way in which they are to
be dealt with, are most clearly set forth; where
the Apostle, having spoken of the typical
majesty of Melchisedec, proceeds to say, "Of
whom we have many things to say, and hard
to be uttered, seeing ye are dull of hearing.
For when for the time ye ought to be teachers,
ye have need that one teach you again which
be the first principles of the oracles of GOD;
and are become such as have need of milk and
not of strong meat. For every one that useth
milk is unskilful in the word of righteousness:
for he is a babe. But strong meat belongeth
unto them that are *of full age.*" And it is to
be noted, first, that this is the same word
($\tau\acute{\epsilon}\lambda\epsilon\iota\omicron\iota$) which has been translated "*perfect*" in
our text; and next, that the Apostle goes on
to define it ;—"them that are of full age, even

<hr>

[21] Galat. iv. 1, sqq.

those who by reason of use have their senses exercised to discern both good and evil."[22]

Thus we are to grow in CHRIST, by the nourishment suited to our growth,—by the milk, or elementary principles of doctrine, and plain rules of childlike obedience and temper : and then, as our faith and knowledge are increased, we are to advance by the stronger meats of the deeper mysteries which have been revealed in CHRIST, and the more difficult measures of firmness in believing, and resistance to temptation,—by the trials, which require more strength than that of infancy, but, where that strength exists first, add further strength and growth, and carry us on to "perfection," to the full stature and vigour of the Christian manhood.

Yet further, in writing to his Ephesian disciples, the Apostle exhibits to us the very type of "the perfect man," "the measure of the stature of the fulness of CHRIST ;" "that we henceforth be no more children, tossed to and fro, and carried about with every wind of doctrine ;... but speaking the truth in love,

---

[22] Hebr. v. 11–14.

may grow up into Him in all things, Which is the Head, even Christ."[23]

Thus we have the gifts in their order,— the life, the nourishment, the discipline. And lastly, we have the standard by which we are to measure ourselves, that Perfect Man unto which we are to grow, revealed to us in the measure of the full stature of the Incarnate Saviour.

And these scriptural illustrations correspond with the earlier divisions of our text: for we have there the "teaching," which leads to perfection in knowledge, by the administration of milk and solid food according to advancement: and we have the "warning," which leads to perfection in holiness, after the model of the perfections of our Father which is in Heaven.

Now, the practical application of all this is twofold;—to each Christian separately, as a member of Christ; to the Church, as His Body. To us these interests ought to be one. But as it is through the reality of our share in the first that we arrive at the per-

---

[23] Ephes. iv. 13, sqq.

ception of the second, let us give our first attention to that which comes most nearly home to us individually.

We are taught, we are warned to be perfect, even as our FATHER Which is in Heaven is perfect. Now the question immediately arises,—Can we be perfect? And who is there, that will dare to say, Yes?—Yet this is our call. Yet this, and nothing less, is our reasonable service. Nay, even if this were achieved, we should be unprofitable servants. We cannot shut our eyes to our duty. We should of ourselves reject any other than a perfect pattern. We can of ourselves see that none other accords with the perfections of GOD. What then is wrought in us by this seeming contradiction? Its effect is to increase the depth and secure the permanence of our penitence. The Christian's sense of his own sin is the measure of his sense of CHRIST's mercy. And his sense of the exalted nature of his duty must be the measure of his sense of sin. Such is the working of our call to perfection, together with our consciousness of inability.

Now, if this were all, the result would be not so much ceaseless penitence, as sheer de-

spair.   But the question has another side ;
and on that side, another answer.   Let us
ask, Shall we be perfect ?   And to this the
answer of faith is, " I thank GOD, through
JESUS CHRIST our LORD."[24]   Not we, but
CHRIST JESUS in us ;—not we of ourselves,
but as members of that Body of His, to which
perfectness is promised.   We shall be perfect (let us say it in faith) : because it is
our call to be so ; and the callings of GOD
are not in vain, not mockeries ; HE is the
GOD, not of the dead, but of the living.   Not
we, indeed, shall be perfect, but the work of
CHRIST, but CHRIST Himself, in us.   And
therefore our strivings after perfection must
be as unceasing as our penitence for our imperfection : because HE it is that worketh in
us mightily ; and therefore we are taught and
encouraged to work, inasmuch as it is not
of our own weak nature that the impossible
effort is required : and because that SPIRIT
Which strives after the attainment of so great
an end, is CHRIST in us the hope of glory ;[25]
—not the REDEEMER only, who once wrought
a mighty work for us on the Cross, and now

[24] Rom. vii. 25.   [25] Coloss. i. 27.

Y

continually intercedes for us at the Father's right hand on high ; but Christ the sender of the Holy Ghost,—Who by His indwelling Spirit is perfecting His good work within us, —raising up Himself in the spirit of each one of us, that we in turn may be built up as lively stones into that spiritual House, which has its unity in Him[26].

This is our perfection ! Because Christ is perfect ; because He is the perfecter of our faith ; because, even in man's nature, He (Who as God needed it not) was made perfect by suffering for us[27] ; because He dwells in us by His Spirit ; because we dwell in Him in His Body, for which He gave Himself, to sanctify and cleanse it, that He might present it to Himself a glorious Church, holy and without blemish.[28]

As His holiness is communicated, and His Spirit is given to all the members of that Body, to quicken and purify them ; so those who retain their faithful hold on Him shall be " presented" in that day, "perfect," not in themselves, but in Him in Whom they have believed.

[26] 1 St. Peter ii. 4, 5, etc.   [27] Hebr. v. 8, 9.
[28] Ephes. v. 25-27.

Then the Ministry will be at an end. Men will have been taught ; they will have been warned. All will be over ; all, except the presentation of every man before the Judge.

What a moment for the pastors ! what a moment for the flocks ! How shall we be presented ? How shall we present you ? Where shall we find our place ? Where will you find yours ? Will it indeed be in that glorious Church, which will be without spot or wrinkle or any such thing ? or will it be among the stains and pollutions which must be cast out of it in its purgation ? Will it be among the perfect, the full-grown men in CHRIST; or will it be among the " children that are corrupters," the babes in understanding, but in malice men ?

Brethren, we must watch for you, teach you, warn you. Heavy indeed is the task and the responsibility. But though your blood may be on the heads of those who should watch for your souls,—remember that it is none the less upon your own heads. It is on your own, whether it be on your Pastors' or not. For, " If thou warn the wicked," saith the LORD, " and he turn not from his wickedness, nor from his wicked way, he shall die in his iniquity ; but thou hast delivered thy soul."[29]

May the SPIRIT of CHRIST guide *us* in teaching and warning, and move *your* hearts to listen and learn ; so that His Word may not return to HIM empty, nor His Work remain imperfect ; but that, both by His blessing on His ministers, and by every operation of His grace on your souls, you may be presented perfect indeed at His coming ; that in that day all the imperfections of our mortality may be swallowed up in HIM Who is our Perfection and our Life !

[29] Ezekiel iii. 18, 19, and xxxiii. 8, 9.

SERMON XIV.

THE BOOK LOST AND FOUND.

Preached on the second Sunday in Advent, 1859.

2 Kings xxii. 8, and 2 Chronicles xxxiv. 15.

I have found the Book of the Law in the House of the LORD.

THE student of God's Word is often told to remember that it is also the word of man,— the word, not of one man, but of many ; that the personal contribution of each human author to the texture of his portion of the work, is to be estimated ; and that the same historical criticism is to be applied to each of the several portions, as is commonly applied to any work which we believe to be uninspired.

And, no doubt, evils have arisen from the

neglect of these warnings. If we do not sufficiently appreciate the variety and the weakness of the human element, we lose a most effectual means of appreciating the Unity and the Perfection of that which is Divine. But while there is something which is almost a truism in the expression of these canons of criticism, there is also something in them which is untrue, if accepted without modification. There are, for instance, points in which our mode of dealing with a book must be ruled by our belief or disbelief of its inspiration. There are points on which we must make up our minds whether or not we are to receive the Scripture history as inspired, before we can decide how we are to proceed in comparing it with other books, or in criticising it like other books.

The facts of the Scripture narrative are stated simply, as the writers assume to know that they took place ;—some being public ; some, private ; some, not external at all, but existing in the inner world of man. Doubtless, investigation merely human might arrive at the knowledge of many of these. But then, we require the uninspired historian to marshal his evidence before he states his conclusions ; and we are entitled to reject the conclusions for which no grounds are shewn. Now, inspiration is independent of any such process as this. An inspired history will indeed carry its own evidence within it, in a fuller harmony and deeper consistency. But it will in many particulars contradict ordinary inferences : both because these are generalized, based upon an average ; and because they can be drawn only from the outside of things. The secret springs, the inmost realities of particular cases, and the idiosyncrasies of individual actors, are (so to speak) the subjects of revelation, in proportion as they are the insoluble problem of uninspired history.

One or two instances of this kind will lead us towards our immediate subject.

To illustrate the difference between the revealed and the human view of the same historical character, we may take the first Herod, as shadowed forth in the Gospel, and as depicted by Josephus. That writer supplies, indeed, horrible facts enough and to spare. But those externals which gave Herod the title of "Great," are vividly (and not unnaturally) present to his mind : and, on the whole, in his pages we see, what doubtless his cotemporaries saw, a monarch of illustrious though chequered character, who reigned energetically and magnificently, if despotically and cruelly ; whose public acts and domestic tragedies might, in the hands of an able vindicator, form a parallel (not altogether to his disadvantage) with the life of our own Eighth Henry, and place the Restorer of the Temple on a level with the Defender of the Faith.[1]

Nor have we any right to cut the knot by simply discrediting Josephus. What men saw, he described. But the few words of Holy Writ give us a glimpse of Herod as GOD saw him.

Again, as an instance of what, in uninspired history, must have been treated as a contradiction between the facts of the case and the character ascribed to the agent, we may take that of St. John, the apostle of love, the friend of his LORD's bosom ; and we may contrast the general tenor of his life and writings, as found in Holy Writ, with the name of Boanerges,

[1] See Josephus, Antiqq. Jud. xvi. 5, 1–4 ; compare xv. 9, 1, 2 ; Bell. Jud. i. 21, etc.

" sons of thunder," which CHRIST assigned to him and his brother[2].

Let the inspiration of the record be granted, and these are so many truths independently revealed. We accept them as such : we seek indeed to trace their consistency and connection ; and are thankful, when we are permitted to succeed. At all events, we know Whom we are believing. But in an uninspired document we should not be justified in taking the matter thus : for, in such a case, the writer would be found to have given his verdict against evidence. And it must be remembered that, without inspiration, there is nothing but this evidence to trust to.

Of this latter kind is the apparent discrepancy between the recorded facts of the reign of Josiah, and the indications of his inward temperament and disposition which are given to us. The facts of his reign, if we could come to their study independently, would lead us, according to ordinary principles of criticism, to characterize him as an ardent, sanguine, energetic man. All seems consistent with this view ;

<hr>

[2] St. Mark iii. 17.

his zeal for religion, his labour in the restoration of the Temple and the reformation of the kingdom ; and the warlike spirit which forced a collision with the power of Egypt, and cost him his life at Megiddo. Activity, forwardness and enterprise seem to mark the man, quite as distinctly as the deep religious principle which hallowed his doings.

Such would be the conclusion from the data of a human historian. Why then do we not draw it ? Because here the superhuman element comes in, to represent his real disposition in a very different light. Huldah "the prophetess"[3] is appropriately introduced, to speak of him as tender, sensitive, and (in a word) feminine in character ; and to promise, as his best reward, that he should be taken early away from the evil to come ; even as an early grave amidst the mourning of the people had been the mercy shewn to Abijah, " because in him there was found some good thing toward the Lord God of Israel in the house of Jeroboam."[4]

It is indeed, when received as a revelation,

3 2 Kings xxii. 14 = 2 Chron. xxxiv. 22.

4 1 Kings xiv. 12, 13.

a marvellous picture of GOD's transforming grace, which ordains strength out of the mouth of babes. But it is not what critical acumen could elicit from the evidence. The philosophical historian must either reject it as a contradiction or accept it as a revelation.

And to us, who do accept it with faith and thankfulness, how full of instruction and edification is the history of Josiah!—At eight years of age he was a king : at fifteen, he had already manifested the earnestness of his personal religion : at nineteen, he began the public reformation of his own kingdom and of the land of Israel : and at five and twenty, as soon as this work was accomplished, he gave himself to the restoration of the Temple.[5]

It was during the progress of this work that a discovery was made, which threw the king and people into perplexity and consternation. " Hilkiah the high-priest said unto Shaphan the scribe, I have found the Book of the Law in the House of the LORD."[6]

Now, we know that the Books of the Law

---

[5] 2 Kings xxii. 1, 3 ; more fully, 2 Chron. xxxiv. 1–8, etc.
[6] 2 Kings xxii. 8 = 2 Chron. xxxiv. 15.

were laid up "in the side of the Ark of the Covenant."[7]   We know of them as the professional study of the Priests and Levites, as being to them both "Law" and "Gospel," the Word of life, and the statutes of the realm. We know that when the future appointment of a king was prophesied and provided for, the first duty enjoined him was, that "when he sitteth on the throne of his kingdom, he shall write him a copy of this Law in a book, out of that which is before the Priests the Levites; and it shall be with him, and he shall read therein all the days of his life."[8]   And when the kingdom had been long established, and a time of slackness had intervened, we read that Jehoshaphat "sent Levites ... and Priests ; and they taught in Judah, and had the Book of the Law of the LORD with them, and went about throughout all the cities of Judah, and taught the people."[9]   And again, after the apostasy of Ahaz, "Hezekiah spake comfortably to the Levites that taught the good knowledge of the LORD ;"[10] and the history of his reformation is full of proof that in his

----

7 Deuter. xxxi. 9, 26.   8 Deuter. xvii. 18, 19.
9 2 Chron. xvii. 8, 9.   10 2 Chron. xxx. 22.

time the Law was known. And yet, after two reigns (but then they were the reigns of Manasseh and Amon[11]), the Book of the Law of the LORD, given to Moses, was " found;"—found, as a thing which has been utterly lost; found, as a book which the Priest and the Scribe needed to read when they found it;—" and Shaphan read it before the king; and it came to pass, when the king heard the words of the Book of the Law, that he rent his clothes."[12]

It has indeed been suggested by Grotius and others, that this was merely the sensation produced by the discovery of the original Roll of the Law, which had been put into the side of the Ark eight centuries before. This may have been the fact. And if this had been all, no doubt it would have created a great sensation. Even now, what excitement, if we might find in Asia or Macedonia the original of an Apostolical Epistle, certified " by the hand of me, Paul, which is the token in every

---

[11] Manasseh reigned fifty-five years, Amon two years ; 2 Kings xxi. 1, 19 = 2 Chron. xxxiii. 1, 21.

[12] 2 Kings xxii. 10, 11 = 2 Chron. xxiv. 18, 19. The Jewish tradition (according to Munster) was that the 28th chapter of Deuteronomy was the passage read.

Epistle.—So I write!"[13] But this is not enough
to explain what took place.   Interesting and
stirring as this would have been, if this had
been all, it would have been an excitement of
joy.   But it was the reading of the Book, not
the finding of it, which had so powerful an
effect.   And that effect was panic and dismay,
because of its contents, its threatenings, the
evil denounced in it against all the sins
which the house of Judah had confessedly
committed.

It is as plain as it is strange, that king,
priest, and people, those who strove to serve
God, and those who served Him not, were ignorant of the Book of His Law! It is, indeed,
difficult to realize to ourselves this state of
things.   It is true that we need not insist on
drawing the largest conclusion from the words
that they might bear.   We may fairly believe
that there were copies of portions, at least, of
the Law scattered here and there.   We may
grant that the priests must have been taught
in those parts which related to the Temple-
worship, and to the ordinary laws of social
and political life.   The cotemporary writings

13 See Coloss. iv. 18 ; 2 Thess. iii. 17.

of Jeremiah show that the schools of the Prophets were never without men of GOD, as thoroughly acquainted with the letter of His Law as filled with the Spirit of HIM who gave it. But, after making all possible allowance, this remains, not to be explained away ;—that of the Law, as a protest against all sin and ungodliness,—as a prophecy of the wrath of GOD if they neglected His worship and His Commandments,—as a moral Law given by GOD, setting before them good and evil, and consequently, life and death,—of all *this*, the nation and its rulers were ignorant ; not only ignorant of its awfulness, and of the imminence of the danger which it threatened ;—but ignorant of the very existence of their Bible, as a book containing the revelation of GOD's wrath against sinners.

Truly, not in vain are we taught to pray, that our "ignorances," as well as our "sins" and "negligences," may be forgiven us !

For not only were these things our ensamples, in the general sense in which all Holy Scriptures are written for our learning :—but even in CHRIST's Church, ay, even in our own

country, the broad lines of this strange history have still more strangely been repeated.
For what, practically, is the difference between a Bible lost, and a Bible of which the
use is lost, a Bible, if found, not understood?
And though in the popular cry about the
" Dark Ages," there is much of ignorance
and arrogance combined,—and though in the
Middle Ages of the Church there were always
those who both could and did study the Bible
with a zeal and knowledge which might well
shame our boastings ; yet most true it is, that
all this bore slight fruit to the poor and simple folk.   Small advantage indeed was it to
the ninety and nine, that Bibles and portions
of the Bible were to be found ; so long as
they were few and costly, written out by
long labour of a man's hand ; so long as these
few were out of their reach for use or even
sight ; so long as they were in languages
which but one in the hundred understood.[14]
The people could not procure them for themselves.   They could not have read and understood them, if they had procured them.   Too
often they were without any one who, like the

<hr>

[14] See Isaiah xxix. 11, sq.

Jewish priests in the days of Ezra, deemed it his duty to interpret.[15]

And so it came to pass, that, when the multiplication of printed books stimulated the thirst for all kinds of knowledge, and especially for that by which men are made wise unto salvation, the Law and the Gospel were so brought into light again, that even the poor might read them, and the unlearned hear them read in their mother tongue. And as it was in Judah, so it was in the days of that king who has been so often called the Josiah of England. Deep was the mourning; deep were the searchings of heart; deep the repentance for the time of ignorance and famine of the Word of the LORD. And from that day, great has been, and is, the zeal,— though even yet too little, and perhaps not always according to knowledge,—to speed the holy work, to evangelize our own population, our colonies, and the heathen; to teach the people, and furnish them with the Word of Life; in faithful hope of that promised day, when such imperfect and partial endeavours

[15] Nehem. viii. 1–8.

shall be superseded, and that which is perfect shall come ; when " they shall teach no more every man his neighbour and every man his brother, saying, Know the LORD : for they shall all know me, from the least of them unto the greatest of them, saith the LORD."[16]

And so far it is well! Thus did Josiah begin by purging not only Jerusalem and Judah, but the land of Israel also,—the cities of Manasseh and Ephraim and Simeon, even unto Naphtali[17] : thus did he go on to repair the house of the LORD in Jerusalem.

But amidst such pleasant reflections on our church-extension and missionary work, a question starts up, " If thou makest thy boast of GOD, and knowest His will, and approvest the things that are more excellent, being instructed out of the Law, and art confident that thou thyself art a guide of the blind, a light of them which are in darkness...., Thou therefore which teachest another, teachest thou not thyself ?"[18]

Josiah and his fellow-workers were not in-

16 Jerem. xxxi. 34.　　　　17 2 Chron. xxxiv. 6, 8.
18 Rom. ii. 17–21.

sensible to this part of their duty. They were not content with putting down false religions throughout the sphere of their influence, and restoring God's House and worship in the beauty of holiness. But "the king went up into the house of the Lord, and all the men of Judah...; and he read in their ears all the words of the book of the Covenant which was found in the house of the Lord. And the king stood by a pillar, and made a covenant before the Lord, to walk after the Lord, and to keep His commandments and His testimonies and His statutes with all their heart and all their soul, to perform the words of this Covenant that were written in this book. And all the people stood to the covenant."[19]

This not only touches the nation, or the Church: it touches every one of us in the nation, in the Church. The same thing which has happened to these, happens to individuals also. Even here, brethren, in this spot, which, if any, is the heart of our country's religious

[19] 2 Kings xxiii. 2, 3 = 2 Chron. xxxiv. 30, 31, 32.

life, are there none of you who have lost the Book of Life?—lost it, how much the more wilfully, how much the more guiltily, because in so many senses you have it?

True; you have it, in the shape, perhaps, in which it was given you when you left your homes, as the best gift of those who loved you best.

You have it, in the unbroken series of readings, in which the words of Apostles and Evangelists, Prophets and Psalmists and holy men of old, are poured into your ears day by day in the course of public worship.

You have it continually urged home to your consciences in this place and other like places. Nor can all the imperfections of the preacher take any thing from the blessedness of the message that he brings.

You have it, in the labours of those who are teaching and guiding you, making its study the beginning and the end of all your studies, and correcting the words of man's wisdom by those which the Holy Ghost teaches.

But amongst all these privileges, how many are there who have it *not*, to any use or profit ; and who have so lost it, as to have an account to give for having had it !

Remember, that it was *in the Temple* that the Book was lost of old.   And so, too often, it is even now.   Unhappily, we cannot deny that there are some among us, who will not hear, will not read ; to whom their Bible is a sealed book, their chapel a rarely trodden floor ; or so trodden, as to be profaned with what the wise man calls " the sacrifice of fools."[20]   And so, while the dew of Heaven falls round them, they are dry as Gideon's fleece.   They are indeed in the temple ; but only as those who sold oxen and sheep, and the changers of money, whom CHRIST drove out of it.

And there are those, who give their bodily presence, and do not of set purpose close their ears.   But they do not open them.   Their heart does not go with them.   They listen to GOD's Word as to an idle tale : and while idle tales remain in their memory, GOD's Word slips away.   Thus the parable of the Sower is daily fulfilled before our eyes, and among ourselves.

[20] Eccles. v. 1.

But, to pass from these cases, which may well be called extreme,—there are other persons, who listen a little; and read a little; and reflect a little; and form something of a resolution to do more—at a convenient season. But, oh, that convenient season! Is it for our imitation that the example of Felix is recorded? When we hear his "Go thy way for this time; when I have a convenient season, I will call for thee;" does not the Apostle's "Behold, *now* is the accepted time, behold, *now* is the day of salvation,"[21] ring in our ears the knell of souls that have not only lost the Gospel, but have flung it away, when it has found them?

Nay, not only such as shrink from the WORD of GOD, lose it here, where all are called upon to study it and shew that they are acquainted with it. You may have it in your hands; you may read it; you may impress it on your memory: and yet in all this, you may be losing it. This is no mere possibility. It is a sad fact of every day. And why? Because you are reading it for your examinations! GOD forbid, indeed, that such a cause should be fairly

<hr>

[21] Acts xxiv. 25; 2 Corinth. vi. 2.

charged with such an effect. But there is a known danger attending all privileges, whether the use of GOD's Word, or the ministry of His Church, or whatever they may be,—the danger of profaning them by familiarity. And those whose study of the Bible has for its be-all and end-all the schools of the University, will lose it in the heart, while they are fixing it in the head. Their heart is hardened, their spiritual sense is dulled. Must we not fear lest " the letter" kill such students of it; because that spirit is quenched within them, which should have been in harmony with the SPIRIT speaking through it ? Nay, more. Call to mind, my dear brethren, the devices, the tricks, even the jests which are sometimes used among you to imprint the details of Scripture on the memory before an examination :—and then think what a curse that is, " Let the things that should have been for their wealth, be unto them an occasion of falling."[22]

And you, who have to teach, who have to examine : let me beseech you, for the sake of

[22] Psalm lxix. 23 (Prayer Book).

those whose future is so much in your hands, to watch your work, and to frame it so as to take this stumblingblock out of their way ;— so teaching, as the oracles of GOD ; so questioning, as to make them see (and their eyes are keen to see) that crude and heartless knowledge is unprofitable for today as well as for tomorrow.

And watch, not least, for and over those who are really giving themselves to the study of that Holy Book : for after all, even in handling, they may lose it. I shall not, I trust, be deemed an enemy to the intelligent study of the text of the Bible, or to the devotion of all faculties of mind to the examination of every word of it. But still I must tell these students, that this, if this be all, is but the dissection of a corpse, while the Life, the Living Word itself, is too subtle for their scalpel. These are they who may most easily be misled into small criticism by the maxim that the books of the Bible are to be subjected to the same treatment as other books. For their general training as scholars and critics tempts them to dwell on points of language, or contro-

versy, or literary interest ; to give themselves
to the form, or the adjuncts, rather than to
the matter of their studies. And if they ac-
quire, as may too easily happen, the habit of
studying the Bible merely or chiefly with scientific and literary views ; of prying into, dissect-
ing, criticising the Word, because it is man's,
as if it were not also GOD'S ; of judging the
Law which is to judge them ; or of looking on
the words which enshrine the facts and mysteries of Redemption from some cloudland of
their own, neither earth nor heaven ; can we
help fearing for such, that they are losing
the Word of Life ? Nay, the nearer they
approach the Person of the REDEEMER, is not
their danger the greater, lest even while they
reach the finger to His hands, and thrust the
hand into His side, they may yet miss the
blessing of believing that which they have
seen with their eyes, which they have looked
upon, and their hands have handled ?[23]

But if these are real dangers,—real to ourselves and to those for whom we have to la-

[23] St. John xx. 27 ; 1 St. John i. 1.

bour, watch and pray,—how deep is our debt of thankfulness for the mercies of HIM Who is ever with us, even when we have most entirely lost the sense of His presence! HE will not let us alone. HE is not content to wait and suffer us to find HIM if we will. In manners and at times the most various and most unlikely, HE comes to meet us, as HE met the recreant prophet of Pethor. He finds us, and makes us find HIM in His Holy Word, even when we hide ourselves from HIM.

A chance allusion, perhaps a scoff, may prick a callous conscience. The lessons of childhood may return to the mind, with the forms of those who are no more, as preachers from the grave. The ambitious student may feel himself rebuked; or the critical overawed; or the sceptical may see that it is CHRIST, and no mere man, whom he has been seeking to entangle in contradictions.

One man may have attended public worship time after time, without feeling that he has carried away a blessing; and at last, on some one day, a portion read in the service or dwelt on by the preacher will fall on his ear and filter into his heart, and awaken his conscience ;— it may be, suddenly, as the Spirit breatheth where It listeth ; it may, more probably, be only in appearance suddenly, after silent and patient working of the Spirit within, as when the hidden life of a seed bursts forth at length into light and sight.

Another may take up the Bible casually ; and he will be guided to a passage which he has never noticed before ; or he may look at one which he has read and heard often, but unheedingly :—and the vision will *now* become plain to his eyes ; the Saviour Himself will stand forth from the page ; and a whisper will reach his heart, as when on the way to Damascus Saul heard the remonstrance of Him Whom he had persecuted.

Another may be listlessly allowing his thoughts to wander ; and all at once some traceless association will bring to mind a word of Christ's speaking, or of the Holy Ghost's inspiring, which shall not merely flash on the darkness of his soul and vanish again, but shall remain as the shining light to guide his steps through life, and cheer his way down to death.

But who can reckon up all the ways in which GOD justifies His saying by the prophet, "I was found of them that sought me not; I was made manifest unto them that asked not after me"?[24] For these are daily miracles, by which HE brings forth old things and new out of His treasures ;—old, even the things of His eternal Godhead and unchanging love ; and yet new, to stir the hearts, to suit the needs of all who will not refuse to hearken.

And now that we see the bearing of this history on ourselves,—how we, in our day of boasted light, and among all our real privileges, may be brought to feel that we have been hitherto living in real, practical ignorance of the Word of GOD,—let us go back to the narrative, and note the effect of the discovery on those who found the Law, and on the king to whom they read it. He rent his clothes, and sent to enquire of the LORD for himself

[24] Isaiah lxv. 1, as quoted in Rom. x. 20 :—compare the version of the LXX.

and for all his people concerning the words of
this book that was found: for (he said) great is
the wrath of the LORD that is kindled against
us, because our fathers have not hearkened
unto the words of this book.[25]

This was the first fruit of their discovery.
The mirror was held up to their faces: and
they were confounded to see the likeness of
themselves, such as their lives in those times
of ignorance had made them.   Yet these were
GOD's people, the children of the kingdom
and of the promises. And, doubtless, they
could tell of the great things which GOD had
done for them; of the difference which HE
had made between them and all the nations;
of the glorious kingdom which they were to
inherit, when their MESSIAH was revealed.
And most, if not all, of us have something to
say, in the words of our Church's and our
parents' teaching, if not in our own, of the
promises of GOD, the preciousness of CHRIST's
blood-shedding, the gifts and graces of the
SPIRIT in His Covenant, the blessings of the
coming of His Kingdom; in short, of all that

[25] 2 Kings xxii. 13 = 2 Chron. xxxiv. 21.

which has been done, or is to be done for us; as if we had only to sit still and receive all, with unwashen hands and hearts uncircumcised. Surely such knowledge is worse than ignorance, if it be not accompanied by the knowledge of the Word as an inworking, a transforming Law, as the power of a heavenly life upon earth!

Well may they, to whom CHRIST comes thus mercifully, follow the example of Josiah and his people! We, indeed, are not accustomed to shew our joy or sorrow in parables of passionate gesture. Yet we cherish, it may be, feelings as true and deep, as those do, who "wear their heart upon their sleeve." If then, we do not rend our clothes and weep, in testimony of contrition; let us at least seek for the deep and living spirit of repentance for the sin which our ignorance has been. Let us seek for the spirit of prayer, that HE, Who has been so long with us and yet we have not known HIM, may at last, in this the holy season of His Advent, come to us as HE has never come before, making our hearts burn within us while HE opens to us the Scriptures, abiding with us till HE has fed us with the bread of life[26],—and only withdrawing from us, to make Himself known more truly as HE is, ascended to His FATHER and our FATHER, gone to prepare a place for us.

Blessed are they to whom their SAVIOUR comes in this way, *early;* who find His Law and delight in it, who find Himself, and bear His yoke in their youth. They have a blessing which will never fail, whatever be the probation which HE has in store for them;—whether they are reared up in His courts, as the child Samuel was, to minister actively before HIM in Church or State, from youth till they are old and grayheaded; or whether the Word comes to them as it came to Josiah, with a gift not really the less precious because we may be less able to appreciate it;—" Because thine heart was tender, and thou didst humble thyself before GOD, when thou heardest His words against this place, and against the inhabitants thereof, and humbledst thyself before ME, and didst rend thy clothes, and weep before ME; I have

[26] St. Luke xxiv. 29–32.

even heard thee also, saith the LORD. Behold, I will gather thee to thy fathers, and thou shalt be gathered to thy grave in peace."[27]

Early or late, when they rest from their labours, their work is done; their crown is won; they are with their LORD!

Blessed LORD, Who hast caused all Holy Scriptures to be written for our learning; Grant that we may in such wise hear them, read, mark, learn, and inwardly digest them, that by patience, and comfort of Thy Holy Word, we may embrace and ever hold fast the blessed hope of everlasting life, which THOU hast given us in our SAVIOUR JESUS CHRIST. *Amen.*

[27] 2 Chron. xxxiv. 27, 28 = 2 Kings xxii. 19, 20.

Albemarle Street, London.
January, 1860.

MR. MURRAY'S

GENERAL LIST OF WORKS.

ABBOTT'S (Rev. J.) Philip Musgrave; or, Memoirs of a Church of England Missionary in the North American Colonies. Post 8vo. *2s. 6d.*

ABERCROMBIE'S (John, M.D.) Enquiries concerning the Intellectual Powers and the Investigation of Truth. *Fifteenth Edition.* Fcap. 8vo. *6s. 6d.*

———————— Philosophy of the Moral Feelings. *Twelfth Edition.* Fcap. 8vo. *4s.*

———————— Pathological and Practical Researches on the Diseases of the Stomach, &c. *Third Edition.* Fcap. 8vo. *6s.*

ACLAND'S (Rev. Charles) Popular Account of the Manners and Customs of India. Post 8vo. *2s. 6d.*

ADDISON'S WORKS. A New Edition, with a New Life and Notes. By Rev. Whitwell Elwin. 4 Vols. 8vo. *In preparation.*

ADOLPHUS'S (J. L.) Letters from Spain, in 1856 and 1857. Post 8vo. *10s. 6d.*

ÆSCHYLUS. (The Agamemnon and Choephoræ.) Edited, with Notes. By Rev. W. Peile, D.D. *Second Edition.* 2 Vols. 8vo. *9s.* each.

ÆSOP'S FABLES. A New Translation. With Historical Preface. By Rev. Thomas James, M.A. With 100 Woodcuts, by John Tenniel and J. Wolf. *26th Thousand.* Post 8vo. *2s. 6d.*

AGRICULTURAL (The) Journal. Of the Royal Agricultural Society of England. 8vo. *10s. Published half-yearly.*

AMBER-WITCH (The). The most interesting Trial for Witchcraft ever known. Translated from the German by Lady Duff Gordon. Post 8vo. *2s. 6d.*

ARABIAN NIGHTS ENTERTAINMENT. Translated from the Arabic, with Explanatory Notes. By E. W. Lane. *A New Edition.* Edited by E. Stanley Poole. With 600 Woodcuts. 3 Vols. 8vo. *42s.*

ARTHUR'S (Little) History of England. By Lady Callcott. *Nineteenth Edition.* With 20 Woodcuts. Fcap. 8vo. *2s. 6d.*

AUNT IDA'S Walks and Talks; a Story Book for Children. By a Lady. Woodcuts. 16mo. *5s.*

AUSTIN'S (Sarah) Fragments from German Prose Writers. With Biographical Notes. Post 8vo. *10s.*

———————— Translation of Ranke's History of the Popes of Rome. *Third Edition.* 2 Vols. 8vo. *24s.*

B

ADMIRALTY PUBLICATIONS; Issued by direction of the Lords
Commissioners of the Admiralty:—

. A MANUAL OF SCIENTIFIC ENQUIRY, for the Use of Travellers
in General. By Various Hands. Edited by Sir JOHN F. HERSCHEL,
Bart. *Third Edition*, revised by Rev. ROBERT MAIN. Woodcuts.
Post 8vo. 9s.

2. AIRY'S ASTRONOMICAL OBSERVATIONS MADE AT GREENWICH.
1836 to 1847. Royal 4to. 50s. each.

—— ASTRONOMICAL RESULTS. 1848 to 1857. 4to. 8s. each.

3. —— APPENDICES TO THE ASTRONOMICAL OBSERVA-
TIONS.
1836.—I. Bessel's Refraction Tables.
    II. Tables for converting Errors of R.A. and N.P.D. } 8s.
       into Errors of Longitude and Ecliptic P.D.
1837.—I. Logarithms of Sines and Cosines to every Ten } 8s.
       Seconds of Time.
    II. Table for converting Sidereal into Mean Solar Time.
1842.—Catalogue of 1439 Stars. 8s.
1845.—Longitude of Valentia. 8s.
1847.—Twelve Years' Catalogue of Stars. 14s.
1851.—Maskelyne's Ledger of Stars. 6s.
1852.—I. Description of the Transit Circle. 5s.
    II. Regulations of the Royal Observatory. 2s.
1853.—Bessel's Refraction Tables. 3s.
1854.—I. Description of the Zenith Tube. 3s.
    II. Six Years' Catalogue of Stars. 10s.
1856.—Description of the Galvanic Apparatus at Greenwich Ob-
servatory. 8s.

4. —— MAGNETICAL AND METEOROLOGICAL OBSERVA-
TIONS. 1840 to 1847. Royal 4to. 50s. each.

—— MAGNETICAL AND METEOROLOGICAL RESULTS.
1848 to 1857. 4to. 8s. each.

5. —— ASTRONOMICAL, MAGNETICAL, AND METEOROLO-
GICAL OBSERVATIONS, 1848 to 1857. Royal 4to. 50s. each.

6. —— REDUCTION OF THE OBSERVATIONS OF PLANETS,
1750 to 1830. Royal 4to. 50s.

7. ———————————————————— LUNAR OBSERVATIONS. 1750
to 1830. 2 Vols. Royal 4to. 50s. each.

8. BERNOULLI'S SEXCENTENARY TABLE. *London*, 1779. 4to.

9. BESSEL'S AUXILIARY TABLES FOR HIS METHOD OF CLEAR-
ING LUNAR DISTANCES. 8vo.

10. ——FUNDAMENTA ASTRONOMIÆ: *Regiomontii*, 1818. Folio. 60s.

11. BIRD'S METHOD OF CONSTRUCTING MURAL QUADRANTS.
London, 1768. 4to. 2s. 6d.

12. —— METHOD OF DIVIDING ASTRONOMICAL INSTRU-
MENTS. *London*, 1767. 4to. 2s. 6d.

13. COOK, KING, AND BAYLY'S ASTRONOMICAL OBSERVATIONS.
London, 1782. 4to. 21s.

14. EIFFE'S ACCOUNT OF IMPROVEMENTS IN CHRONOMETERS.
4to. 2s.

15. ENCKE'S BERLINER JAHRBUCH, for 1830. *Berlin*, 1828. 8vo. 9s.

16. GROOMBRIDGE'S CATALOGUE OF CIRCUMPOLAR STARS.
4to. 10s.

17. HANSEN'S TABLES DE LA LUNE. 4to. 20s.

17. HARRISON'S PRINCIPLES OF HIS TIME-KEEPER. PLATES.
1767. 4to. 5s.

18. HUTTON'S TABLES OF THE PRODUCTS AND POWERS OF
NUMBERS. 1781. Folio. 7s. 6d.

19. LAX'S TABLES FOR FINDING THE LATITUDE AND LONGI-
TUDE. 1821. 8vo. 10s.

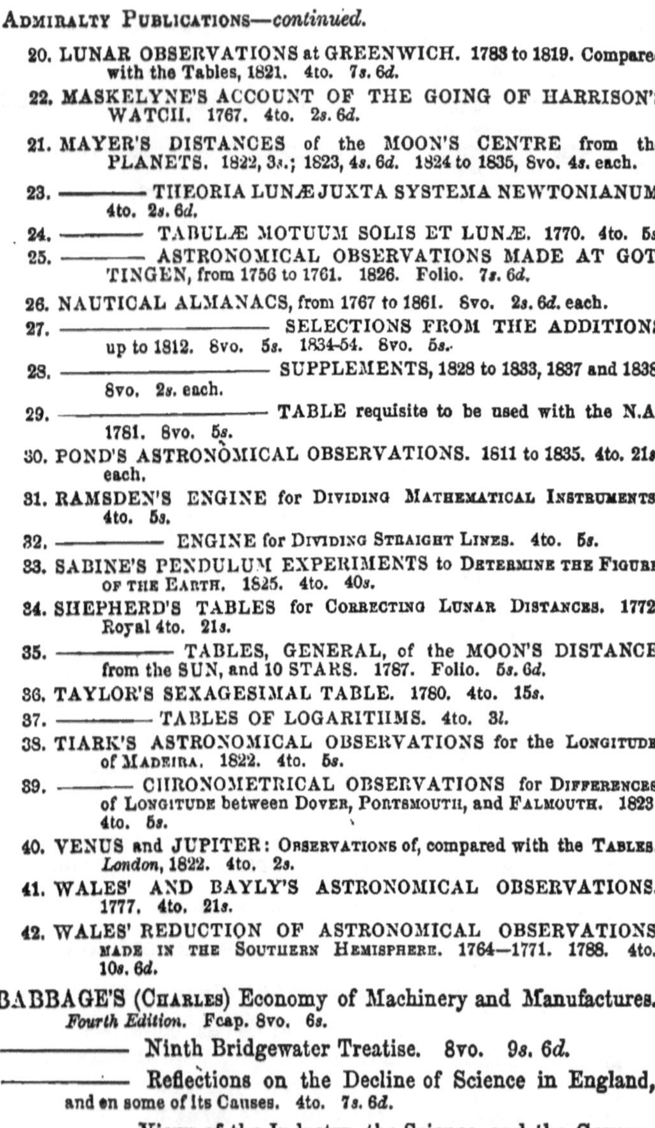

Admiralty Publications—*continued.*

20. LUNAR OBSERVATIONS at GREENWICH. 1783 to 1819. Compared with the Tables, 1821. 4to. 7s. 6d.

22. MASKELYNE'S ACCOUNT OF THE GOING OF HARRISON'S WATCH. 1767. 4to. 2s. 6d.

21. MAYER'S DISTANCES of the MOON'S CENTRE from the PLANETS. 1822, 3s.; 1823, 4s. 6d. 1824 to 1835, 8vo. 4s. each.

23. ———— THEORIA LUNÆ JUXTA SYSTEMA NEWTONIANUM 4to. 2s. 6d.

24. ———— TABULÆ MOTUUM SOLIS ET LUNÆ. 1770. 4to. 5s.

25. ———— ASTRONOMICAL OBSERVATIONS MADE AT GOT-TINGEN, from 1756 to 1761. 1826. Folio. 7s. 6d.

26. NAUTICAL ALMANACS, from 1767 to 1861. 8vo. 2s. 6d. each.

27. ————————— SELECTIONS FROM THE ADDITIONS up to 1812. 8vo. 5s. 1834-54. 8vo. 5s.

28. ————————— SUPPLEMENTS, 1828 to 1833, 1837 and 1838. 8vo. 2s. each.

29. ————————— TABLE requisite to be used with the N.A. 1781. 8vo. 5s.

30. POND'S ASTRONOMICAL OBSERVATIONS. 1811 to 1835. 4to. 21s. each.

31. RAMSDEN'S ENGINE for DIVIDING MATHEMATICAL INSTRUMENTS. 4to. 5s.

32. ———— ENGINE for DIVIDING STRAIGHT LINES. 4to. 5s.

33. SABINE'S PENDULUM EXPERIMENTS to DETERMINE THE FIGURE OF THE EARTH. 1825. 4to. 40s.

34. SHEPHERD'S TABLES for CORRECTING LUNAR DISTANCES. 1772. Royal 4to. 21s.

35. ———— TABLES, GENERAL, of the MOON'S DISTANCE from the SUN, and 10 STARS. 1787. Folio. 5s. 6d.

36. TAYLOR'S SEXAGESIMAL TABLE. 1780. 4to. 15s.

37. ———— TABLES OF LOGARITHMS. 4to. 3l.

38. TIARK'S ASTRONOMICAL OBSERVATIONS for the LONGITUDE of MADEIRA. 1822. 4to. 5s.

39. ———— CHRONOMETRICAL OBSERVATIONS for DIFFERENCES of LONGITUDE between DOVER, PORTSMOUTH, and FALMOUTH. 1823. 4to. 5s.

40. VENUS and JUPITER: OBSERVATIONS of, compared with the TABLES. *London*, 1822. 4to. 2s.

41. WALES' AND BAYLY'S ASTRONOMICAL OBSERVATIONS. 1777. 4to. 21s.

42. WALES' REDUCTION OF ASTRONOMICAL OBSERVATIONS MADE IN THE SOUTHERN HEMISPHERE. 1764—1771. 1788. 4to. 10s. 6d.

BABBAGE'S (CHARLES) Economy of Machinery and Manufactures. *Fourth Edition.* Fcap. 8vo. 6s.

———— Ninth Bridgewater Treatise. 8vo. 9s. 6d.

———— Reflections on the Decline of Science in England, and on some of its Causes. 4to. 7s. 6d.

———— Views of the Industry, the Science, and the Government of England, 1851. *Second Edition.* 8vo. 7s. 6d.

BAIKIE'S (W. B.) Narrative of an Exploring Voyage up the Rivers Quorra and Tshadda in 1854. Map. 8vo. 16s.

BANKES' (George) Story of Corfe Castle, with documents relating to the Time of the Civil Wars, &c. Woodcuts. Post 8vo. 10s. 6d.

BASSOMPIERRE'S Memoirs of his Embassy to the Court of England in 1626. Translated with Notes. 8vo. 9s. 6d.

BARROW'S (Sir John) Autobiographical Memoir, including Reflections, Observations, and Reminiscences at Home and Abroad. From Early Life to Advanced Age. Portrait. 8vo. 16s.

—————— **Voyages of Discovery and Research within the** Arctic Regions, from 1818 to the present time. Abridged and arranged from the Official Narratives. 8vo. 15s.

—————— **(Sir George) Ceylon; Past and Present. Map.** Post 8vo. 6s. 6d.

—————— **(John) Naval Worthies of Queen Elizabeth's Reign,** their Gallant Deeds, Daring Adventures, and Services in the infant state of the British Navy. 8vo. 14s.

—————— **Life and Voyages of Sir Francis Drake. With nume-** rous Original Letters. Post 8vo. 2s. 6d.

BEES AND FLOWERS. Two Essays. By Rev. Thomas James. Reprinted from the "Quarterly Review." Fcap. 8vo. 1s. each.

BELL'S (Sir Charles) Mechanism and Vital Endowments of the Hand as evincing Design. *Sixth Edition.* Woodcuts. Post 8vo. 7s. 6d.

BENEDICT'S (Jules) Sketch of the Life and Works of Felix Mendelssohn Bartholdy. *Second Edition.* 8vo. 2s. 6d.

BERTHA'S Journal during a Visit to her Uncle in England. Containing a Variety of Interesting and Instructive Information. *Seventh Edition.* Woodcuts. 12mo. 7s. 6d.

BIRCH'S (Samuel) History of Ancient Pottery and Porcelain : Egyptian, Assyrian, Greek, Roman, and Etruscan. With 200 Illustra- 2 Vols. Medium 8vo. 42s.

BLUNT'S (Rev. J. J.) Principles for the proper understanding of the Mosaic Writings, stated and applied, together with an Incidental Argument for the truth of the Resurrection of our Lord. Being the tions. Hulsean Lectures for 1832. Post 8vo. 6s. 6d.

—————— **Undesigned Coincidences in the Writings of the Old** and New Testament, an Argument of their Veracity : with an Appendix containing Undesigned Coincidences between the Gospels, Acts, and Josephus. *Sixth Edition.* Post 8vo. 7s. 6d.

—————— **History of the Church in the First Three Centuries.** *Second Edition.* 8vo. 9s. 6d.

—————— **Parish Priest; His Duties, Acquirements and Obliga-** tions. *Third Edition.* Post 8vo. 7s. 6d.

—————— **Lectures on the Right Use of the Early Fathers.** *Second Edition.* 8vo. 15s.

—————— **Plain Sermons Preached to a Country Congregation.** *Second Edition.* 2 Vols. Post 8vo. 7s. 6d. each.

BLACKSTONE'S COMMENTARIES on the Laws of England. A New Edition, adapted to the present state of the law. By R. MALCOLM KERR, LL.D. 4 Vols. 8vo. 42s.

———————————————— FOR STUDENTS. Being those Portions of the above work which relate to the BRITISH CONSTITUTION and the RIGHTS OF PERSONS. By R. MALCOLM KERR, LLD. *Second Thousand.* Post 8vo. 9s.

BLAINE (ROBERTON) on the Laws of Artistic Copyright and their Defects, for Artists, Engravers, Printsellers, &c. 8vo. 3s. 6d.

BOOK OF COMMON PRAYER. With 1000 Illustrations of Borders, Initials, and Woodcut Vignettes. *A New Edition.* Medium 8vo. 21s. *cloth,* 31s. 6d. *calf,* or 42s. *morocco.*

BOSWELL'S (JAMES) Life of Dr. Johnson. Including the Tour to the Hebrides. Edited by Mr. CROKER. *Third Edition.* Portraits. Royal 8vo. 10s. sewed, 12s. cloth.

BORROW'S (GEORGE) Lavengro; The Scholar—The Gipsy—and the Priest. Portrait. 3 Vols. Post 8vo. 30s.

———————— Romany Rye; a Sequel to Lavengro. *Second Edition.* 2 Vols. Post 8vo. 21s.

———————— Bible in Spain; or the Journeys, Adventures, and Imprisonments of an Englishman in an Attempt to circulate the Scriptures in the Peninsula. 3 Vols. Post 8vo. 27s., or *Popular Edition.* 16mo, 6s.

———————— Zincali, or the Gipsies of Spain; their Manners, Customs, Religion, and Language. 2 Vols. Post 8vo. 18s., or *Popular Edition.* 16mo, 6s.

BRAY'S (MRS.) Life of Thomas Stothard, R.A. With Personal Reminiscences. Illustrated with Portrait and 60 Woodcuts of his chief works. 4to.

BREWSTER'S (SIR DAVID) Martyrs of Science, or the Lives of Galileo, Tycho Brahe, and Kepler. *Fourth Edition.* Fcap. 8vo. 4s. 6d.

———————— More Worlds than One. The Creed of the Philosopher and the Hope of the Christian. *Eighth Edition.* Post 8vo. 6s.

———————— Stereoscope: its History, Theory, Construction, and Application to the Arts and to Education. Woodcuts. 12mo. 5s. 6d.

———————— Kaleidoscope: its History, Theory, and Construction, with its application to the Fine and Useful Arts. *Second Edition.* Woodcuts. Post 8vo. 5s. 6d.

BRITISH ASSOCIATION REPORTS. 8vo. York and Oxford, 1831-32, 13s. 6d. Cambridge, 1833, 12s. Edinburgh, 1834, 15s. Dublin, 1835, 13s. 6d. Bristol, 1836, 12s. Liverpool, 1837, 16s. 6d. Newcastle, 1838, 15s. Birmingham, 1839, 13s. 6d. Glasgow, 1840, 15s. Plymouth, 1841, 13s. 6d. Manchester, 1842, 10s. 6d. Cork, 1843, 12s. York, 1844. 20s. Cambridge, 1845, 12s. Southampton, 1846, 15s. Oxford, 1847, 18s. Swansea, 1848, 9s. Birmingham, 1849, 10s. Edinburgh, 1850, 15s. Ipswich, 1851, 16s. 6d. Belfast, 1852, 15s. Hull, 1853, 10s. 6d. Liverpool, 1854, 18s. Glasgow, 1855, 15s.; Cheltenham, 1856, 18s; Dublin, 1857, 15s; Leeds 1858, 20s.

BRITISH CLASSICS. A New Series of Standard English
Authors, printed from the most correct text, and edited with elucidatory notes. Published occasionally in demy 8vo. Volumes.

Already Published.

GOLDSMITH'S WORKS. Edited by Peter Cunningham, F.S.A.
Vignettes. 4 Vols. 30s.

GIBBON'S DECLINE AND FALL OF THE ROMAN EMPIRE.
Edited by William Smith, LL.D. Portrait and Maps. 8 Vols. 60s.

JOHNSON'S LIVES OF THE ENGLISH POETS. Edited by Peter
Cunningham, F.S.A. 3 Vols. 22s. 6d.

BYRON'S POETICAL WORKS. Edited, with Notes. 6 vols. 45s.

In Preparation.

WORKS OF POPE. Edited, with Notes.

WORKS OF DRYDEN. Edited, with Notes.

HUME'S HISTORY OF ENGLAND. Edited, with Notes.

LIFE, LETTERS, AND JOURNALS OF SWIFT. By John Forster.

WORKS OF SWIFT. Edited by John Forster.

BROUGHTON'S (Lord) Journey through Albania and other
Provinces of Turkey in Europe and Asia, to Constantinople, 1809—10.
Third Edition. Maps and Woodcuts. 2 Vols. 8vo. 30s.

———————— Visits to Italy, from the Year 1816 to 1824.
Second Edition. 2 vols. Post 8vo. 18s.

BUBBLES FROM THE BRUNNEN OF NASSAU. By an Old
Man. *Sixth Edition.* 16mo. 5s.

BUNBURY'S (C. J. F.) Journal of a Residence at the Cape of Good
Hope; with Excursions into the Interior, and Notes on the Natural
History and Native Tribes of the Country. Woodcuts. Post 8vo. 9s.

BUNYAN (John) and Oliver Cromwell. Select Biographies. By
Robert Southey. Post 8vo. 2s. 6d.

BUONAPARTE'S (Napoleon) Confidential Correspondence with his
Brother Joseph, sometime King of Spain. *Second Edition.* 2 vols. 8vo.
26s.

BURGHERSH'S (Lord) Memoir of the Operations of the Allied
Armies under Prince Schwarzenberg and Marshal Blucher during the
latter end of 1813—14. 8vo. 21s.

———————— Early Campaigns of the Duke of Wellington in
Portugal and Spain. 8vo. 8s. 6d.

BURGON'S (Rev. J. W.) Portrait of a Christian Gentleman: a
Memoir of the late Patrick Fraser Tytler, author of "The History of
Scotland." *Second Edition.* Post 8vo. 9s.

BURN'S (Lieut-Col.) French and English Dictionary of Naval
and Military Technical Terms. *Third Edition.* Crown 8vo. 15s.

BURNS' (Robert) Life. By John Gibson Lockhart. Fifth
Edition. Fcap. 8vo. 3s.

BURR'S (G. D.) Instructions in Practical Surveying, Topographical Plan Drawing, and on sketching ground without Instruments.
Third Edition. Woodcuts. Post 8vo. 7s. 6d.

BUXTON'S (Sir Fowell) Memoirs. With Selections from his Correspondence. By his Son. Portrait. *Fifth Edition.* 8vo. 16*s.* The same, Post 8vo. 8*s.* 6*d.*; or, an *Abridged Edition*, Portrait, Fcap. 8vo. 2*s.*

BYRON'S (Lord) Life, Letters, and Journals. By Thomas Moore. Plates. 6 Vols. Fcap. 8vo. 18*s.*

———— Life, Letters, and Journals. By Thomas Moore. With Portraits. Royal 8vo. 9*s.*, or 10*s.* 6*d.* in cloth.

———— Poetical Works. Portrait. 6 Vols. Demy 8vo. 45*s.*

———— Poetical Works. Plates. 10 Vols. Fcap. 8vo. 30*s.*

———— Poetical Works. With Engravings. Royal 8vo. 9*s.*, or 10*s.* 6*d.* in cloth.

———— Poetical Works. Printed in small but beautifully clear type. Portrait. Crown 8vo. 9*s.*

———— Poetical Works. 8 Vols. 24mo. 20*s.*

———— Childe Harold's Pilgrimage. Illustrated, with 80 Wood Engravings. Crown 8vo. 21*s.*

———— Childe Harold. Crown 8vo. 10*s.* 6*d.*

———— Childe Harold. 24mo. 2*s.* 6*d.*

———— Childe Harold. Portrait and Titles. Fcap. 8vo. 1*s.*

———— Childe Harold. Portrait. Post 8vo. 6*d.*

———— Dramas. 2 Vols. 24mo. 5*s.*

———— Tales and Poems. 24mo. 2*s.* 6*d.*

———— Miscellaneous. 2 Vols. 24mo. 5*s.*

———— Don Juan and Beppo. 2 Vols. 24mo. 5*s.*

———— Beauties. Poetry and Prose. Portrait, Fcap. 8vo. 3*s.* 6*d.*

CARNARVON'S (Lord) Portugal, Gallicia, and the Basque Provinces. From Notes made during a Journey to those Countries. *Third Edition.* Post 8vo. 6*s.*

———— Archæology of Berkshire. Fcap. 8vo. 1*s.*

CAMPBELL'S (Lord) Lives of the Lord Chancellors and Keepers of the Great Seal of England. From the Earliest Times to the Death of Lord Eldon in 1838. *Fourth Edition.* 10 Vols. Crown 8vo. 6*s.* each.

———— Life of Lord Chancellor Bacon. Fcap. 8vo. 2*s.* 6*d.*

———— Lives of the Chief Justices of England. From the Norman Conquest to the Death of Lord Tenterden. *Second Edition.* 3 Vols. 8vo. 42*s.*

———— Shakspeare's Legal Acquirements Considered. 8vo. 5*s.* 6*d.*

———— (George) Modern India. A Sketch of the System of Civil Government. With some Account of the Natives and Native Institutions. *Second Edition.* 8vo. 16*s.*

———— India as it may be. An Outline of a proposed Government and Policy. 8vo. 12*s.*

———— (Thos.) Short Lives of the British Poets. With an Essay on English Poetry. Post 8vo. 6*s.*

CALVIN'S (John) Life. With Extracts from his Correspondence
By Thomas H. Dyer. Portrait. 8vo. 15s.

CALLCOTT'S (Lady) Little Arthur's History of England.
Nineteenth Edition. With 20 Woodcuts. Fcap. 8vo. 2s. 6d.

CARMICHAEL'S (A. N.) Greek Verbs. Their Formations,
Irregularities, and Defects. *Second Edition.* Post 8vo. 8s. 6d.

CASTLEREAGH (The) DESPATCHES, from the commencement
of the official career of the late Viscount Castlereagh to the close of his
life. Edited by the Marquis of Londonderry. 12 Vols. 8vo. 14s. each.

CATHCART'S (Sir George) Commentaries on the War in Russia
and Germany, 1812-13. Plans. 8vo. 14s.

———————— Military Operations in Kaffraria, which led to the
Termination of the Kaffir War. *Second Edition.* 8vo. 12s.

CAVALCASELLE (G. B.) Notices of the Early Flemish Painters;
Their Lives and Works. Woodcuts. Post 8vo. 12s.

CHANTREY (Sir Francis). Winged Words on Chantrey's Wood-
cocks. Edited by Jas. P. Muirhead. Etchings. Square 8vo. 10s. 6d.

CHARMED ROE (The); or, The Story of the Little Brother and
Sister. By Otto Speckter. Plates. 16mo. 5s.

COBBOLD'S (Rev. R. H.) Pictures of the Chinese drawn by themselves. With Descriptions. Plates. Crown 8vo. 9s.

CLAUSEWITZ'S (Carl Von) Campaign of 1812, in Russia.
Translated from the German by Lord Ellesmere. Map. 8vo. 10s. 6d.

CLIVE'S (Lord) Life. By Rev. G. R. Gleig, M.A. Post 8vo. 6s.

COLERIDGE (Samuel Taylor). Specimens of his Table-Talk.
Fourth Edition. Portrait. Fcap. 8vo. 6s.

———————— (Henry Nelson) Introductions to the Study of
the Greek Classic Poets. *Third Edition.* Fcap. 8vo. 5s. 6d.

COLONIAL LIBRARY. [See Home and Colonial Library.]

COOKERY (Domestic). Founded on Principles of Economy and
Practical Knowledge, and adapted for Private Families. *New Edition.*
Woodcuts. Fcap. 8vo. 5s.

CORNWALLIS (The) Papers and Correspondence during the
American War,—Administrations in India,—Union with Ireland, and
Peace of Amiens. Edited by Charles Ross. *Second Edition.* 3 Vols.
8vo. 63s.

CRABBE'S (Rev. George) Life, Letters, and Journals. By his Son.
Portrait. Fcap. 8vo. 3s.

———————— Poetical Works. Plates. 8 Vols. Fcap. 8vo. 24s.

———————— Poetical Works. Plates. Royal 8vo. 10s. 6d.

CRAIK'S (G. L.) Pursuit of Knowledge under Difficulties.
New Edition. 2 Vols. Post 8vo. 12s.

CURZON'S (Hon. Robert) Visits to the Monasteries of the Levant.
Fourth Edition. Woodcuts. Post 8vo. 15s.

———————— Armenia and Erzeroum. A Year on the Frontiers of
Russia, Turkey, and Persia. *Third Edition.* Woodcuts. Post 8vo. 7s. 6d.

CUNNINGHAM'S (ALLAN) Life of Sir David Wilkie. With his Journals and Critical Remarks on Works of Art. Portrait. 3 Vols. 8vo. 42s.

———————— Poems and Songs. Now first collected and arranged, with Biographical Notice. 24mo 2s. 6d.

———————— (CAPT. J. D.) History of the Sikhs. From the Origin of the Nation to the Battle of the Sutlej. *Second Edition.* Maps. 8vo. 15s.

———————— (PETER) London—Past and Present. A Handbook to the Antiquities, Curiosities, Churches, Works of Art, Public Buildings, and Places connected with interesting and historical associations. *Second Edition.* Post 8vo. 16s.

———————— Modern London. A complete Guide for Visitors to the Metropolis. Map. 16mo. 5s.

———————— Westminster Abbey. Its Art, Architecture, and Associations. Woodcuts. Fcap. 8vo. 1s.

———————— Works of Oliver Goldsmith. Edited with Notes. Vignettes. 4 vols. 8vo. 30s. (Murray's British Classics.)

———————— Lives of Eminent English Poets. By SAMUEL JOHNSON, LL.D. Edited with Notes. 3 vols. 8vo. 22s. 6d. (Murray's British Classics.)

CROKER'S (J. W.) Progressive Geography for Children. *Fifth Edition.* 18mo. 1s. 6d.

———————— Stories for Children, Selected from the History of England. *Fifteenth Edition.* Woodcuts. 16mo. 2s. 6d.

———————— Boswell's Life of Johnson. Including the Tour to the Hebrides. *Third Edition.* Portraits. Royal 8vo. 10s. sowed, or 12s. cloth.

———————— LORD HERVEY'S Memoirs of the Reign of George the Second, from his Accession to the death of Queen Caroline. Edited with Notes. *Second Edition.* Portrait. 2 Vols. 8vo. 21s.

———————— Essays on the Early Period of the French Revolution. Reprinted from the Quarterly Review. 8vo. 15s.

———————— Historical Essay on the Guillotine. Fcap. 8vo. 1s.

CROMWELL (OLIVER) and John Bunyan. By ROBERT SOUTHEY. Post 8vo. 2s. 6d.

CROWE'S (J. A.) Notices of the Early Flemish Painters; their Lives and Works. Woodcuts. Post 8vo. 12s.

CURETON (REV. W.) Remains of a very Ancient Recension of the Four Gospels in Syriac, hitherto unknown in Europe. Discovered, Edited, and Translated. 4to. 24s.

DARWIN'S (CHARLES) Journal of Researches into the Natural History and Geology of the Countries visited during a Voyage round the World. Post 8vo. 8s. 6d.

———————— Origin of Species by Means of Natural Selection; or, the Preservation of Favoured Races in the Struggle for Life. Post 8vo. 14s.

DAVIS'S (SIR J. F.) China: A General Description of that Empire and its Inhabitants, down to 1857. *New Edition.* Woodcuts. 2 Vols. Post 8vo. 14s.

DAVY'S (SIR HUMPHRY) Consolations in Travel; or, Last Days of a Philosopher. *Fifth Edition.* Woodcuts. Fcap. 8vo. 6s.

———————— Salmonia; or, Days of Fly Fishing. With some Account of the Habits of Fishes belonging to the genus Salmo. *Fourth Edition.* Woodcuts. Fcap. 8vo. 6s.

ELLESMERE'S (LORD) Two Sieges of Vienna by the Turks.
Translated from the German. Post 8vo. 2s. 6d.

———————— **Second Campaign of Radetzky in Piedmont.**
The Defence of Temeswar and the Camp of the Ban. From the German.
Post 8vo. 6s. 6d.

———————— **Campaign of 1812 in Russia, from the German**
of General Carl Von Clausewitz. Map. 8vo. 10s. 6d.

———————— **Pilgrimage, and other Poems. Crown 4to. 24s.**

———————— **Essays on History, Biography, Geography, and**
Engineering. 8vo. 12s.

ELPHINSTONE'S (HON. MOUNTSTUART) History of India—the
Hindoo and Mahomedan Periods. *Fourth Edition.* With an Index.
Map. 8vo. 18s.

ELWIN'S (REV. W.) Lives of Eminent British Poets. From
Chaucer to Wordsworth. 4 Vols. 8vo. *In Preparation.*

ENGLAND (HISTORY OF) from the Peace of Utrecht to the Peace
of Versailles, 1713—83. By LORD MAHON. *Library Edition,* 7 Vols.
8vo, 93s.; or, *Popular Edition,* 7 Vols. Post 8vo. 35s.

———————— **From the First Invasion by the Romans,**
down to the 14th year of Queen Victoria's Reign. By MRS. MARKHAM.
98*th Edition.* Woodcuts. 12mo. 6s.

———————— **As IT IS : Social, Political, and Industrial, in the**
19th Century. By W. JOHNSTON. 2 Vols. Post 8vo. 18s.

———————— **and France under the House of Lancaster. With an**
Introductory View of the Early Reformation. *Second Edition.* 8vo. 15s.

ENGLISHWOMAN IN AMERICA. Post 8vo. 10s. 6d.

———————— **RUSSIA : or, Impressions of Manners**
and Society during a Ten Years' Residence in that Country. *Fifth
Thousand.* Woodcuts. Post 8vo. 10s. 6d.

EOTHEN ; or, Traces of Travel brought Home from the East.
A New Edition. Post 8vo. 7s. 6d.

ERSKINE'S (CAPT., R.N.) Journal of a Cruise among the Islands
of the Western Pacific, including the Fejees, and others inhabited by
the Polynesian Negro Races. Plates. 8vo. 16s.

ESKIMAUX (THE) and English Vocabulary, for the use of Travellers
in the Arctic Regions. 16mo. 3s. 6d.

ESSAYS FROM "THE TIMES." Being a Selection from the
LITERARY PAPERS which have appeared in that Journal. *Seventh
Thousand.* 2 vols. Fcap. 8vo. 8s.

EXETER'S (BISHOP OF) Letters to the late Charles Butler, on the
Theological parts of his Book of the Roman Catholic Church; with
Remarks on certain Works of Dr. Milner and Dr. Lingard, and on some
parts of the Evidence of Dr. Doyle. *Second Edition.* 8vo. 16s.

FAIRY RING (THE), A Collection of TALES and STORIES for Young
Persons. From the German. By J. E. TAYLOR. Illustrated by RICHARD
DOYLE. *Second Edition.* Fcap. 8vo.

FALKNER'S (FRED.) Muck Manual for the Use of Farmers. A
Treatise on the Nature and Value of Manures. *Second Edition,* with a
Glossary of Terms and an Index. Fcap. 8vo. 5s.

FAMILY RECEIPT-BOOK. A Collection of a Thousand Valuable
and Useful Receipts. Fcap. 8vo. 5s. 6d.

FANCOURT'S (Col.) History of Yucatan, from its Discovery
to the Close of the 17th Century. With Map. 8vo. 10s. 6d.

FARRAR'S (Rev. A. S.) Science in Theology. Sermons Preached
before the University of Oxford. 8vo. 9s.

FEATHERSTONHAUGH'S (G. W.) Tour through the Slave States
of North America, from the River Potomac, to Texas and the Frontiers
of Mexico. Plates. 2 Vols. 8vo. 26s.

FELLOWS' (Sir Charles) Travels and Researches in Asia Minor,
more particularly in the Province of Lydia. *New Edition.* Plates. Post
8vo. 9s.

FERGUSSON'S (James) Palaces of Nineveh and Persepolis
Restored: an Essay on Ancient Assyrian and Persian Architecture.
With 45 Woodcuts. 8vo. 16s.

———————— Handbook of Architecture. Being a Concise
and Popular Account of the Different Styles prevailing in all Ages
and Countries in the World. With a Description of the most remarkable Buildings. *Fourth Thousand.* With 850 Illustrations. 8vo. 26s.

FERRIER'S (T. P.) Caravan Journeys in Persia, Affghanistan,
Herat, Turkistan, and Beloochistan, with Descriptions of Meshed, Balk,
and Candahar, and Sketches of the Nomade Tribes of Central Asia.
Second Edition. Map. 8vo. 21s.

———————— History of the Afghans. Map. 8vo. 21s.

FEUERBACH'S Remarkable German Crimes and Trials. Translated from the German by Lady Duff Gordon. 8vo. 12s.

FISHER'S (Rev. George) Elements of Geometry, for the Use of
Schools. *Fifth Edition.* 18mo. 1s. 6d.

———————— First Principles of Algebra, for the Use of Schools.
Fifth Edition. 18mo. 1s. 6d.

FLOWER GARDEN (The). An Essay. By Rev. Thos. James.
Reprinted from the "Quarterly Review." Fcap. 8vo. 1s.

FORD'S (Richard) Handbook for Spain, Andalusia, Ronda, Valencia,
Catalonia, Granada, Gallicia, Arragon, Navarre, &c. *Third Edition.*
2 Vols. Post 8vo. 30s.

———— Gatherings from Spain. Post 8vo. 6s.

FORSTER'S (John) Historical & Biographical Essays. 2 Vols.
Post 8vo. 21s.
I. The Grand Remonstrance, 1641.
II. The Plantagenets and the Tudors.
III. Civil Wars & Oliver Cromwell.
IV. Daniel De Foe.
V. Sir Richard Steele.
VI. Charles Churchill.
VII. Samuel Foote.

FORSYTH'S (William) Hortensius, or the Advocate: an Historical
Essay on the Office and Duties of an Advocate. Post 8vo. 12s.

———————— History of Napoleon at St. Helena. From the
Letters and Journals of Sir Hudson Lowe. Portrait and Maps. 3 Vols.
8vo. 45s.

FORTUNE'S (Robert) Narrative of Two Visits to China, between
the years 1843-52, with full Descriptions of the Culture of the Tea
Plant. *Third Edition.* Woodcuts. 2 Vols. Post 8vo. 18s.

———————— Residence among the Chinese: Inland, on the
Coast, and at Sea, during 1853-56. Woodcuts. 8vo. 16s.

FRANCE (History of). From the Conquest by the Gauls to the
Death of Louis Philippe. By Mrs. Markham. *56th Thousand.* Woodcuts. 12mo. 6s.

FRENCH (The) in Algiers; The Soldier of the Foreign Legion—and the Prisoners of Abd-el-Kadir. Translated by Lady Duff Gordon. Post 8vo. 2s. 6d.

GALTON'S (Francis) Art of Travel; or, Hints on the Shifts and Contrivances available in Wild Countries. *Third Edition, enlarged.* Woodcuts. Post 8vo. 7s. 6d.

GEOGRAPHICAL (The) Journal. Published by the Royal Geographical Society of London. 8vo.

GERMANY (History of). From the Invasion by Marius, to the present time. On the plan of Mrs. Markham. *Fifteenth Thousand.* Woodcuts. 12mo. 6s.

GIBBON'S (Edward) Decline and Fall of the Roman Empire. *A New Edition.* Preceded by his Autobiography. Edited with Notes by Dr. Wm. Smith. Maps. 8 Vols. 8vo. 60s.

———— The Student's Gibbon; Being the History of the Decline and Fall, Abridged, incorporating the Researches of Recent Commentators. By Dr. Wm. Smith. *Sixth Thousand.* Woodcuts. Post 8vo. 7s. 6d.

GIFFARD'S (Edward) Deeds of Naval Daring; or, Anecdotes of the British Navy. 2 Vols. Fcap. 8vo. 5s.

GISBORNE'S (Thomas) Essays on Agriculture. *Third Edition.* Post 8vo.

GLADSTONE'S (W. E.) Prayers arranged from the Liturgy for Family Use. *Second Edition.* 12mo. 2s. 6d.

GOLDSMITH'S (Oliver) Works. A New Edition. Printed from the last editions revised by the Author. Edited by Peter Cunningham. Vignettes. 4 Vols. 8vo. 30s. (Murray's British Classics.)

GLEIG'S (Rev. G. R.) Campaigns of the British Army at Washington and New Orleans. Post 8vo. 2s. 6d.

———— Story of the Battle of Waterloo. Compiled from Public and Authentic Sources. Post 8vo. 5s.

———— Narrative of Sir Robert Sale's Brigade in Afghanistan, with an Account of the Seizure and Defence of Jellalabad. Post 8vo. 2s. 6d.

———— Life of Robert Lord Clive. Post 8vo. 5s.

———— Life and Letters of General Sir Thomas Munro. Post 8vo. 5s.

GORDON'S (Sir Alex. Duff) Sketches of German Life, and Scenes from the War of Liberation. From the German. Post 8vo. 6s.

———— (Lady Duff) Amber-Witch: the most interesting Trial for Witchcraft ever known. From the German. Post 8vo. 2s. 6d.

———— French in Algiers. 1. The Soldier of the Foreign Legion. 2. The Prisoners of Abd-el-Kadir. From the French. Post 8vo. 2s. 6d.

————Remarkable German Crimes and Trials. From the German of Fuerbach. 8vo. 12s.

GRANT'S (Asahel) Nestorians, or the Lost Tribes; containing Evidence of their Identity, their Manners, Customs, and Ceremonies; with Sketches of Travel in Ancient Assyria, Armenia, and Mesopotamia; and Illustrations of Scripture Prophecy. *Third Edition.* Fcap 8vo. 6s.

GRENVILLE (The) PAPERS. Being the Public and Private Correspondence of George Grenville, his Friends and Contemporaries, during a period of 30 years.— Including his DIARY OF POLITICAL EVENTS while First Lord of the Treasury. Edited, with Notes, by W. J. SMITH. 4 Vols. 8vo. 16s. each.

GREEK GRAMMAR FOR SCHOOLS. Abridged from Matthiæ. By the BISHOP OF LONDON. *Ninth Edition,* revised by Rev. J. EDWARDS. 12mo. 3s.

GREY'S (SIR GEORGE) Polynesian Mythology, and Ancient Traditional History of the New Zealand Race. Woodcuts. Post 8vo. 10s. 6d.

GROTE'S (GEORGE) History of Greece. From the Earliest Times to the close of the generation contemporary with the death of Alexander the Great. *Third Edition.* Maps and Index. 12 vols. 8vo. 16s. each.

———— (MRS.) Memoir of the Life of the late Ary Scheffer. Portrait, 8vo. (Nearly Ready.)

GROSVENOR'S (LORD ROBERT) Leaves from my Journal during the Summer of 1851. *Second Edition.* Plates. Post 8vo. 3s. 6d.

GUSTAVUS VASA (History of), King of Sweden. With Extracts from his Correspondence. Portrait. 8vo. 10s. 6d.

HALLAM'S (HENRY) Constitutional History of England, from the Accession of Henry the Seventh to the Death of George the Second. *Seventh Edition.* 3 Vols. 8vo. 30s.

———————— History of Europe during the Middle Ages. *Tenth Edition.* 3 Vols. 8vo. 30s.

———————— Introduction to the Literary History of Europe, during the 16th, 17th, and 18th Centuries. *Fourth Edition.* 3 Vols. 8vo. 36s.

———————— Literary Essays and Characters. Selected from the last work. Fcap. 8vo. 2s.

———————— Historical Works. Containing the History of England,—The Middle Ages of Europe,—and the Literary History of Europe. *Complete Edition.* 10 Vols. Post 8vo. 6s. each.

HAMILTON'S (JAMES) Wanderings in Northern Africa, Benghazi, Cyrene, the Oasis of Siwah, &c. *Second Edition.* Woodcuts. Post 8vo. 12s.

———————— (WALTER) Hindostan, Geographically, Statistically, and Historically. Map. 2 Vols. 4to. 94s. 6d.

HAMPDEN'S (BISHOP) Essay on the Philosophical Evidence of Christianity, or the Credibility obtained to a Scripture Revelation from its Coincidence with the Facts of Nature. 8vo. 9s. 6d.

HARCOURT'S (EDWARD VERNON) Sketch of Madeira; with Map and Plates. Post 8vo. 8s. 6d.

HART'S ARMY LIST. (*Quarterly and Annually.*) 8vo.

HAY'S (J. H. DRUMMOND) Western Barbary, its wild Tribes and savage Animals. Post 8vo. 2s. 6d.

HEBER (BISHOP) Parish Sermons; on the Lessons, the Gospel, or the Epistle, for every Sunday in the Year, and for Week-day Festivals. *Sixth Edition.* 2 Vols. Post 8vo. 16s.

———————— Sermons Preached in England. *Second Edition.* 8vo. 9s. 6d.

———————— Hymns written and adapted for the Weekly Church Service of the Year. *Twelfth Edition.* 16mo. 2s.

———————— Poetical Works. *Fifth Edition.* Portrait. Fcap. 8vo. 7s. 6d.

———————— Journey through the Upper Provinces of India, From Calcutta to Bombay, with a Journey to Madras and the Southern Provinces. 2 Vols. Post 8vo. 12s.

HAND-BOOK OF TRAVEL-TALK; or, Conversations in English, German, French, and Italian. 18mo. 3s. 6d.

———————— NORTH GERMANY—HOLLAND, BELGIUM, and the Rhine to Switzerland. Map. Post 8vo. 10s.

———————— SOUTH GERMANY—Bavaria, Austria, Salzberg, the Austrian and Bavarian Alps, the Tyrol, and the Danube, from Ulm to the Black Sea. Map. Post 8vo. 10s.

———————— PAINTING—the German, Flemish, and Dutch Schools. From the German of KUGLER. *A New Edition.* Edited by DR. WAAGEN. Woodcuts. Post 8vo. (*In the Press.*)

———————— SWITZERLAND—the Alps of Savoy, and Piedmont. Maps. Post 8vo. 9s.

———————— FRANCE—Normandy, Brittany, the French Alps, the Rivers Loire, Seine, Rhone, and Garonne, Dauphiné, Provence, and the Pyrenees. Maps. Post 8vo. 10s.

———————— SPAIN—Andalusia, Ronda, Granada, Valencia, Catalonia, Gallicia, Arragon, and Navarre. Maps. 2 Vols. Post 8vo. 30s.

———————— PORTUGAL, LISBON, &c. Map. Post 8vo. 9s.

———————— PAINTING—SPANISH AND FRENCH SCHOOLS. By SIR EDMUND HEAD, BART. Woodcuts. Post 8vo. 12s.

———————— NORTH ITALY—Florence, Sardinia, Genoa, the Riviera, Venice, Lombardy, and Tuscany. Map. Post 8vo. 2 Vols. 12s.

———————— CENTRAL ITALY—SOUTH TUSCANY and the PAPAL STATES. Map. Post 8vo. 7s.

———————— ROME—AND ITS ENVIRONS. Map. Post 8vo. 9s.

———————— SOUTH ITALY—Naples, Pompeii, Herculaneum, Vesuvius, &c. Map. Post 8vo. 10s.

———————— SICILY. Map. Post 8vo. (*In the Press.*)

———————— PAINTING—the Italian Schools. From the German of KUGLER. Edited by Sir CHARLES EASTLAKE, R.A. Woodcuts. 2 Vols. Post 8vo. 30s.

———————— EARLY ITALIAN PAINTERS AND PROGRESS OF PAINTING IN ITALY. By Mrs. JAMESON. Woodcuts. Post 8vo. 12s.

———————— BIOGRAPHICAL DICTIONARY OF ITALIAN PAINTERS. With a Chart. Post 8vo. 6s. 6d.

———————— GREECE—the Ionian Islands, Albania, Thessaly, and Macedonia. Maps. Post 8vo. 15s.

———————— TURKEY—MALTA, ASIA MINOR, CONSTANTINOPLE, Armenia, Mesopotamia, &c. Maps. Post 8vo.

———————— EGYPT—Thebes, the Nile, Alexandria, Cairo, the Pyramids, Mount Sinai, &c. Map. Post 8vo. 15s.

———————— SYRIA AND PALESTINE; the Peninsula of Sinai, Edom, and the Syrian Desert. Maps. 2 Vols. Post 8vo. 24s.

———————— BOMBAY AND MADRAS. Map. 2 Vols. Post 8vo. 24s.

———————— DENMARK—NORWAY and SWEDEN. Maps. Post 8vo. 15s.

———————— RUSSIA—THE BALTIC AND FINLAND. Maps. Post 8vo. 12s.

HANDBOOK OF LONDON, Past and Present. Alphabetically
arranged. *Second Edition.* Post 8vo. 16*s.*
—————— MODERN LONDON. A Guide to all objects
of interest in the Metropolis. Map. 16mo. 5*s.*
—————— ENVIRONS OF LONDON.. Including a Circle of
30 Miles round St. Paul's. Maps. Post 8vo. (*In preparation.*)
—————— DEVON AND CORNWALL. Maps. Post 8vo.
7*s.* 6*d.*
—————— WILTS, DORSET, AND SOMERSET. Map. Post
8vo. 7*s.* 6*d.*
—————— KENT AND SUSSEX. Map. Post 8vo. 10*s.*
—————— SURREY, HANTS, and the Isle of Wight.
Maps. Post 8vo. 7*s.* 6*d.*
—————— WESTMINSTER ABBEY—its Art, Architecture,
and Associations. Woodcuts. 16mo. 1*s.*
—————— SOUTHERN CATHEDRALS OF ENGLAND.
Woodcuts. Post 8vo. (*Nearly Ready.*)
—————— PARIS. Post 8vo. (*In preparation.*)
—————— FAMILIAR QUOTATIONS. Chiefly from English
Authors. *Third Edition.* Fcap. 8vo. 5*s.*
—————— ARCHITECTURE. Being a Concise and Popular
Account of the Different Styles prevailing in all Ages and Countries.
By James Fergusson. *Fourth Thousand.* With 850 Illustrations.
8vo. 26*s.*
—————— ARTS OF THE MIDDLE AGES AND RE-
naissance. By M. Jules Labarte. With 200 Illustrations. 8vo. 18*s.*

HEAD'S (Sir Francis) Rough Notes of some Rapid Journeys across
the Pampas and over the Andes. Post 8vo. 2*s.* 6*d.*
—————— Descriptive Essays : contributed to the " Quarterly
Review." 2 Vols. Post 8vo. 18*s.*
—————— Bubbles from the Brunnen of Nassau. By an Old Man.
Sixth Edition. 16mo. 5*s.*
—————— Emigrant. *Sixth Edition.* Fcap. 8vo. 2*s.* 6*d.*
—————— Stokers and Pokers; or, the London and North-Western
Railway. Post 8vo. 2*s.* 6*d.*
—————— Defenceless State of Great Britain. Post 8vo. 12*s.*
—————— Faggot of French Sticks; or, Sketches of Paris.
New Edition. 2 Vols. Post 8vo. 12*s.*
—————— Fortnight in Ireland. *Second Edition.* Map. 8vo. 12*s.*
—————— (Sir George) Forest Scenes and Incidents in Canada.
Second Edition. Post 8vo. 10*s.*
—————— Home Tour through the Manufacturing Districts of
England, Scotland, and Ireland, including the Channel Islands, and the
Isle of Man. *Third Edition.* 2 Vols. Post 8vo. 12*s.*
—————— (Sir Edmund) Handbook of Painting—the Spanish
and French Schools. With Illustrations. Post 8vo.
—————— Shall and Will; or, Two Chapters on Future Auxiliary
Verbs. *Second Edition, Enlarged.* Fcap. 8vo. 4*s.*

HEIRESS (The) in Her Minority; or, The Progress of Character.
By the Author of "Bertha's Journal." 2 Vols. 12mo. 18s.

HERODOTUS. A New English Version. Edited with Notes,
and Essays. By Rev. G. Rawlinson, assisted by Sir Henry
Rawlinson, and Sir J. G. Wilkinson. Maps and Woodcuts. 4 Vols.
8vo. 18s. each.

HERVEY'S (Lord) Memoirs of the Reign of George the Second,
from his Accession to the Death of Queen Caroline. Edited, with Notes
by Mr. Croker. Second Edition. Portrait. 2 Vols. 8vo. 21s.

HICKMAN'S (Wm.) Treatise on the Law and Practice of Naval
Courts Martial. 8vo. 10s. 6d.

HILLARD'S (G. S.) Six Months in Italy. 2 Vols. Post 8vo. 16s.

HISTORY OF ENGLAND AND FRANCE under the House
of Lancaster. With an Introductory View of the Early Reformation.
Second Edition. 8vo. 15s.

HOLLAND'S (Rev. W. B.) Psalms and Hymns, selected and
adapted to the various Solemnities of the Church. Third Edition. 24mo.
1s. 3d.

HOLLWAY'S (J. G.) Month in Norway. Fcap. 8vo. 2s.

HONEY BEE (The). An Essay. By Rev. Thomas James.
Reprinted from the "Quarterly Review." Fcap. 8vo. 1s.

HOOK'S (Dean) Church Dictionary. Eighth Edition. 8vo. 16s.

——— Discourses on the Religious Controversies of the Day.
8vo. 9s.

——— (Theodore) Life. By J. G. Lockhart. Reprinted from the
"Quarterly Review." Fcap. 8vo. 1s.

HOOKER'S (Dr. J. D.) Himalayan Journals; or, Notes of an Oriental
Naturalist in Bengal, the Sikkim and Nepal Himalayas, the Khasia
Mountains, &c. Second Edition. Woodcuts. 2 vols. Post 8vo. 18s.

HOOPER'S (Lieut.) Ten Months among the Tents of the Tuski;
with Incidents of an Arctic Boat Expedition in Search of Sir John
Franklin. Plates, 8vo. 14s.

HORACE (Works of). Edited by Dean Milman. With 300
Woodcuts. Crown 8vo. 21s.

——— (Life of). By Dean Milman. Woodcuts, and coloured
Borders. 8vo. 9s.

HOSPITALS AND SISTERHOODS. By a Lady. Fcap. 8vo.
3s. 6d.

HOUSTOUN'S (Mrs.) Yacht Voyage to Texas and the Gulf of
Mexico. Plates. 2 Vols. Post 8vo. 21s.

HOME AND COLONIAL LIBRARY. Complete in 70 Parts.

Post 8vo, 2s. 6d. each, or bound in 34 Volumes, cloth.

CONTENTS OF THE SERIES.

THE BIBLE IN SPAIN. By George Borrow.
JOURNALS IN INDIA. By Bishop Heber.
TRAVELS IN THE HOLY LAND. By Captains Irby and Mangles.
THE SIEGE OF GIBRALTAR. By John Drinkwater.
MOROCCO AND THE MOORS. By J. Drummond Hay.
LETTERS FROM THE BALTIC. By a Lady.
THE AMBER-WITCH. By Lady Duff Gordon.
OLIVER CROMWELL & JOHN BUNYAN. By Robert Southey.
NEW SOUTH WALES. By Mrs. Meredith.
LIFE OF SIR FRANCIS DRAKE. By John Barrow.
FATHER RIPA'S MEMOIRS OF THE COURT OF CHINA.
A RESIDENCE IN THE WEST INDIES. By M. G. Lewis.
SKETCHES OF PERSIA. By Sir John Malcolm.
THE FRENCH IN ALGIERS. By Lady Duff Gordon.
VOYAGE OF A NATURALIST. By Charles Darwin.
HISTORY OF THE FALL OF THE JESUITS.
LIFE OF LOUIS PRINCE OF CONDE. By Lord Mahon.
GIPSIES OF SPAIN. By George Borrow.
THE MARQUESAS. By Hermann Melville.
LIVONIAN TALES. By a Lady.
MISSIONARY LIFE IN CANADA. By Rev. J. Abbott.
SALE'S BRIGADE IN AFFGHANISTAN. By Rev. G. R. Gleig.
LETTERS FROM MADRAS. By a Lady.
HIGHLAND SPORTS. By Charles St. John.
JOURNEYS ACROSS THE PAMPAS. By Sir F. B. Head.
GATHERINGS FROM SPAIN. By Richard Ford.
SIEGES OF VIENNA BY THE TURKS. By Lord Ellesmere.
SKETCHES OF GERMAN LIFE. By Sir A. Gordon.
ADVENTURES IN THE SOUTH SEAS. By Hermann Melville.
STORY OF BATTLE OF WATERLOO. By Rev. G. R. Gleig.
A VOYAGE UP THE RIVER AMAZON. By W. H. Edwards.
THE WAYSIDE CROSS. By Capt. Milman.
MANNERS & CUSTOMS OF INDIA. By Rev. C. Acland.
CAMPAIGNS AT WASHINGTON. By Rev. G. R. Gleig.
ADVENTURES IN MEXICO. By G. F. Ruxton.
PORTUGAL AND GALLICIA. By Lord Carnarvon.
LIFE OF LORD CLIVE. By Rev. G. R. Gleig.
BUSH LIFE IN AUSTRALIA. By H. W. Haygarth.
THE AUTOBIOGRAPHY OF HENRY STEFFENS.
SHORT LIVES OF THE POETS. By Thomas Campbell.
HISTORICAL ESSAYS. By Lord Mahon.
LONDON & NORTH-WESTERN RAILWAY. By Sir F. B. Head.
ADVENTURES IN THE LIBYAN DESERT. By Bayle St. John.
A RESIDENCE AT SIERRA LEONE. By a Lady.
LIFE OF GENERAL MUNRO. By Rev. G. R. Gleig.
MEMOIRS OF SIR FOWELL BUXTON. By his Son.

HUME (The Student's). A History of England, from the Invasion of Julius Cæsar. Based on Hume's History, and continued to 1858. *Tenth Thousand.* Woodcuts. Post 8vo. 7s. 6d.

HUTCHINSON (Colonel) on Dog-Breaking; the most expeditious, certain, and easy Method, whether great Excellence or only Mediocrity be required. *Third Edition.* Woodcuts. Post 8vo. 9s.

HUTTON'S (H. E.) Principia Græca; an Introduction to the Study of Greek. Comprehending Grammar, Delectus, and Exercise-book, with Vocabularies. 12mo. 2s. 6d.

IRBY AND MANGLES' Travels in Egypt, Nubia, Syria, and the Holy Land, including a Journey round the Dead Sea, and through the Country east of the Jordan. Post 8vo. 2s. 6d.

JAMES' (Rev. Thomas) Fables of Æsop. A New Translation, with Historical Preface. With 100 Woodcuts by Tenniel and Wolf. *Twenty-sixth Thousand.* Post 8vo. 2s. 6d.

JAMESON'S (Mrs.) Memoirs of the Early Italian Painters, and of the Progress of Italian Painting in Italy. *New Edition, revised and enlarged.* With very many Woodcuts. Post 8vo. 12s. (*Uniform with Kugler's Handbooks.*)

JAPAN AND THE JAPANESE. Described from the Accounts of Recent Dutch Travellers. *New Edition.* Post 8vo. 6s.

JARDINE'S (David) Narrative of the Gunpowder Plot. *New Edition.* Post 8vo. 7s. 6d.

JERVIS'S (Capt.) Manual of Operations in the Field, for the Use of Officers. Post 8vo. 9s. 6d.

JESSE'S (Edward) Favorite Haunts and Rural Studies; or Visits to Spots of Interest in the Vicinity of Windsor and Eton. Woodcuts. Post 8vo. 12s.

———— Scenes and Occupations of Country Life. With Recollections of Natural History. *Third Edition.* Woodcuts. Fcap. 8vo. 6s.

———— Gleanings in Natural History. With Anecdotes of the Sagacity and Instinct of Animals. *Eighth Edition.* Fcap. 8vo. 6s.

JOHNSON'S (Dr. Samuel) Life: By James Boswell. Including the Tour to the Hebrides. Edited by the late Mr. Croker. *Third Edition.* Portraits. Royal. 8vo. 10s. sewed; 12s. cloth.

———— Lives of the most eminent English Poets. Edited by Peter Cunningham. 3 vols. 8vo. 22s. 6d. (Murray's British Classics.)

JOHNSTON'S (Wm.) England: Social, Political, and Industrial, in 19th Century. 2 Vols. Post 8vo. 18s.

JOURNAL OF A NATURALIST. *Fourth Edition.* Woodcuts. Post 8vo. 9s. 6d.

JOWETT'S (Rev. B.) Commentary on St. Paul's Epistles to the Thessalonians, Galatians, and Romans. *Second Edition.* 2 Vols. 8vo. 30s.

JONES' (Rev. R.) Literary Remains. With a Prefatory Notice. By Rev. W. Whewell, D.D. Portrait. 8vo. 14s.

KEN'S (Bishop) Life. By A Layman. *Second Edition.* Portrait. 2 Vols. 8vo. 18s.

———— (Bishop) Exposition of the Apostles' Creed. Extracted from his "Practice of Divine Love." *New Edition.* Fcap. 1s. 6d.

———— Approach to the Holy Altar. Extracted from his "Manual of Prayer" and "Practice of Divine Love." *New Edition.* Fcap. 8vo 1s. 6d.

c 2

KING'S (Rev. S. W.) Italian Valleys of the Alps; a Tour through all the Romantic and less-frequented "Vals" of Northern Piedmont, from the Tarentaise to the Gries. With Illustrations. Crown 8vo. 18s.

KING EDWARD VIth's Latin Grammar; or, an Introduction to the Latin Tongue, for the Use of Schools. *12th Edition*. 12mo. 3s. 6d.

——————————— First Latin Book; or, the Accidence, Syntax and Prosody, with an English Translation for the Use of Junior Classes. *Third Edition*. 12mo. 2s.

KINGLAKE'S (A. W.) History of the War in the Crimea. Based chiefly upon the Private Papers of Field Marshal Lord Raglan, and other authentic materials. Vols. I. and II. 8vo.

KNAPP'S (J. A.) English Roots and Ramifications; or, the Derivation and Meaning of Divers Words. Fcap. 8vo. 4s.

KUGLER'S (Dr. Franz) Handbook to the History of Painting (the Italian Schools). Translated from the German. Edited, with Notes, by Sir Charles Eastlake. *Third Edition*. Woodcuts. 2 Vols. Post 8vo. 30s.

——————— (the German, Dutch, and Flemish Schools). Translated from the German. *A New Edition*. Edited, with Notes. By Dr. Waagen. Woodcuts. Post 8vo. *Nearly Ready*.

LABARTE'S (M. Jules) Handbook of the Arts of the Middle Ages and Renaissance. With 200 Woodcuts. 8vo. 18s.

LABORDE'S (Leon de) Journey through Arabia Petræa, to Mount Sinai, and the Excavated City of Petræa,—the Edom of the Prophecies. *Second Edition*. With Plates. 8vo. 18s.

LANE'S (E. W.) Arabian Nights. Translated from the Arabic, with Explanatory Notes. *A New Edition*. Edited by E. Stanley Poole. With 600 Woodcuts. 3 Vols. 8vo. 42s.

———————— Manners and Customs of the Modern Egyptians. A *New Edition*, with Additions and Improvements by the Author. Edited by E. Stanley Poole. Woodcuts. 8vo. 18s.

LATIN GRAMMAR (King Edward the VIth's.) For the Use of Schools. *Twelfth Edition*. 12mo. 3s. 6d.

——————— First Book (King Edward VI.); or, the Accidence, Syntax, and Prosody, with English Translation for Junior Classes. *Third Edition*. 12mo. 2s.

LAYARD'S (A. H.) Nineveh and its Remains. Being a Narrative of Researches and Discoveries amidst the Ruins of Assyria. With an Account of the Chaldean Christians of Kurdistan; the Yezedis, or Devil-worshippers; and an Enquiry into the Manners and Arts of the Ancient Assyrians. *Sixth Edition*. Plates and Woodcuts. 2 Vols. 8vo. 36s.

——————————— Nineveh and Babylon; being the Result of a Second Expedition to Assyria. *Fourteenth Thousand*. Plates. 8vo. 21s. Or Fine Paper, 2 Vols. 8vo. 30s.

——————— Popular Account of Nineveh. *15th Edition*. With Woodcuts. Post 8vo. 5s.

LESLIE'S (C. R.) Handbook for Young Painters. With Illustrations. Post 8vo. 10s. 6d.

——————— Life of Sir Joshua Reynolds. With an Account of his Works, and a Sketch of his Cotemporaries. Fcap. 4to. *In the Press*.

LEAKE'S (Col. W. Martin) Topography of Athens, with Remarks on its Antiquities; to which is added, the Demi of Attica. *Second Edition.* Plates. 2 Vols. 8vo. 50s.

—— Travels in Northern Greece. Maps. 4 Vols. 8vo. 60s.

—— Disputed Questions of Ancient Geography. Map. 8vo. 6s. 6d.

—— Numismata Hellenica. A Catalogue of Greek Coins. With Map and Appendix. 4to. 63s.

—— A Supplement to Numismata Hellenica; Completing a descriptive Catalogue of Twelve Thousand Greek Coins, with Notes Geographical and Historical. 4to.

—— Peloponnesiaca: A Supplement to Travels in the Morea. 8vo. 15s.

—— Thoughts on the Degradation of Science in England. 8vo. 3s. 6d.

LETTERS FROM THE SHORES OF THE BALTIC. By a Lady. Post 8vo. 2s. 6d.

—— Madras; or, First Impressions of Life and Manners in India. By a Lady. Post 8vo. 2s. 6d.

—— Sierra Leone, written to Friends at Home. By a Lady. Edited by Mrs. Norton. Post 8vo. 6s.

—— Head Quarters; or, The Realities of the War in the Crimea. By a Staff Officer. *Popular Edition.* Plans. Post 8vo. 6s.

LEXINGTON (The) PAPERS; or, Some Account of the Courts of London and Vienna at the end of the 17th Century. Edited by Hon. H. Manners Sutton. 8vo. 14s.

LEWIS' (Sir G. C.) Essay on the Government of Dependencies. 8vo. 12s.

—— Glossary of Provincial Words used in Herefordshire and some of the adjoining Counties. 12mo. 4s. 6d.

—— (Lady Theresa) Friends and Contemporaries of the Lord Chancellor Clarendon, illustrative of Portraits in his Gallery. With a Descriptive Account of the Pictures, and Origin of the Collection. Portraits. 3 Vols. 8vo. 42s.

—— (M. G.) Journal of a Residence among the Negroes in the West Indies. Post 8vo. 2s. 6d.

LIDDELL'S (Dean) History of Rome. From the Earliest Times to the Establishment of the Empire. With the History of Literature and Art. *Library Edition.* 2 Vols. 8vo. 28s.

—— STUDENT'S HISTORY OF ROME. Abridged from the Larger Work. *Fifteenth Thousand.* With 100 Woodcuts. Post 8vo. 7s. 6d.

LINDSAY'S (Lord) Lives of the Lindsays; or, a Memoir of the Houses of Crawford and Balcarres. With Extracts from Official Papers and Personal Narratives. *Second Edition.* 3 Vols. 8vo. 24s.

—— Report of the Claim of James, Earl of Crawford and Balcarres, to the Original Dukedom of Montrose, created in 1488. Folio. 15s.

LITTLE ARTHUR'S HISTORY OF ENGLAND. By Lady Callcott. *Nineteenth Edition.* With 20 Woodcuts. Fcap. 8vo. 2s. 6d.

LIVINGSTONE'S (Rev. Dr.) Missionary Travels and Researches in South Africa; including a Sketch of Sixteen Years' Residence in the Interior of Africa, and a Journey from the Cape of Good Hope to Loanda on the West Coast; thence across the Continent, down the River Zambesi, to the Eastern Ocean. *Thirtieth Thousand.* Map, Plates, and Index. 8vo. 21*s.*

LIVONIAN TALES.—The Disponent.—The Wolves.—The Jewess. By the Author of "Letters from the Baltic." Post 8vo. 2*s.* 6*d.*

LOCKHART'S (J. G.) Ancient Spanish Ballads. Historical and Romantic. Translated, with Notes. *Illustrated Edition.* 4to. 21*s.* Or, *Popular Edition.* Post 8vo. 2*s.* 6*d.*

———————— **Life of Robert Burns.** *Fifth Edition.* Fcap. 8vo. 3*s.*

LOUDON'S (Mrs.) Instructions in Gardening for Ladies. With Directions and Calendar of Operations for Every Month. *Eighth Edition.* Woodcuts. Fcap. 8vo. 5*s.*

———————— **Modern Botany; a Popular Introduction to the** Natural System of Plants. *Second Edition.* Woodcuts. Fcap. 8vo. 6*s.*

LOWE'S (Sir Hudson) Letters and Journals, during the Captivity of Napoleon at St. Helena. By William Forsyth. Portrait. 3 Vols. 8vo. 45*s.*

LUCKNOW: A Lady's Diary of the Siege. Written for Friends at Home. *Fourth Thousand.* Fcap. 8vo. 4*s.* 6*d.*

LYELL'S (Sir Charles) Principles of Geology; or, the Modern Changes of the Earth and its Inhabitants considered as illustrative of Geology. *Ninth Edition.* Woodcuts. 8vo. 18*s.*

———————— **Visits to the United States, 1841-46.** *Second Edition.* Plates. 4 Vols. Post 8vo. 24*s.*

MAHON'S (Lord) History of England, from the Peace of Utrecht to the Peace of Versailles, 1713–83. *Library Edition.* 7 Vols. 8vo. 93*s.* *Popular Edition.* 7 Vols. Post 8vo. 35*s.*

———————— **"Forty-Five;" a Narrative of the Rebellion in Scot**land. Post 8vo. 3*s.*

———————— **History of British India from its Origin till the Peace** of 1783. Post 8vo. 3*s.* 6*d.*

———————— **History of the War of the Succession in Spain.** *Second Edition.* Map. 8vo. 15*s.*

———————— **Spain under Charles the Second; or, Extracts from the** Correspondence of the Hon. Alexander Stanhope, British Minister at Madrid from 1690 to 1700. *Second Edition.* Post 8vo. 6*s.* 6*d.*

———————— **Life of Louis Prince of Condé, surnamed the Great.** Post 8vo. 6*s.*

———————— **Life of Belisarius.** *Second Edition.* Post 8vo. 10*s.* 6*d.*

———————— **Historical and Critical Essays.** Post 8vo. 6*s.*

———————— **Story of Joan of Arc.** Fcap. 8vo. 1*s.*

———————— **Addresses Delivered at Manchester, Leeds, and Bir**mingham. Fcap. 8vo. 1*s.*

McCLINTOCK'S (Capt.) Narrative of the Discovery of the Fate of Sir John Franklin and his Companions, in the Arctic Seas. With Preface, by Sir Roderick Murchison. Map and Illustrations. 8vo. 16*s.*

McCOSH (Rev. Dr.) On the intuitive Convictions of the Mind. 8vo.

M^cCULLOCH'S (J. R.) Collected Edition of RICARDO's Political Works. With Notes and Memoir. *Second Edition.* 8vo. 16*s.*

MALCOLM'S (SIR JOHN) Sketches of Persia. *Third Edition.* Post 8vo. 6*s.*

MANSEL'S (REV. H. L.) Bampton Lectures. The Limits of Religious Thought Examined. *Fourth and cheaper Edition.* Post 8vo. 7*s.* 6*d.*

———— Examination of Professor Maurice's Strictures on the Bampton Lectures of 1858. *Second Edition* 8vo. 2*s.* 6*d.*

MANTELL'S (GIDEON A.) Thoughts on Animalcules; or, the Invisible World, as revealed by the Microscope. *Second Edition.* Plates. 16mo. 6*s.*

MANUAL OF SCIENTIFIC ENQUIRY, Prepared for the Use of Officers and Travellers. By various Writers. *Third Edition revised* by the Rev. R. MAIN. Maps. Post 8vo. 9*s.* (*Published by order of the Lords of the Admiralty.*)

MARKHAM'S (MRS.) History of England. From the First Invasion by the Romans, down to the fourteenth year of Queen Victoria's Reign. 118*th Edition.* Woodcuts. 12mo. 6*s.*

———— History of France. From the Conquest by the Gauls, to the Death of Louis Philippe. *Sixtieth Edition.* Woodcuts. 12mo. 6*s.*

———— History of Germany. From the Invasion by Marius, to the present time. *Fifteenth Edition.* Woodcuts. 12mo. 6*s.*.

———— History of Greece. From the Earliest Times to the Roman Conquest. With the History of Literature and Art. By Dr. WM. SMITH. *Twentieth Thousand.* Woodcuts. 12mo. 7*s.* 6*d.* (*Questions.* 12mo. 2*s.*)

———— History of Rome, from the Earliest Times to the Establishment of the Empire. With the History of Literature and Art. By DEAN LIDDELL. *Fifteenth Thousand.* Woodcuts. 12mo. 7*s.* 6*d.*

MARKLAND'S (J. H.) Reverence due to Holy Places. *Third Edition.* Fcap. 8vo. 2*s.*

MARRYAT'S (JOSEPH) History of Modern and Mediæval Pottery and Porcelain. With a Description of the Manufacture, a Glossary, and a List of Monograms. *Second Edition.* Plates and Woodcuts. 8vo. 31*s.* 6*d.*

MATTHIÆ'S (AUGUSTUS) Greek Grammar for Schools. Abridged from the Larger Grammar. By Blomfield. *Ninth Edition.* Revised by EDWARDS. 12mo. 3*s.*

MAUREL'S (JULES) Essay on the Character, Actions, and Writings of the Duke of Wellington. *Second Edition.* Fcap. 8vo. 1*s.* 6*d.*

MAWE'S (H. L.) Journal of a Passage from the Pacific to the Atlantic, crossing the Andes in the Northern Provinces of Peru, and descending the great River Maranon. 8vo. 12*s.*

MAXIMS AND HINTS for an Angler, and the Miseries of Fishing. By RICHARD PENN. *New Edition.* Woodcuts. 12mo. 1*s.*

MAYO'S (DR.) Pathology of the Human Mind. Fcap. 8vo. 5*s.* 6*d.*

MELVILLE'S (HERMANN) Typee and Omoo; or, Adventures amongst the Marquesas and South Sea Islands. 2 Vols. Post 8vo.

MENDELSSOHN'S (FELIX BARTHOLDY) Life. By JULES BENEDICT. 8vo. 2*s.* 6*d.*

MEREDITH'S (Mrs. Charles) Notes and Sketches of New South
Wales, during a Residence from 1839 to 1844. Post 8vo. 2s. 6d.

———— —— Tasmania, during a Residence of Nine Years.
With Illustrations. 2 Vols. Post 8vo. 18s.

MERRIFIELD (Mrs.) on the Arts of Painting in Oil, Miniature,
Mosaic, and Glass; Gilding, Dyeing, and the Preparation of Colours
and Artificial Gems, described in several old Manuscripts. 2 Vols. 8vo.
30s.

MILLS (Arthur) India in 1858: A Summary of the Existing
Administration—Political, Fiscal, and Judicial; with Laws and Public
Documents, from the earliest to the present time. Second Edition. With
Coloured Revenue Map. 8vo. 10s. 6d.

MITCHELL'S. (Thomas) Plays of Aristophanes. With English
Notes. 8vo.—1. CLOUDS, 10s.—2. WASPS, 10s.—3. FROGS, 15s.

MILMAN'S (Dean) History of Christianity, from the Birth of
Christ to the Extinction of Paganism in the Roman Empire. 3 Vols.
8vo. 36s.

———— —— History of Latin Christianity; including that of the
Popes to the Pontificate of Nicholas V. Second Edition. 6 Vols. 8vo. 72s.

———— —— Character and Conduct of the Apostles considered as
an Evidence of Christianity. 8vo. 10s. 6d.

———— —— Life and Works of Horace. With 300 Woodcuts.
New Edition. 2 Vols. Crown 8vo. 30s.

———— —— Poetical Works. Plates. 3 Vols. Fcap. 8vo. 18s.

———— —— Fall of Jerusalem. Fcap. 8vo. 1s.

———— —— (Capt. E. A.) Wayside Cross; or, the Raid of Gomez.
A Tale of the Carlist War. Post 8vo. 2s. 6d.

MODERN DOMESTIC COOKERY. Founded on Principles of
Economy and Practical Knowledge, and adapted for Private Families.
New Edition. Woodcuts. Fcap. 8vo. 5s.

MOLTKE'S (Baron) Russian Campaigns on the Danube and the
Passage of the Balkan, 1828—9. Plans. 8vo. 14s.

MONASTERY AND THE MOUNTAIN CHURCH. By Author
of "Sunlight through the Mist." Woodcuts. 16mo. 4s.

MOORE'S (Thomas) Life and Letters of Lord Byron. 6 Vols.
Fcap. 8vo. 18s.

———— —— Life and Letters of Lord Byron. With Portraits.
Royal 8vo. 9s. sewed, or 10s. 6d. in cloth.

MOZLEY'S (Rev. J. B.) Treatise on the Augustinian Doctrine of
Predestination. 8vo. 14s.

———— —— Primitive Doctrine of Baptismal Regeneration. 8vo. 7s. 6d.

MUCK MANUAL (The) for the Use of Farmers. A Practical Treatise
on the Chemical Properties, Management, and Application of Manures.
By Frederick Falkner. Second Edition. Fcap. 8vo. 5s.

MUNDY'S (Gen.) Pen and Pencil Sketches during a Tour
in India. Third Edition. Plates. Post 8vo. 7s. 6d.

MUNRO'S (General Sir Thomas) Life and Letters. By the Rev.
G. R. Gleig. Post 8vo. 6s.

MURCHISON'S (Sir Roderick) Russia in Europe and the Ural Mountains; Geologically Illustrated. With Coloured Maps, Plates, Sections, &c. 2 Vols. Royal 4to.

———————— Siluria ; or, a History of the Oldest Rocks containing Organic Remains. *Third Edition.* Map and Plates. 8vo. 42s.

MURRAY'S (Capt. A.) Naval Life and Services of Admiral Sir Philip Durham. 8vo. 5s. 6d.

MURRAY'S RAILWAY READING. For all classes of Readers.

[The following are published :]

Wellington. By Lord Ellesmere'. 6d.
Nimrod on the Chase, 1s.
Essays from "The Times." 2 Vols. 8s.
Music and Dress. 1s.
Layard's Account of Nineveh. 5s.
Milman's Fall of Jerusalem. 1s.
Mahon's "Forty-Five." 3s.
Life of Theodore Hook. 1s.
Deeds of Naval Daring. 2 Vols. 5s.
The Honey Bee. 1s.
James' Æsop's Fables. 2s. 6d.
Nimrod on the Turf. 1s. 6d.
Oliphant's Nepaul. 2s. 6d.
Art of Dining. 1s. 6d.
Hallam's Literary Essays. 2s.
Mahon's Joan of Arc. 1s.
Head's Emigrant. 2s. 6d.
Nimrod on the Road. 1s.
Wilkinson's Ancient Egyptians. 12s.
Croker on the Guillotine. 1s.
Hollway's Norway. 2s.
Maurel's Wellington. 1s. 6d.
Campbell's Life of Bacon. 2s. 6d.
The Flower Garden. 1s.
Lockhart's Spanish Ballads. 2s. 6d.
Lucas on History. 6d.
Beauties of Byron. 3s.
Taylor's Notes from Life. 2s.
Rejected Addresses. 1s.
Penn's Hints on Angling. 1s.

MUSIC AND DRESS. Two Essays, by a Lady. Reprinted from the "Quarterly Review." Fcap. 8vo. 1s.

NAPIER'S (Sir Wm.) English Battles and Sieges of the Peninsular War. *Third Edition.* Portrait. Post 8vo. 10s. 6d.

——————— Life and Opinions of General Sir Charles Napier ; chiefly derived from his Journals, Letters, and Familiar Correspondence. *Second Edition.* Portraits. 4 Vols. Post 8vo. 48s.

NAUTICAL ALMANACK (The). Royal 8vo. 2s. 6d. (*Published by Authority.*)

NAVY LIST (The Quarterly). (*Published by Authority.*) Post 8vo. 2s. 6d.

NELSON (The Pious Robert), his Life and Times. By Rev. C. T. Secretan, M.A. Portrait. 8vo. 12s.

NEWBOLD'S (Lieut.) Straits of Malacca, Penang, and Singapore. 2 Vols. 8vo. 26s.

NEWDEGATE'S (C. N.) Customs' Tariffs of all Nations ; collected and arranged up to the year 1855. 4to. 30s.

NICHOLLS' (Sir George) History of the British Poor : Being an Historical Account of the English, Scotch, and Irish Poor Law : in connection with the Condition of the People. 4 Vols. 8vo.

The work may be had separately :—
English Poor-Laws. 2 Vols. 8vo. 28s.
Irish Poor. 8vo. 14s.—Scotch Poor. 8vo. 12s.

——— (Rev. H. G.) Historical and Descriptive Account of the Forest of Dean, derived from Personal Observation and other Sources, Public, Private, Legendary, and Local. Woodcuts, &c. Post 8vo. 10s. 6d.

NICOLAS' (Sir Harris) Historic Peerage of England. Exhibiting, under Alphabetical Arrangement, the Origin, Descent, and Present State of every Title of Peerage which has existed in this Country since the Conquest. Being a New Edition of the "Synopsis of the Peerage." Revised, Corrected, and Continued to the Present Time. By William Courthope, Somerset Herald. 8vo. 30s.

NIMROD On the Chace—The Turf—and The Road. Reprinted from the "Quarterly Review." Woodcuts. Fcap. 8vo. 3s. 6d.

O'CONNOR'S (R.) Field Sports of France; or, Hunting, Shooting, and Fishing on the Continent. Woodcuts. 12mo. 7s. 6d.

OLIPHANT'S (LAURENCE) Journey to Katmandu, with Visit to the Camp of the Nepaulese Ambassador. Fcap. 8vo. 2s. 6d.

OWEN'S (PROFESSOR) Manual of Fossil Mammals. Including the substance of the course of Lectures on Osteology and Palæontology of the class Mammalia, delivered at the Metropolitan School of Science, Jermyn Street. Illustrations. 8vo. [In the Press.

OXENHAM'S (REV. W.) English Notes for Latin Elegiacs; designed for early Proficients in the Art of Latin Versification, with Prefatory Rules of Composition in Elegiac Metre. *Third Edition.* 12mo. 4s.

PAGET'S (JOHN) Hungary and Transylvania. With Remarks on their Condition, Social, Political, and Economical. *Third Edition.* Woodcuts. 2 Vols. 8vo. 18s.

PARIS' (Dr.) Philosophy in Sport made Science in Earnest; or, the First Principles of Natural Philosophy inculcated by aid of the Toys and Sports of Youth. *Eighth Edition.* Woodcuts. Post 8vo. 9s.

PARKYNS' (MANSFIELD) Personal Narrative of Three Years' Residence and Adventures in Abyssinia. Woodcuts. 2 Vols. 8vo. 30s.

PEEL'S (SIR ROBERT) Memoirs. Left in MSS. Edited by EARL STANHOPE and the Right Hon. EDWARD CARDWELL. 2 Vols. Post 8vo. 7s. 6d. each.

PEILE'S (REV. DR.) Agamemnon and Choephoræ of Æschylus. A New Edition of the Text, with Notes. *Second Edition.* 2 Vols. 8vo. 9s. each.

PENN'S (RICHARD) Maxims and Hints for an Angler, and the Miseries of Fishing. To which is added, Maxims and Hints for a Chess-player. *New Edition.* Woodcuts. Fcap. 8vo. 1s.

PENROSE'S (REV. JOHN) Faith and Practice; an Exposition of the Principles and Duties of Natural and Revealed Religion. Post 8vo. 8s. 6d.

———— (F. C.) Principles of Athenian Architecture, and the Optical Refinements exhibited in the Construction of the Ancient Buildings at Athens, from a Survey. With 40 Plates. Folio. 5l. 5s. (*Published under the direction of the Dilettanti Society.*)

PERCY'S (JOHN, M.D.) Metallurgy; or, the Art of Extracting Metals from their Ores and adapting them to various purposes of Manufacture. Illustrations. 8vo. [In the Press.

PERRY'S (SIR ERSKINE) Bird's-Eye View of India. With Extracts from a Journal kept in the Provinces, Nepaul, &c. Fcap. 8vo. 5s.

PHILLIPS' (JOHN) Memoirs of William Smith, LL.D. (the Geologist). Portrait. 8vo. 7s. 6d.

———— Geology of Yorkshire, The Yorkshire Coast, and the Mountain-Limestone District. Plates 4to. Part I., 20s. – Part II., 30s.

———— Rivers, Mountains, and Sea Coast of Yorkshire. With Essays on the Climate, Scenery, and Ancient Inhabitants of the Country. *Second Edition*, with 36 Plates. 8vo. 15s.

PHILPOTT'S (BISHOP) Letters to the late Charles Butler, on the Theological parts of his "Book of the Roman Catholic Church;" with Remarks on certain Works of Dr. Milner and Dr. Lingard, and on some parts of the Evidence of Dr. Doyle. *Second Edition.* 8vo. 16s.

PHIPPS' (HON. EDMUND) Memoir, Correspondence, Literary and Unpublished Diaries of Robert Plumer Ward. Portrait. 2 Vols. 8vo. 28s.

POPE'S (ALEXANDER) Works. An entirely New Edition. Edited, with Notes. 8vo. [In the Press.

PORTER'S (Rev. J. L.) Five Years in Damascus. With Travels to
Palmyra, Lebanon, and other Scripture Sites. Map and Woodcuts.
2 vols. Post 8vo. 21s.

———— Handbook for Syria and Palestine: including an Account
of the Geography, History, Antiquities, and Inhabitants of these Countries,
the Peninsula of Sinai, Edom, and the Syrian Desert. Maps. 2 Vols.
Post 8vo. 24s.

———— (Mrs.) Rational Arithmetic for Schools and for
Private Instruction. 12mo. 3s. 6d.

PRAYER-BOOK (The Illustrated), with 1000 Illustrations of Borders, Initials, Vignettes, &c. Medium 8vo. Cloth, 21s.; Calf, 31s. 6d.;
Morocco, 42s.

PRECEPTS FOR THE CONDUCT OF LIFE. Exhortations to
a Virtuous Course and Dissuasions from a Vicious Career. Extracted
from the Scriptures. *Second Edition.* Fcap. 8vo. 1s.

PRINSEP'S (Jas.) Essays on Indian Antiquities, Historic,
Numismatic, and Palæographic, with Tables, illustrative of Indian
History, Chronology. Modern Coinages, Weights, Measures, &c.
Edited by Edward Thomas. Illustrations. 2 Vols. 8vo. 52s. 6d.

PROGRESS OF RUSSIA IN THE EAST. An Historical Summary, continued to the Present Time. With Map by Arrowsmith.
Third Edition. 8vo. 6s. 6d.

PUSS IN BOOTS. With 12 Illustrations; for Old and Young.
By Otto Speckter. *A New Edition.* 16mo. 1s. 6d.

QUARTERLY REVIEW (The). 8vo. 6s.

RANKE'S (Leopold) Political and Ecclesiastical History of the
Popes of Rome, during the Sixteenth and Seventeenth Centuries. Translated from the German by Mrs. Austin. *Third Edition.* 2 Vols. 8vo. 24s.

RAWLINSON'S (Rev. George) Herodotus. A New English
Version. Edited with Notes and Essays. Assisted by Sir Henry
Rawlinson and Sir J. G. Wilkinson. Maps and Woodcuts. 4 Vols.
8vo. 18s. each.

———— Historical Evidences of the truth of the Scripture
Records stated anew, with special reference to the Doubts and Discoveries
of Modern Times; being the Bampton Lectures for 1859. 8vo. 14s.

REJECTED ADDRESSES (The). By James and Horace Smith.
With Biographies of the Authors, and additional Notes. *New Edition,
with the Author's latest Corrections.* Fcap. 8vo. 1s., or *Fine Paper,* with
Portrait. Fcap. 8vo. 5s.

RENNIE'S (James) Insect Architecture. To which are added
Chapters on the Ravages, the Preservation, for Purposes of Study, and
the Classification of Insects. *New Edition.* Woodcuts. Post 8vo. 5s.

RICARDO'S (David) Political Works. With a Notice of his
Life and Writings. By J. R. M'Culloch. *New Edition.* 8vo. 16s.

RIPA'S (Father) Memoirs during Thirteen Years' Residence at the
Court of Peking, in the Service of the Emperor of China. Translated
from the Italian. By Fortunato Prandi. Post 8vo. 2s. 6d.

ROBERTSON'S (Rev. J. C.) History of the Christian Church, From
the Apostolic Age to the Pontificate of Gregory the Great, a.d. 590.
Second and Revised Edition. Vol. 1. 8vo. 16s.

———— Second Period, from a.d. 590 to the Concordat of
Worms. a.d. 1123. Vol. 2. 8vo. 18s.

———— Becket, Archbishop of Canterbury; a Biography.
Illustrations. Post 8vo. 9s.

ROBINSON'S (Rev. Dr.) Biblical Researches in the Holy Land.
Being a Journal of Travels in 1838, and of Later Researches in 1852.
With New Maps. 3 Vols. 8vo. 36s.
₊ The " Later Researches" *may be had separately.* 8vo. 15s.

ROMILLY'S (Sir Samuel) Memoirs and Political Diary. By his
Sons. *Third Edition.* Portrait. 2 Vols. Fcap. 8vo. 12s.

ROSS'S (Sir James) Voyage of Discovery and Research in the
Southern and Antarctic Regions during the years 1839-43. Plates.
2 Vols. 8vo. 36s.

ROWLAND'S (David) Manual of the English Constitution; a
Review of its Rise, Growth, and Present State. Post 8vo. 10s. 6d.

RUNDELL'S (Mrs.) Domestic Cookery, founded on Principles
of Economy and Practice, and adapted for Private Families. *New and
Revised Edition.* Woodcuts. Fcap. 8vo. 5s.

RUSSIA ; A Memoir of the Remarkable Events which attended
the Accession of the Emperor Nicholas. By Baron M. Korff, Secretary
of State. 8vo. 10s. 6d. *(Published by Imperial Command.)*

RUXTON'S (George F.) Travels in Mexico ; with Adventures
among the Wild Tribes and Animals of the Prairies and Rocky Mountains. Post 8vo. 6s.

SALE'S (Lady) Journal of the Disasters in Affghanistan. *Eighth
Edition.* Post 8vo. 12s.

———— (Sir Robert) Brigade in Affghanistan. With an Account of
the Seizure and Defence of Jellalabad. By Rev. G. R. Gleig. Post 8vo. 2s. 6d.

SANDWITH'S (Humphry) Narrative of the Siege of Kars
and of the Six Months' Resistance by the Turkish Garrison under
General Williams. *Seventh Thousand.* Post 8vo. 3s. 6d.

SCOTT'S (G. Gilbert) Remarks on Secular and Domestic
Architecture, Present and Future. *Second Edition.* 8vo. 9s.

SCROPE'S (William) Days of Deer-Stalking in the Forest of Atholl ;
with some Account of the Nature and Habits of the Red Deer. *Third
Edition.* Woodcuts. Crown 8vo. 20s.

Days and Nights of Salmon Fishing in the Tweed ;
with a short Account of the Natural History and Habits of the Salmon.
Second Edition. Woodcuts. Royal 8vo. 31s. 6d.

———— (G. P.) Memoir of Lord Sydenham, and his Administration in Canada. *Second Edition.* Portrait. 8vo. 9s. 6d.

———— Geology and Extinct Volcanos of Central France.
Second Edition, revised and enlarged. Illustrations. Medium 8vo. 30s.

SHAFTESBURY (Lord Chancellor), Memoirs of his Early Life.
With his Letters, Speeches, and other Papers. By W. D. Christie.
Portrait. 8vo. 10s. 6d.

SHAW'S (Thos. B.) Outlines of English Literature, for the Use of
Young Students. Post 8vo. 12s.

SIERRA LEONE ; Described in a Series of Letters to Friends at
Home. By A Lady. Edited by Mrs. Norton. Post 8vo. 6s.

SMILES' (Samuel) Life of George Stephenson. *Fifth Edition.*
Portrait. 8vo. 16s.

———— Story of the Life of Stephenson. With Woodcuts.
Fifth Thousand. Post 8vo. 6s.

———— Self Help. With Illustrations of Character and Conduct.
Post 8vo. 6s.

SOMERVILLE'S (Mary) Physical Geography. *Fourth Edition.*
Portrait. Post 8vo. 9s.

———————— Connexion of the Physical Sciences. *Ninth
Edition.* Woodcuts. Post 8vo. 9s.

SOUTH'S (John F.) Household Surgery ; or, Hints on Emergen-
cies. *Seventeenth Thousand.* Woodcuts. Fcp. 8vo. 4s. 6d.

SOUTHEY'S (Robert) Book of the Church ; with Notes containing the Authorities, and an Index. *Seventh Edition.* Post 8vo. 7s. 6d.

———————— Lives of John Bunyan & Oliver Cromwell. Post 8vo. 2s. 6d.

SMITH'S (Wm., LL.D.) Dictionary of Greek and Roman Antiquities. *Second Edition*. With 500 Woodcuts. 8vo. 42s.

———— Smaller Dictionary of Greek and Roman Antiquities. Abridged from the above work. *Fourth Edition*. With 200 Woodcuts. Crown 8vo. 7s. 6d.

———— Dictionary of Greek and Roman Biography and Mythology. With 500 Woodcuts. 3 Vols. 8vo. 5l. 15s. 6d.

———— Dictionary of Greek and Roman Geography. With Woodcuts. 2 Vols. 8vo. 80s.

———— Atlas of Ancient Geography. 4to. [*In preparation.*

———— Classical Dictionary for the Higher Forms in Schools. Compiled from the above two works. *Fifth Edition*. With 750 Woodcuts. 8vo. 18s.

———— Smaller Classical Dictionary. Abridged from the above work. *Fifth Edition*. With 200 Woodcuts. Crown 8vo. 7s. 6d.

———— Latin - English Dictionary. Based upon the Works of Forcellini and Freund. *Seventh Thousand*. 8vo. 21s.

———— Smaller Latin-English Dictionary. Abridged from the above work. *Sixteenth Thousand*. Square 12mo. 7s 6d.

———— English-Latin Dictionary. 8vo. & 12mo. [*In preparation.*

———— Mediæval Latin-English Dictionary. Selected from the great work of Ducange. 8vo. [*In preparation.*

———— Dictionary of the Bible, including its Antiquities, Biography, Geography, and Natural History. Woodcuts. Vol. 1. 8vo. 42s. [*Nearly ready.*

———— Gibbon's History of the Decline and Fall of the Roman Empire. Edited, with Notes. Portrait and Map. 8 Vols. 8vo. 60s. (Murray's British Classics.)

———— Student's Gibbon; being the History of the Decline and Fall, Abridged. Incorporating the Researches of Recent Commentators. *Sixth Thousand*. Woodcuts. Post 8vo. 7s. 6d.

———— Student's History of Greece; from the Earliest Times to the Roman Conquest. With the History of Literature and Art. *Twentieth Thousand*. Woodcuts. Crown 8vo. 7s. 6d. (Questions. 12mo. 2s.)

———— Smaller History of Greece for Junior Classes. Woodcuts. 12mo. 3s. 6d.

———— Student's Hume. A History of England from the Invasion of Julius Cæsar. Based on Hume's History, and continued to 1858. *Tenth Thousand*. Woodcuts. Post 8vo. 7s. 6d.

———— Student's History of Rome; from the Earliest Times to the Establishment of the Empire. With the History of Literature and Art. By H. G. Liddell, D.D. *Fifteenth Thousand*. Woodcuts. Crown 8vo. 7s. 6d.

———— Principia Latina; a First Latin Course, comprehending Grammar, Delectus, and Exercise Book, with Vocabularies, for the lower forms in Public and Private Schools. 12mo. 3s. 6d.

———— Principia Græca; an Introduction to the Study of Greek. Comprehending Grammar, Delectus, and Exercise-book with Vocabularies. For the Lower Forms. By H. E. Hutton, M.A. 12mo. 2s. 6d.

———— (Wm. Jas.) Grenville Letters and Diaries, including Mr. Grenville's Diary of Political Events, while First Lord of the Treasury. Edited, with Notes. 4 Vols. 8vo. 64s.

———— (James & Horace) Rejected Addresses. *Twenty-third Edition*. Fcap. 8vo. 1s., or *Fine Paper*, with Portrait. Fcap. 8vo. 5s.

———— (Thomas Assheton) Reminiscences of his Life and Pursuits. By Sir Eardley Wilmot. Illustrations. 8vo.

SPECKTER'S (OTTO) Puss in Boots, suited to the Tastes of Old
and Young. *A New Edition*. With 12 Woodcuts. Square 12mo. 1*s.* 6*d.*
———————— Charmed Roe; or, the Story of the Little Brother
and Sister. Illustrated. 16mo.

STANLEY'S (Rev. A. P.) ADDRESSES AND CHARGES OF THE LATE
BISHOP STANLEY. With a Memoir of his Life. *Second Edition*. 8vo. 10*s.* 6*d.*
———————— Sermons preached in Canterbury Cathedral, on the
Unity of Evangelical and Apostolical Teaching. Post 8vo. 7*s.* 6*d.*
———————— Commentary on St. Paul's Epistles to the Corin-
thians, with Notes and Dissertations. *Second, and revised Edition*. 8vo. 18*s.*
———————— Historical Memorials of Canterbury. The Landing of
Augustine—The Murder of Becket—The Black Prince—The Shrine of
Becket. *Third Edition*. Woodcuts. Post 8vo. 7*s.* 6*d.*
———————— Sinai and Palestine, in Connexion with their History.
Sixth Edition. Map. 8vo. 16*s.*

ST. JOHN'S (CHARLES) Wild Sports and Natural History of the
Highlands. Post 8vo. 6*s.*
———————— (BAYLE) Adventures in the Libyan Desert and the
Oasis of Jupiter Ammon. Woodcuts. Post 8vo. 2*s.* 6*d.*

STEPHENSON'S (GEORGE) Life. The Railway Engineer. By
SAMUEL SMILES. *Fifth Edition*. Portrait. 8vo. 16*s.*
———————— The Story of his Life. By SAMUEL SMILES. *Fifth
Thousand*. Woodcuts. Post 8vo. 6*s.*

STOTHARD'S (THOS., R. A.) Life. With Personal Reminiscences.
By Mrs. BRAY. With Portrait and 60 Woodcuts. 4to.

STREET'S (G. E.) Brick and Marble Architecture of Italy, in the
Middle Ages. Plates. 8vo. 21*s.*

STRIFE FOR THE MASTERY. Two Allegories. With Illustrations. Crown 8vo. 6*s.*

SWIFT'S (JONATHAN) Life, Letters and Journals. By JOHN
FORSTER. 8vo. *In Preparation*.
———————— Works. Edited, with Notes. By JOHN FORSTER. 8vo.
In Preparation.

SYDENHAM'S (LORD) Memoirs. With his Administration in
Canada. By G. POULET SCROPE, M.P. *Second Edition*. Portrait. 8vo. 9*s.* 6*d.*

SYME'S (JAS.) Principles of Surgery. *Fourth Edition*. 8vo. 14*s.*

TAYLOR'S (HENRY) Notes from Life. Fcap 8vo. 2*s.*
———————— (J. E.) Fairy Ring. A Collection of Stories for Young
Persons. From the German. With Illustrations by RICHARD DOYLE.
Second Edition. Woodcuts. Fcap. 8vo.

TENNENT'S (SIR J. E.) Christianity in Ceylon. Its Introduction
and Progress under the Portuguese, Dutch, British, and American Missions. With an Historical Sketch of the Brahmanical and Buddhist
Superstitions. Woodcuts. 8vo. 14*s.*

THOMSON'S (DR. A. S.) Story of New Zealand; Past and Present
—Savage and Civilised. Maps and Illustrations. 2 Vols. Post 8vo. 24*s.*

THREE-LEAVED MANUAL OF FAMILY PRAYER; arranged
so as to save the trouble of turning the Pages backwards and forwards.
Royal 8vo. 2*s.*

TICKNOR'S (GEORGE) History of Spanish Literature. With Criti-
cisms on particular Works, and Biographical Notices of Prominent
Writers. *Second Edition*. 3 Vols. 8vo. 24*s.*

TOCQUEVILLE'S (M. DE) State of France before the Revolution,
1789, and on the Causes of that Event. Translated by HENRY REEVE,
Esq. 8vo. 14*s.*

TREMENHEERE'S (H. S.) Political Experience of the Ancients, in its bearing on Modern Times. Fcap. 8vo. 2s. 6d.

———————————— Notes on Public Subjects, made during a Tour in the United States and Canada. Post 8vo. 10s. 6d.

———————————— Constitution of the United States compared with our own. Post 8vo. 9s. 6d.

TWISS' (HORACE) Public and Private Life of Lord Chancellor Eldon, with Selections from his Correspondence. Portrait. *Third Edition*. 2 Vols. Post 8vo. 21s.

TYNDALL'S (JOHN) Glaciers of the Alps. Being a Narrative of various Excursions among them, and an Account of Three Years' Observations and Experiments on their Motion, Structure, and General Phenomena. Post 8vo. *In the Press*.

TYTLER (PATRICK FRASER), A Memoir of. By his Friend, REV. J. W. BURGON, M.A. *Second Edition*. 8vo. 9s.

UBICINI'S (M. A.) Letters on Turkey and its Inhabitants—the Moslems, Greeks, Armenians, &c. Translated by LADY EASTHOPE. 2 Vols. Post 8vo. 21s.

VAUGHAN'S (REV. DR.) Sermons preached in Harrow School. 8vo. 10s. 6d.

———————————— New Sermons. 12mo. 5s.

VENABLES' (REV. R. L.) Domestic Scenes in Russia during a Year's Residence, chiefly in the Interior. *Second Edition*. Post 8vo. 5s.

VOYAGE to the Mauritius and back, touching at the Cape of Good Hope, and St. Helena. By Author of "PADDIANA." Post 8vo. 9s. 6d.

WAAGEN'S (DR.) Treasures of Art in Great Britain. Being an Account of the Chief Collections of Paintings, Sculpture, Manuscripts, Miniatures, &c. &c., in this Country. Obtained from Personal Inspection during Visits to England. 3 Vols. 8vo. 36s.

———————————— Galleries and Cabinets of Art in England. Being an Account of more than Forty Collections, visited in 1854-56 and never before described. With Index. 8vo. 18s.

WADDINGTON'S (DEAN) Condition and Prospects of the Greek Church. *New Edition*. Fcap. 8vo. 3s. 6d.

WAKEFIELD'S (E. J.) Adventures in New Zealand. With some Account of the Beginning of the British Colonisation of the Island. Map. 2 Vols. 8vo. 28s.

WALKS AND TALKS. A Story-book for Young Children. By AUNT IDA. With Woodcuts. 16mo. 5s.

WARD'S (ROBERT PLUMER) Memoir, Correspondence, Literary and Unpublished Diaries and Remains. By the HON. EDMUND PHIPPS. Portrait. 2 Vols. 8vo. 28s.

WATT'S (JAMES) Life. Incorporating the most interesting passages from his Private and Public Correspondence. By JAMES P. MUIRHEAD, M.A. *Second Edition*. Portraits and Woodcuts. 8vo. 16s.

———— Origin and Progress of his Mechanical Inventions. Illustrated by his Correspondence with his Friends. Edited by J. P. MUIRHEAD. Plates. 3 vols. 8vo. 45s., or Large Paper. 3 Vols. 4to.

WILKIE'S (SIR DAVID) Life, Journals, Tours, and Critical Remarks on Works of Art, with a Selection from his Correspondence. By ALLAN CUNNINGHAM. Portrait. 3 Vols. 8vo. 42s.

WOOD'S (LIEUT.) Voyage up the Indus to the Source of the River Oxus, by Kabul and Badakhshan. Map. 8vo. 14s.

WELLINGTON'S (The Duke of) Despatches during his various
Campaigns. Compiled from Official and other Authentic Documents. By
Col. Gurwood, C.B. *New Enlarged Edition.* 8 Vols. 8vo. 21*s*. each.

———————— Supplementary Letters, Despatches, and other
Papers relating to India. Edited by his Son. 4 Vols. 8vo. 20*s*. each.

———————— Civil Correspondence and Memoranda, while
Chief Secretary for Ireland, from 1807 to 1809. 8vo. 20*s*.

———————— Selections from his Despatches and General
Orders. By Colonel Gurwood. 8vo. 18*s*.

———————— Speeches in Parliament. 2 Vols. 8vo. 42*s*.

WILKINSON'S (Sir J. G.) Popular Account of the Private Life,
Manners, and Customs of the Ancient Egyptians. *New Edition.*
Revised and Condensed. With 500 Woodcuts. 2 Vols. Post 8vo. 12*s*.

———————— Dalmatia and Montenegro; with a Journey to
Mostar in Hertzegovina, and Remarks on the Slavonic Nations. Plates
and Woodcuts. 2 Vols. 8vo. 42*s*.

———————— Handbook for Egypt.—Thebes, the Nile, Alexandria, Cairo, the Pyramids, Mount Sinai, &c. Map. Post 8vo. 15*s*.

———————— On Colour, and on the Necessity for a General
Diffusion of Taste among all Classes; with Remarks on laying out
Dressed or Geometrical Gardens. With Coloured Illustrations and
Woodcuts. 8vo. 18*s*.

———————— (G. B.) Working Man's Handbook to South Australia; with Advice to the Farmer, and Detailed Information for the
several Classes of Labourers and Artisans. Map. 18mo. 1*s*. 6*d*.

WILSON'S (Rev. D., late Lord Bishop of Calcutta) Life, with
Extracts from his Letters and Journals. By Rev. Josiah Bate-
man, M.A. Portrait and Illustrations. 2 Vols. 8vo. 28*s*.

———————— (Genl. Sir Robert) Journal, while employed at the
Head Quarters of the Russian Army on a special mission during the
Invasion of Russia, and Retreat of the French Army, 1812. 8vo.

WORDSWORTH'S (Rev. Dr.) Athens and Attica. Journal of a
Tour. *Third Edition.* Plates. Post 8vo. 8*s*. 6*d*.

———————— Greece: Pictorial, Descriptive, and Historical,
with a History of Greek Art, by G. Scharf, F.S.A. *New Edition.* With
600 Woodcuts. Royal 8vo. 28*s*.

———————— King Edward VIth's Latin Grammar, for the
Use of Schools. 12*th Edition*, revised. 12mo. 3*s*. 6*d*.

———————— First Latin Book, or the Accidence, Syntax
and Prosody, with English Translation for Junior Classes. *Third
Edition.* 12mo. 2*s*.

WORNUM (Ralph). A Biographical Dictionary of Italian Painters:
with a Table of the Contemporary Schools of Italy. By a Lady.
Post 8vo. 6*s*. 6*d*.

———————— Epochs of Painting Characterised; a Sketch
of the History of Painting, showing its gradual and various development from the earliest ages to the present time. *New Edition*, Woodcuts. Post 8vo. 6*s*.

WROTTESLEY'S (Lord) Thoughts on Government and Legislation.
Post 8vo. 7*s*. 6*d*.

YOUNG'S (Dr. Thos.) Life and Miscellaneous Works, edited by Dean
Peacock and John Leitch. Portrait and Plates. 4 Vols. 8vo. 15*s*. each.

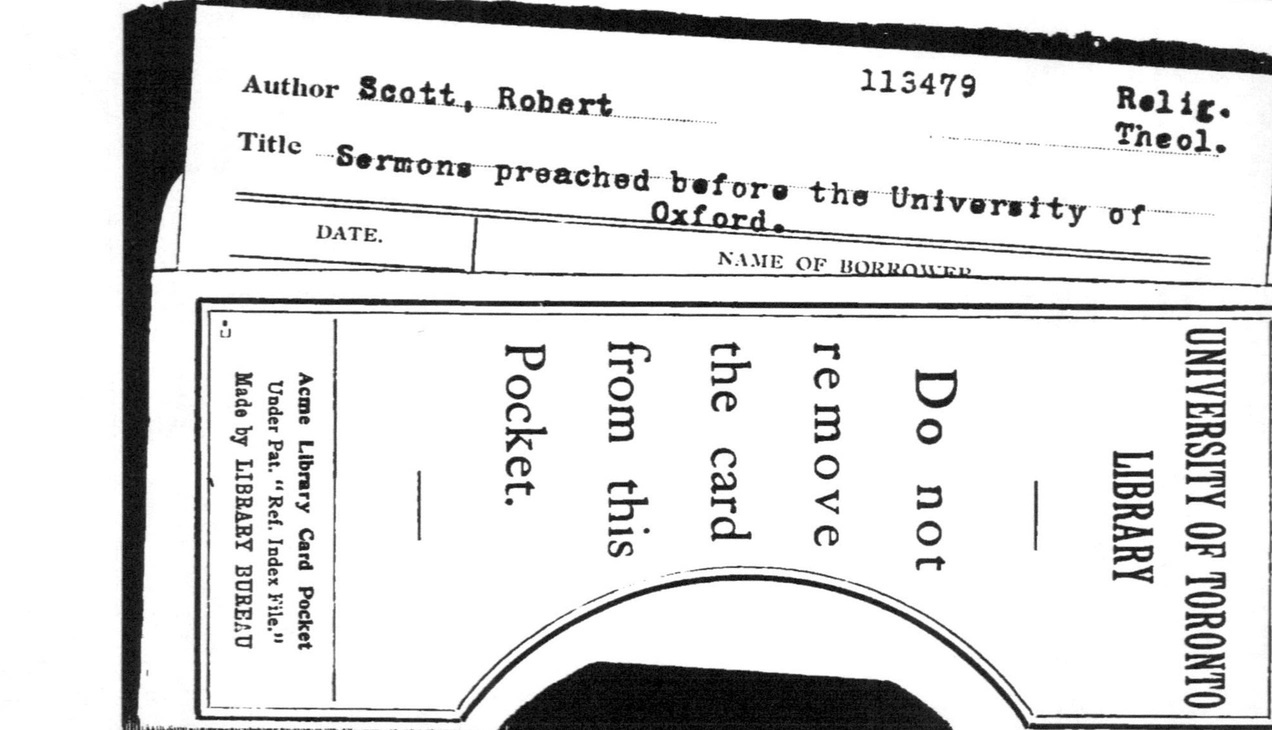